MICHIGAN

A STATE OF ENVIRONMENTAL JUSTICE?

EDITED BY Bunyan Bryant
and Elaine Hockman

NEW YORK

MICHIGAN

A STATE OF ENVIRONMENTAL JUSTICE?

EDITED BY Bunyan Bryant

and Elaine Hockman

© 2011 Bunyan Bryant, Elaine Hockman. All rights reserved.

ISBN 978-1-61448-029-7 Paperback
ISBN 978-1-61448-030-3 EPub
Library of Congress Control Number: 2011928333

Published by:
MORGAN JAMES PUBLISHING
The Entrepreneurial Publisher
5 Penn Plaza, 23rd Floor
New York City, New York 10001
(212) 655-5470 Office
(516) 908-4496 Fax
www.MorganJamesPublishing.com

Cover Design by:
Rachel Lopez
rachel@r2cdesign.com

In an effort to support local communities, raise awareness and funds, Morgan James Publishing donates one percent of all book sales for the life of each book to Habitat for Humanity.
Get involved today, visit
www.HelpHabitatForHumanity.org.

Contents

Contributors

Bunyan Bryant, Ph.D. is instrumental in establishing the School's Environmental Justice Specialization that focuses on the differential impact of environmental contaminants on people of color and low-income communities. He is also the co-founder and Director of the Environmental Justice Initiative for research and retrieval/dissemination conferences. Research and conferences include both a domestic and international foci, particularly on climate justice. Areas of teaching include Small Group Organization and Advocacy Planning (SNRE 495), Research for Environmental Justice (SNRE 594), and Environmental Justice: Domestic and International (SNRE 492).

Amy Holmes-Chavez currently serves as Associate Director for Planning and External Relations for the Division of Adult and Community Health at the Centers for Disease Control and Prevention's (CDC) National Center for Chronic Disease Prevention and Health Promotion in Atlanta, Georgia. Amy joined CDC in 1996 where she served in various roles in the National Center for Chronic Disease Prevention and Health Promotion's Office of Planning, Evaluation, and Legislation, including serving as team leader for the office's legislative team from 2001- 2002. In 1999, Amy served in two CDC field assignments to the North Carolina Department of Health and Human Services in Raleigh, North Carolina, and to the DeKalb County Board of Health in Atlanta, Georgia. Prior to joining CDC, Amy worked with migrant farm worker youth in Michigan, as a community health educator with migrant farm workers in Virginia, and worked in local health planning in Michigan. Amy received a Master of Public Health degree from the University of Michigan in 1996 with dual concentrations in Health Behavior/Health Education and Public Health Policy and Administration; she received a B.A. degree in Sociology from the University of Michigan in 1992.

Elaine Hockman, Ph.D. is an Adjunct Assistant Professor at the School of Natural Resources and Environment and Manager of the Research Support Laboratory at Wayne State University. She is a methodologist, with a Ph.D. in Psychology and Education, specializing in research design, statistics, and measurements. Her main interest in environmental justice is empirical research to provide objective evidence, understanding, and solutions to environmental justice by working in partnership with academics and the larger community on the salient issues and the conditions they define.

Paul Mohai, Ph.D. is a co-founder of the Environmental Justice Specialization at the University of Michigan. Over the years he has been a major contributor to the growing body of quantitative research examining the disproportionate impact of environmental hazards on people of color and people of low-income. Current research includes national-level studies that examine the role that environmental factors play in accounting for racial and socioeconomic disparities in health. He was a co-organizer of the historic 1990 "Michigan Conference on Race and the Incidence of Environmental Hazards" with colleague Dr. Bunyan Bryant.

Charles Morris is a Catholic priest and pastor. His interest in environmental justice stems from the health, educational, and economic effects of toxins on people of color and low-income groups. He is interested in measuring the differential impacts of various kinds of pollution on people of color and low-income communities.

Alice Nabalamba received her Ph.D. from the School of Planning at the University of Waterloo in 2001. Her current research focuses on the spatial and socio-demographic characteristics of environmental pollutants in Canadian communities.

Kathy Nemsick Rehill has a Master's of Science Degree in Resource Policy and Behavior from the University of Michigan's School of Natural Resources and Environment and a Bachelors of Arts degree in Government from the University of Notre Dame. She began her career in the public interest sector as a community organizer in the Peace Corps in Senegal, West Africa. Kathy has over thirteen years of experience working for non-profit environmental groups, primarily on water pollution policy. Kathy is currently a grant-writing consultant for several national environmental groups and a full-time mother of two children.

1

INTRODUCTION

Bunyan Bryant and Elaine Hockman

...the question is not growth, but how do we grow in sustainable ways that ensure distributive justice, and in ways that support cultural and biological diversity. We need a Marshall Plan, similar to the one crafted for the war-torn cities of Europe after World War II, and the services of the National Guard and as many volunteers as possible to help clean up our cities to make them environmentally benign and livable. We need a health care program, particularly for those people living near these noxious facilities. Too often people are subsidizing the profits of industries with their health and health-care medical bills.

There are several reasons for this book. It is to bring people's attention to the impact of the by-products of growth and development in the state of Michigan: who wins and who loses? While economic growth has been good for some, it has been devastating for others; the by-products of growth and development have threatened the lives of people who breathe polluted air, drink contaminated water, and whose children play on polluted soil. Because of the legacy of racism and classism in the state of Michigan, poor people are forced to live and work in areas with the greatest negative environmental impact. Let us be clear right from the beginning. We are not against economic growth and development; we are against certain kinds of economic growth and development—i.e., growth and development that expose people to unnecessary environmental harms. We feel it is possible to have economic growth and development and environmental protection and we will explore this possibility later on in the book. Even though this book is focused on Michigan, we feel this state is a prime example of environmental injustice because it has a large industrial sector, a large number of toxic inventory citations, Superfund sites, brownfields, and hazardous waste disposal facilities located disproportionately in racially segregated communities and in communities of poverty.

Another reason for this book is to focus the reader's attention on the devastating environmental problems faced by low-income people and people of color and the need to address them now rather than later. Later might be too late since thousands of people suffer from toxic-induced and aggravated diseases, including respiratory problems and a variety of cancers, linked to ambient air quality and a variety of toxic exposures. This book challenges the myth that blacks are disinterested in the environment—a myth that is blatantly not true. People of color have always been interested in clean, safe, and productive environments and an improved quality of live. Lessons we draw from Michigan can be easily applied to the nation as a whole.

Several audiences should read this book. Policymakers, regardless of level of government, should read it to help them become more aware of and concerned about the depth and breath of environmental problems so that they can make more informed policy decisions. This book should be read by corporate executives, regardless of corporate size or hierarchy, and regardless of their political persuasion, because it challenges them to alter their harmful production practices. It should be read by academics interested in researching problems of environmental injustice and thus making their findings readily available to policymakers and the broader public. It should be read by laypeoples to help them protect themselves and their communities against decisions that would do them harm. Although the quantitative analysis in this book does not prove cause and effect, it does show significant associations that support the already growing body of knowledge demonstrating the connection between health status and where people live. We feel that such demonstrations could be the foundations for key environmental policies.

Again, let us be clear. There are no easy answers to the questions raised in this book. Over the years companies have spewed out toxic poisons from smokestacks, dumped hazardous waste into our waterways, and buried toxins in the depths of our land without thinking of their harmful effects. It will take billions of dollars to right past wrongs and to protect communities from future wrongs. This book focuses not only on what the private and public sectors are doing but also on what they are not doing. Why is the government not cleaning up hazardous waste sites, particularly those in minority communities? Why is the government refusing to enforce environmental regulations to provide equal protection of the law? We will attempt to answer these and other questions in this book.

Michigan is not unique; the pollution problems experienced here in Michigan haunt people in states throughout the country, even though the pollution may take on different forms. We have created a racially segregated state and one with considerable number of toxic inventory citations, Superfund sites, brownfields, and hazardous waste disposal facilities, and one where a considerable number of people live in poverty. We must not despair; we can make a difference if we set our minds to it. Again the question is not growth, but how do we grow in sustainable ways that ensure distributive justice, and in ways that support cultural and biological diversity. We need a Marshall Plan, similar to the one crafted for the war-torn cities of Europe after World War II, and the services of the National Guard and as many volunteers as possible to help cleanup our cities to make them environmentally benign and livable. We need a health care program, particularly for those people living near these noxious facilities. Too often people are subsidizing the profits of industries with their health and health-care medical bills. All too often those living in proximity to hazardous waste facilities are the least protected by insurance. Perhaps their health condition will improve somewhat, since Congress has passed a health care bill making health insurance affordable regardless of a person's income or prior condition. But the real protection against illness is related to structural inequalities, poverty and the environmental conditions under which people are forced to live.

Lay people should demand that cumulative impact analysis be made before additional siting in the area, and that industry pick up the cost for citizen participation and analysis. Since the automobile is responsible for over 50 percent of societal pollution, citizen groups should demand more mass transit systems.

Why is it important to solve these most pressing problems? Because at the rate we are going we are squandering our biological capital. We are spoiling the global nest and causing considerable sickness and death. Our economy and quality of life depend upon healthy people, and healthy people depend upon a healthy environment.

During the 1940s, one of the largest wartime conversions took place in the history of the state. Automobile factories were converted to produce tanks and bombers. Blacks and whites migrated from the South to the North to work in the plants. Jobs in the North provided an unprecedented opportunity to make more money than ever. Even following the war, blacks and whites continued to migrate to work in the automobile factories. Jobs were plentiful, earnings high, and a high school diploma was not required. Workers could realize the American dream of buying their own home and sending their children to college. All this could be done with little or no skills.

But while Michigan industry produced social "goods," it also produced social "bads." In those days the spoilage of the land and ambient air, and the harmful effects to personal health and the environment, were seldom on the radar screen. Today all that has changed because people are more aware of the negative health impacts of environmental pollution. Today people at risk are demanding environmental regulations to protect their communities against harm. Historically, corporate managers have attempted to blame their economic woes on environmental regulations. If workers chose to side with environmentalists or if they chose to embrace environmental regulations, then corporate managers would often threaten them with dismissal, claiming that to adhere to such regulations would be too time consuming and cut too deeply into profit margins. Therefore, the employers said, they would have to close shop and move to distant ports for cheaper resources, cheaper labor, and fewer environmental regulations.

This line of argument is all based upon the fact that the cost of production increases as more environmental restrictions impair the creation of goods and services. But employers seldom advance the argument that environmental regulations protect people, their health, and the environment. With good intention, former Gov. John Engler and Russell Harding, director of the Council for Environmental Quality, have very successfully used this basic economic argument in their campaign against EPA and environmental organizations dedicated to environmental protection. Both Engler and Harding believed that the economy can be stimulated by dismantling environmental regulations. Arguments used by Engler and Harding, buttressed by anecdotal evidence, were very convincing. Numerous examples can be cited to demonstrate that environmental regulations reduce jobs, take a bite out of the economy, and leave workers impoverished and dependent. Undoubtedly jobs will be lost because old and inefficient industries cannot afford to retrofit their equipment to be environmentally benign.

Although this argument is convincing and simplistic, it is only part of the story. The dismantling of regulations only shifts the cost of production from industry to people. When these costs are externalized, people pay for the price of production in the form of health care bills for treatment of a variety of toxic-induced or aggravated diseases. Is it fair for people to bear the costs of production that should be borne by corporations? Another part of the story in support of environmental regulations: In 1992, Bezdek reported that since the 1960s spending to protect the environment has been growing three times faster than the gross domestic product (GDP). Because of the largesse of the spending to protect the environment, a whole new industry has developed—an industry that has contributed immensely to economic growth and development. Meyer (1992) reported that cities with ambitious environmental regulations had the highest level of economic growth. Other studies reported that pollution control measures had little or no effect on trading of goods and services or economic competitiveness (Leonard, 1989; Tobey, 1990; Porter, 1990; Cropper and Oates, 1992). In 1998, the U.S. Bureau of Labor Statistics reported that employers attributed 0.1 percent of all layoffs to environmentally related decisions (Forwarded from Lee, 1990). Even at the international level we see environmental regulations having a positive effect.

At the international level creative responses to stringent environmental regulations can be good for the economy. In the 1980s, Germany and Japan, with the most stringent environmental regulations in the world, experienced robust economies; profit was substantial and jobs were in abundance. Environmental regulations forced the managers of corporations in these countries to be creative. Instead of spending large sums of money to fight these regulations, they used that time and energy to develop pollution abatement control technology, and at this point they are cornering the world market on such technology. The State of California has been forced to adhere to strict environmental regulations, and at certain times it has experienced an economic boom. Although they have a ways to go, Californians enjoy much cleaner air now than four decades ago. Even now, the Obama administration believes that spending to protect the environment will create more jobs and a healthy economy.

There are several reasons why environmental regulations are good for the economy and good for the people of Michigan. Environmental regulations force companies to be competitive and to re-engineer their technology to be more energy efficient, cost effective, and thus squander fewer amounts of our precious biological capital. The production of more efficient goods and services would cut our waste stream significantly, leaving less toxic waste, which is often destined for disposal facilities located in people of color communities. While state government officials believe that environmental regulations diminish the wealth of a nation, these regulations in fact transfer wealth from polluters to pollution controllers, and to less polluting firms. It is this biological capital that undergirds the economic and social institutions of the state. Once this capital is squandered, so are the lives of its citizens. Today many companies in Michigan owe both their profit, and even their very existence, to environmental protection spending. These are companies that profit from the production and sale of pollution abatement and control technology to help industry become cleaner and more energy efficient. Conventional wisdom ignores the benefits that may be produced by environmental programs and policies—programs and polices that result in cleaner and healthier air, water, and land for the people of Michigan.

Throughout this book, we will address the issues of racism, environmental racism, environmental equity, and environmental justice. As more articles appear in professional journals and the popular press, there is growing need for more definitive and operational definitions of these terms. The definitions are not carved in stone, and will undoubtedly be fine-tuned as we continue the discourse in coming years. While the first definition that follows is based upon the conceptual thinking of Terry (1970) and Katz (1978), the second, third, and fourth definitions are based upon our own conceptual thinking to date. Environmental racism, equity, and justice are yet to be defined in the professional literature in any precise way. The definition of hazardous waste is from the work of Miller (1988). We hope the definitions put forth in this chapter will provide a conceptual framework for a substantive discourse on the differential environmental impacts experienced by people of color and people of low-income here in the state of Michigan. We start with defining racism as practiced in this country.

Racism: When we speak of racism we refer to the systematic use of cultural norms and values, institutional rules, regulations, and policies, unfair historical accounts, and individual attitudes and opinions used to arbitrarily exclude, dominate, humiliate, insult, and deny opportunities to people of color based upon prescribed biological characteristics. Racism may be thought of as a pattern of decisions or policies at both the individual and institutional level to relegate, consciously or unconsciously, people of color to deplorable working, living, and schooling conditions (Katz, 1978; Terry, 1970).

Environmental Racism: Environmental racism is an extension of racism; it is when those institutional rules, regulations, and policies of government or corporate decisions are used to select arbitrarily people of color communities for least undesirable land uses (LULUs), based in part or solely upon the racial and socio-economic characteristics of those neighborhoods. We have thus observed a national pattern of disproportionately higher numbers of fugitive emissions, hazardous waste and disposal facilities, and sewage treatment plants in people of color and people of low-income communities than in more affluent white communities.

Environmental Equity: We may think of environmental equity as the equal protection of environmental laws. Environmental laws should be equally enforced to ensure proper siting and timely cleanups of hazardous waste and polluting industries, regardless of whether the community is affluent or regardless of its racial or ethnic make-up.

Environmental Justice: Environmental justice is much broader than environmental equity. It refers to those cultural norms and values, institutional rules, regulations, and policies or decisions that support sustainable communities, where people can interact with confidence that their environment is safe, nurturing, and productive. Environmental justice is served when people can realize their highest potential, without experiencing discrimination based on race, class, ethnicity or national origin. Environmental justice is supported by decent paying and safe jobs; quality schools and recreation; decent housing and adequate health care; democratic decision-making and personal empowerment; and communities free of violence, drugs, and poverty. These are communities where both cultural and biological diversity are respected and highly revered, and where distributive justice prevails.

Hazardous Waste: Hazardous waste may be defined as any discarded material that may pose a substantial threat to human beings or the environment when managed improperly. Such waste can exist in solid, liquid, or gaseous form; it may also include ignitable, corrosive, or dangerously reactive substances. Examples of such waste are lead, mercury, acids, cyanides, herbicides and pesticides, solvents from dry cleaners, arsenic, cadmium, soil contaminated with PCBs, dioxins, fly and ground ash from incinerators, infectious waste from hospitals and research laboratories, radioactive materials, and obsolete explosives, and nerve gas stockpiled by the Defense Department (Miller, 1988).

Why the State of Michigan is Important in Studying Environmental Injustice?

There are many reasons why Michigan is a good site to study environmental justice. First, because of the manufacturing sector, Michigan has 77 hazardous waste sites listed on the Environmental Protection Agency's national priority

Table 1. Estimated Annual Cardiopulmonary Deaths in the MSA from PM-10 and the Number of Deaths from Car Accidents.

Metropolitan Statistical Area	Average Annual Mean PM-10 Concentration (1990-1994) (ug/m³)	Estimated Annual Cardiopulmonary Deaths Attributable to Particulate Air Pollution				Adult Cardio-Pulmonary Deaths (1989)	Deaths from Auto Accidents (1989)
		Point Estimate	Range		Deaths per 100,000 Population		
DETROIT, MI	33.2	2,123	1,265	- 2,906	49	18,695	626
FLINT, MI	24.1	118	69	- 163	23	2,011	116
GRAND RAPIDS, MI	26.0	166	98	- 230	28	2,371	123
SAGINAW, MI	25.6	66	39	- 91	29	971	89
TOLEDO, OH-MI	26.3	257	152	- 355	32	3,569	191

Point estimates are derived from the risk ratio reported in the American Cancer Society (ACS) study. Ranges are derived from 95-percent confidence intervals around the risk ratio in the ACS study.

Metropolitan Statistical Areas are as defined by the Office of Management and Budget for 1980, except for New England, where areas are New England County Metropolitan Areas.

Natural Resources Defense Council. (no date) Retrieved April 14, 2003 from the Natural Resources Defense Council Web site: *http://www.nrdc.org/air/pollution/bt/MI.asp*

list, making it the fifth worst state in the country for the number of listed sites (Statistical Abstract, 1992). Although Michigan has lost a number of industries over the years, it is still considered a major industrial state. According to the 1989 Toxic Release Inventory, 74,122,909 pounds of chemicals were emitted in Michigan. Of these emissions, 80% of them end up in the air. Additionally, Table 1 above shows some startling facts regarding the five cities within the Standard Metropolitan Statistical Area (SMSA). It shows that particulate air pollution (PM-10) contributes significantly to mortality. For the purpose of comparison the table 1 above also shows the total number of cardiopulmonary deaths in the MSA and the number of deaths from car accidents.

Every year in Michigan older power plants trigger 18,500 asthma attacks, many of which occur in children. Eleven thousand of these attacks would be avoided if these plants were forced to comply with the law and install pollution controls. Due to the exposure of power plant pollution, Michigan citizens lose 159,000 workdays. However, sixty percent fewer lost workdays and 523 fewer deaths would be avoided by enacting the Clean Power Act which would require old and antiquated power plants to limit their pollutants (Natural Resources Defense Council, no date).

Although the state of Michigan not only produces 50 million cubic yards of solid waste annually, (Michigan Waste Industries Association, no date), but the state up until 2006 imported millions of tons of trash from Canada and surrounding areas (Roper and van Guilder, 2006). Even though this was a big victory, Michigan's trash generating abilities will continue to grow--i.e., more slowly thus indicating that the siting and expansion of landfills will perhaps continue to be a growth area. There is more. In 1999, Michigan registered 18 unhealthy air days, second only to Pennsylvania (Minnesota Issue Watch, 2002). According to SEMCOG, Michigan has on the average 10 ozone action days per-season and had as many as 25 in (1999). In 2003, when Michigan smog pollution levels ranked 11th worst in the nation, smog levels in the Detroit Metropolitan Area exceeded EPA's health standards ranking the city 25th for the worst smog pollution among U.S. major cities (PIRGIM, 2004). Polluted waterways, and weak enforcement of pollution control laws are all threats to the health of the people of Michigan. Second, the accumulation structure is dominated by the automobile and related industries, particularly in the southeastern part of the State. The social structure of accumulation cannot exist unless there are safe, easy, and relatively inexpensive ways of disposing of toxic and hazardous waste or protecting our air, water, and land. The landscape in the southeastern part of the state is not only dominated by the automobile industry, but it has more landfills and incinerators and hazardous disposal facilities than perhaps any other place in the state.

Third, of the approximately 1,291,706 blacks, making up 13.9% of the State's population, about 60% live in Detroit. Compared to the white population, the geographic distribution of blacks is highly concentrated. As of 1990, while almost two-thirds of Michigan's white population lived in urban areas, almost the entire black population (97.1%) lived in urban areas. Approximately, 80% of Detroiters are black. Outside of the city of Detroit, large numbers of blacks live in Flint, Benton Harbor, Pontiac, and Grand Rapids, giving Michigan the reputation of being the most segregated state in the union with respect to race, and one of the most segregated by income (Rusk, 1993). Detroit, next to Benton Harbor, a city of 12,000 people, is the most segregated city in the State.

Fourth, the next largest population group is the Hispanics (201,596), who make up about 2% of the state population. Although Hispanics in the United States originate from more than a dozen Spanish-speaking countries, the largest group of Hispanics (about 69%) in Michigan are of Mexican origin. Although their percentage in the state population is small, they also tend to live in close proximity to toxic and hazardous waste more so than their more affluent white counterparts. A part of this population is invisible because each summer they work in the fields to harvest crops, spending long hours at back-breaking labor. They are often engulfed in pesticides and suffer from a number of health problems associated with their jobs. Also there is a sizable Arab population in the Dearborn area. They are over exposed to toxins from Ford Motor and other surrounding companies. Over the years, government health agencies have expressed considerable concerns about the health conditions of minorities.

Fifth, the University of Michigan School of Natural Resources and Environment has played a key role in researching and bringing currency to the disproportionate impacts of environmental hazards on people of color and low-income groups. In 1990, Bryant and Mohai invited scholar-activists to write and present papers at a retrieval/dissemination conference on Race and the Incidence of Environmental Hazards. The outcome of this conference led to a book called *Race and the Incidence of Environmental Hazards*, and a series of high-level policy meetings with EPA Administrators William K. Reilly and Carol Browner. This conference and other scholar-activists played a key role in getting President Clinton to sign the Environmental Justice Executive Order 12898. In 1990, Mohai and Bryant were co-principal investigators of the Detroit Area Study, which has served as the basis for several articles for peer-review journals.

Sixth, Michigan is the home of both very liberal and conservative tendencies. Over the years the labor movement has championed liberal causes such as increased wages and improved workplace safety conditions for workers; it has bargained for increased retirement packages and fringe benefits. It has been at the forefront of decent welfare and mental health programs for workers and the surrounding community. Yet on the other hand, George Wallace won the Michigan democratic primary in the 1960s. School buses were fire bombed in the 1970s to prevent school desegregation. In the early 1970s, the principal of Willow Run High School was tarred and feathered because of his liberal educational views. With the exception of Ohio, Michigan has more than twice the number of hate groups as compared to most other Midwestern states (Center for New Community, 2001).

The case study and research chapters included in this book describe only a few of the struggles that people in Michigan waged against toxins and those responsible for them. That struggle continues to take place in the cities of Inkster and Hamtramck, and in Augustna, Sumpter, and many other townships. The defeat of the proposed medical waste incinerator in Highland Park and the phase out of the Ford Hospital Medical Waste Incinerator are victories that should be celebrated. As more and more low-income and minority communities become aware of their vulnerability, and as they become aware of numerous environmental stressors in their communities, they may be motivated to resist government and corporate attempts to use their communities for waste disposal sites. Hazardous and toxic waste may shape both the civil rights and the environment movement in the 21st Century. Many groups in Michigan are struggling to make their communities safe from toxins. The solutions to the problems experienced by people in Michigan are perhaps no different than problems experienced by people in other communities throughout the country. In the past, Michigan took the lead for industrial growth, and in the future the state could take the lead in the manufacture of pollution abatement and control technology as a way of creating decent paying and safe jobs. For all these reasons, Michigan is an excellent site for study.

Chapter 2, by Bryant and Hockman, provides an overview of environmental justice issues. This overview includes a review of the literature, the role of the social structure of accumulation in the production of hazardous waste and its disposal, the problem of the disproportionate burden of hazardous waste on low-income communities and communities of color as reflected by two national studies, the development of competition among countries and states, and the feelings of distrust, anger, and fear of those populations who live close to polluting facilities.

Chapter 3, by Bryant and Mohai, is based upon the Detroit Area Study; it reports findings related to African-American awareness of environmental issues and differences and similarities between black and white perception of more abstract environmental issues such as acid rain, depletion of the ozone layer, and loss of places for fish and wildlife to live, as well as quality of life issues.

Chapter 4, by Hockman, Bryant, and Morris, describes the data from which several of the quantitative studies are based. They discuss methodology issues, demographic variables, unit of analysis, ecological fallacy, measurement and causality issues. They also discuss the various denials of corporations and how these denials are used as a defensive posture to prevent them from taking responsibility for their action. An introduction to chapters 5 through 12 will be taken up in the Methodology chapter. At the end of the Methodology chapter an introduction to the remaining chapters will be presented.

Statistics used in the studies confirm many of the beliefs voiced by citizens. Although we are not able to prove causality, we believe that the overexposure of toxins does make people vulnerable to health risks. In the following pages we present the information so you can draw your own conclusions. A special thanks go to the students who labored hard to write the chapters included in this volume. Although the data collection and analysis focused primarily on the southeastern part of the state of Michigan and the Flint area, these data and the analysis based upon these data are more than 20 years old. However, we feel that very little has changed over the years in the state of Michigan. In fact things may have gotten worse. But we feel that mistakes made in the past can be helpful to policymakers, researchers and environmental activists in the future. Also we feel that the quantitative analysis and case studies written in this book can serve as a base or reference point from which future studies can be compared or assessed.

It is difficult to do a study as rigorously as one would like to, and to conclude findings in which one has complete confidence. Two of the 13 chapters are based on primary data sources from the 1990 Detroit Area Study, while 8 chapters in the book are based upon secondary data sources. We had to assume that these secondary data resources were collected and reported rigorously by the state. We feel this book will make a significant contribution in helping us understand the nature of the environmental justice problem here in Michigan. And perhaps our understanding of these problems may have implications for the nation as a whole.

2

ENVIRONMENTAL JUSTICE: OVERVIEW

Bunyan Bryant and Elaine Hockman

Many of the problems of pollution we face today are augmented by the social structure of accumulation. This structure consists of the political system, organized labor, the market system supported by government protection, laws, entitlements, subsidies, certain rights and guarantees—all of which are designed and integrated to maintain order and to ensure profits. It is an accumulation structure that allows the accumulation of profits and the allocation of services at considerable costs to nature. While the structure supports the accumulation of profits, it also supports the accumulation of millions of tons of waste that must be disposed of safely every year.

Perhaps no other society in the history of the world has produced as much gross national product as the United States. At the same time, perhaps no other society has produced as much waste. Although we are only six percent of the world's population, U.S. citizens utilize approximately 40 percent of the world's resources, and we are responsible for approximately 40 percent of the world's pollution. As the nation grows and develops economically, we will use a greater share of the world's resources and produce a greater share of the world's pollution. We produce not only chemicals that deplete the ozone layer and chemicals that cause global warming, but we produce chemicals that create acid rain and other pollutants that significantly destroy the environment. Even though we hear much talk of sustainable development, these rumblings are only on the margins; they do not impact significantly our growth and development ethic. In May 1999, at the Cobo Convention Center in Detroit, the President's Council on Sustainable Development had its National Town Hall meeting. The question is what will be the long-term effect of this town hall meeting? Although encouraged, we are also practical because we recognize the lack of political will and the widespread bureaucratic inertia that impede progress. Although that now may be changing.

Furthermore, some supporters of sustainable development neglect the concept of justice; they fail to incorporate environmental justice within their vocabulary in any meaningful way. This leads us to ask: sustainability for whom? Who benefits and who benefits the most? Unless sustainable develop ment deals with the issue of justice forthrightly, ideas of sustainability will perhaps always be viewed with suspicion, particularly by communities of color and low-income groups.

Review of the Literature

Multiple studies and social protests show that people of color are dispro- portionately overburdened with environmental hazards. The general public, policymakers, social scientists, and others are now showing more concern. Empirical validation by a host of studies now suggests that we can no longer assume that environmental hazards impact everyone in society more or less equally. Evidence has been mounting to suggest that low-income groups and people of color are significantly affected more so than are their white, often more affluent counterparts (Asch and Seneca, 1978; Berry, 1977; Bullard, 1990; Commission for Racial Justice, 1987; Faber, 2002; Harrison, 1975; Kruvant, 1975; U.S. General Accounting Office, 1983; Council on Environmental Qual- ity, 1971; Freeman, 1972; Gelobter, 1988; Gianessi et al., 1979; West, 1992a; Zupan, 1973; Lavelle and Coyle, 1992; Morello-Frosch, et al. 2002; Pine et al., 2000; Burke, 1993; Wilson, 2002). The overwhelming majority of these studies have shown that not only are people of color and low-income groups disproportionately burdened by elevated levels of pollutants, but they have led researchers to investigate who the primary beneficiaries are (Asch and Seneca, 1978; Gelobter, 1988; Kruvant, 1975; Zupan, 1973; Lavelle and Coyle, 1992).

Even though uniform standards exist, it took 20% longer for Superfund sites in communities of color to be placed on the national priority list compared with more affluent white communities. The fines in white communities for violating Resource Conservation and Recovery Act (RCRA) regulations were six times greater than in minority communities (Lavelle and Coyle 1992). Such policy implementation clearly indicates that if one lives in a poor and/or minority com- munity, the probability is greater that the government will fail to provide equal protection. Yet, the enforcement of uniform air standards via the Clean Air Act has provided people of color and the inner city poor the greatest improvements in air quality. However, that improvement does not necessarily mean that the quality of the air is satisfactory compared with more affluent white areas. Even though improvements have been made in urban ambient air quality, it may still be below acceptable standards.

Other studies showing the relationship between race and the siting of toxic disposal facilities include the following: In 1983, the United States General Accounting Office (GAO) found that three out of four of the largest landfills (75%) in EPA's Region 4 were in predominantly African-American communities.

In 1987, a nationwide study sponsored by the Commission of Racial Justice of the United Church of Christ found that the majority (54.2%) of all Americans lived near uncontrolled (illegal) hazardous waste sites.

This study showed that while 56.3% of all people of color lived near an uncontrolled hazardous waste site, 53.6% of all whites lived near them. Although people of color were slightly more burdened, both groups were significantly exposed. While uncontrolled[1] hazardous waste sites were more equally distributed in communities regardless of color, the study reported that twice the percentage of commercial hazardous waste sites (where siting decisions were made in the public or corporate sector) were found in people of color communities compared with their white counterparts (23.7% vs. 12.3%).

Goldman (1994) reviewed 64 studies and found an overwhelming body of empirical evidence that people of color and lower-income groups face disproportionate environmental impacts in the United States. He reported that racial disparities were found more frequently than income disparities with respect to various kinds of environmental concerns . When race and income were compared, race proved more important in nearly three-quarters of the statistical tests (22 out of 30).

The research results of the 1990 Detroit Area Study (DAS) were consistent with most of the literature cited above. Although there were 21 commercial hazardous waste facilities in the state of Michigan, 16 (76%) of them were located within the tri-county (Wayne, Oakland, and Macomb) area in the southeastern part of the state. Of the 16, half were located within the city limits of Detroit. Yet as indicated by the U.S. Census Bureau data, the percentages of minorities for the tri-county area was approximately 21 percent African American, while the city of Detroit was approximately 80% African American. Therefore, we concluded that commercial hazardous waste facilities are disproportionately concentrated in areas heavily populated by minorities. This study found that a heavier concentration of minorities and people below the poverty line lived within a mile of commercial hazardous waste facilities. However, as the spatial distance increased from these facilities, there was a corresponding decrease in the percentages of minorities and low-income people.

Although the overwhelming number of studies claim that race was a greater explanatory variable than income, several studies concluded the opposite (Morris and Perle, 1996; Markham and Rufa, 1997). Bowen, et al. (1995) found that in Cuyahoga County, Ohio, white residents were more likely to live in tracts containing higher concentrations of toxic release. Anderton et al. (1994) posited that if one uses census tracts as the unit of analysis, Treatment Storage

---

[1]   Uncontrolled hazardous waste sites are referred to in the study as illegal waste sites.

and Disposal Facilities (TSDFs) are no more likely to be located in tracts with higher percentages of blacks than in any other tracts. In the tri-county area of Detroit, Tomboulian et al. (1995) found that industrial land use was a far more powerful indicator of environmental pollution than were racial factors. Yandle and Burton (1996) found that hazardous waste sites were originally placed in areas that were predominantly poor but also predominantly white. Been (1994) raises the question of whether the disproportionate burdens of locally undesirable land uses (LULUs) were due to siting decisions or to discrimination in the housing market. Boerner and Lambert (1995) expressed methodological concerns with current environmental equity research because of the lack of a meaningful definition of what constitutes a minority population.

Mounting evidence is emerging that long-term exposure to hazardous environmental conditions may result in serious risk to public health. While Geschwind, et al. (1992) found that women who lived near hazardous waste sites had significantly higher numbers of children born with birth defects, Wang, et al. (1997) linked low-birth weight to air pollution in China. Koren and Utell (1997) linked significant increases in asthma with polluted ambient air quality. Also Pershagen and Simonato (1990) and Steingraber (1997) and Cushman (1997) strongly linked cancers with the presence of chemicals in the environment.

Social science literature indicates that the political and economic vulnerability of people of color and low-income groups may be key explanatory variables for the spatial location of toxic and hazardous waste in certain communities. The potential to become politically active to protect their community from toxins is enhanced by access to resources such as time, money, information, content, organizational skills, and knowledge of the geopolitical system (McCarthy and Zald, 1977; Jenkins, 1983). Can what has been termed as learned helplessness and alienation be overcome? Can political efficacy, personal efficacy, and internal control be improved upon to lower the political and economic vulnerability of certain groups of people? (For more information on these terms, see Gamson, 1968; Orr, 1974; Craig, 1979; Orum, 1974; Rotter, 1966, 1975). Groups with the fewest resources may perhaps be least likely to become politically active, yet they may be motivated to overcome their sense of powerlessness because of perceived risk to themselves and their families. Acts of protest or threat orientation may become resources within themselves in order to compensate for resources lacking in other areas. Confidence that their actions will make a difference is important for people to mobilize themselves. People more than ever are taking to the streets to protest high-risk situations and to improve their quality of life.

The Social Structure of Accumulation

Many of the problems of pollution we face today are augmented by the social structure of accumulation. This structure consists of the political system, organized labor, the market system supported by government protection, laws, entitlements, subsidies, certain rights and guarantees—all of which are designed and integrated to maintain order and to ensure profits. It is an accumulation structure that allows the accumulation of profits and the allocation of services at considerable costs to nature. While the structure supports the accumulation of profits, it also supports the accumulation of millions of tons of waste that must be disposed of safely every year. In every industrialized society the accumulation structure emphasizes profit-making more than waste-making. To make a profit and remain competitive, businesses are compelled to put forth their best possible product. Unfortunately, the drive to make a profit does not compel businesses to spend an equivalent amount of time and money in developing the best possible means of waste disposal. The accumulation structure seems to be more attentive to social "goods" driven by the market and less attentive to social "bads" which are seldom driven by the market. Economists often refer to social "bads" as externalities because the true cost of production is not factored into the price of the product. For example, if the true cost of production were factored into automobile production, perhaps we would have an accumulation structure that would result in fewer pollutants and healthier communities. We would also have fewer toxic-induced and aggravated diseases that require out-of-pocket money for medical health care bills. Government and corporate sectors are attempting to bring social "bads" into the market place in the form of tradeable emissions, which will be discussed more fully later on.

At least 7.6 billion pounds of hazardous waste were burned in the United States in 1989 by more than 1,100 incinerators, cement and aggregate kilns, and industrial boilers. With the encouragement of government regulations, this network of incinerators and related technologies had been growing. Yet state and federal governments have made little or no attempt to assess the total health and environmental impact of pollutants released by them (Costner and Thornton, 1990).

Although waste disposal systems are an integral part of the accumulation system, such disposal systems have been inadequate. Even with state-of-the-art incinerators, heavy metals, unburned waste, and products of incomplete combustion (PICs) often form new chemicals during incineration. Metals that are not destroyed in the incineration process—19 of them have been identified so far—are in turn released in forms that are more dangerous than the original waste. An average-size commercial incinerator burning hazardous waste with an average metal content emits approximately 204,000 pounds per year and annually deposits another 670,000 pounds of metals in residual ashes and liquids (Costner and Thornton, 1990). Even though an incinerator may achieve 99.99 percent destruction and removal efficiency, that highly efficient incinerator still releases approximately 7,000 pounds of unburned chemicals into the air annually. Some of the products of incomplete combustion formed during incineration are far more dangerous to health and well-being than are others. In some cases, dioxins, furans, PCBs, and other complex organochlorines are among the most toxic and persistent. Despite the knowledge that low exposures to many metals, organochlorines, and other pollutants have been known to cause cancer, birth defects, reproductive dysfunction, neurological damage and respiratory ailments, we continue to operate incinerators as if there were no evidence that pointed to their harmful effects. Also while the idea of incinerators seems to be a good one in that they reduce waste to 60 to 90 percent of the original weight, they still produce approximately 342 million pounds of ash residues per year. These residues are then buried in landfills even though they are known to contain PICs, PCBs, and other hazardous waste (Costner and Thornton, 1990).

Activist citizens have expressed concern not only about the potential dangers of smokestack emissions, but also about the downward migration of these hazardous emissions and bottom ash into the soil structure and into the underground water table. Because contaminated underground water takes years to cleanse itself, it will eventually pollute the water table for miles around, affecting not only poor communities where landfills are often located but the more affluent ones as well.

Something has to be done with incinerators and the waste produced by society. This dilemma will be increasingly difficult to resolve, particularly in the face of the exponential growth of hazardous waste. To deal with hazardous waste in an environmentally sound way, we must also deal with the market system. While most of the emphasis has been placed upon growing an economy, increasing jobs and incomes, very little attention has been placed upon the growing of waste. For the social structure of accumulation to survive, we must find acceptable, safe, and relatively inexpensive ways to deal with the millions of tons of solid and toxic waste generated each year. If we fail to bring our waste stream under control, it will undermine the system of accumulation that has been carefully spun over the last three hundred years or more.

There have been more landfills and incinerators in action or in the planning stage in southeastern Michigan than in most other parts of the state. This is due in large measure to the industrial character of this region, the automobile manufacturing capital of the nation. Because southeastern Michigan has a number of commercial hazardous waste facilities or polluting or toxic inventory sites in operation or in the planning stage, this region is a particularly important one for study. From our interviews with people directly affected by commercial hazardous waste facilities, we hope to glean important insights that will be helpful in solving the conflict between local community groups and those who want to dump. We hope to obtain insights from people's struggles, insights that will in turn be helpful to other groups throughout the country.

With a population approaching a million people, Detroit is Wayne County's and the state's largest city. It is approximately 80 percent black and has been the site of a declining automobile industry. When the Greater Detroit Resource Recovery Facility in downtown Detroit was built in the 1980s it was the largest incinerator in the world. It was built to keep industry in Detroit and to encourage other businesses to relocate there, increasing job opportunities for the unemployed, thus helping to revitalize the city. The incinerator was designed to receive and process 4,000 tons of raw waste each day, using state-of-the-art equipment. Of the 4,000 tons, 2,500 tons of Refuse Derived Fuel was to be burned per day in two of the facility's three boilers (the third one is a backup). Each can produce 387,000 pounds of steam per hour, 24 hours per day, seven days a week, supplying electricity to over 35,000 homes exclusively from garbage. What turned out to be a novel idea for policymakers became a nightmare for those living near the incinerator and for those who were concerned about the variety of hazardous waste emitted in the fly ash from stacks of the incinerator and from the bottom ash buried in Sumpter Township about 20 miles from downtown Detroit, in the southernmost corner of Wayne County. We hasten to add that environmental justice is more than resistance to incinerators and landfills, it is also resistance to polluting industries of all types and sizes that disproportionately impact communities of color and low-income in negative ways. Environmental justice is concerned about those in poverty who are vulnerable to one of the worst forms of pollution and lead poisoning that attacks the nervous system of our youngsters—particularly those in inner cities or who live in houses built before 1978. The task of environmental justice advocates is to challenge the accumulation system to be more just and humane. As you read the following pages keep in mind how the social structure of accumulation may apply to the concept of environmental justice.

Competition among Countries, and States

Following World War II, the United States subsidized not only the European accumulation structure through the Marshall Plan, but it also subsidized the Japanese accumulation structure to a point where both of these economies have come of age and are now competing with the U.S. in the world market. Increased labor costs, competition from foreign automobile industries, along with the energy crisis of the 1970s, were key contributors to the decline of the structure of accumulation and the Detroit automotive industry. The energy crisis caught American car companies at the height of big car production. Responding mainly to the high costs of gasoline, consumers rejected the big gas-guzzlers made by American companies and turned instead to smaller, more gasoline-efficient foreign cars. The foreign car invasion cost many American workers their jobs. Since the time of the energy crisis, the automobile companies have had their ups and downs. Even though the American automobile companies have rebounded in recent years, with the help of government subsidies, the industry is now a very different one. Although automobile production will continue to increase, it will do so with fewer human workers because computer-driven machines, increased outsourcing and corporate downsizing, displacing thousands of workers.

The Greater Resource Recovery Facility was one of many things Detroit tried in order to create a climate supportive of profitability and jobs. Another major undertaking was the city's underwriting of the destruction of the Poletown neighborhood so that General Motors could build a modern automobile plant. The city was bending over backwards to attract and keep the automobile industry alive in Detroit, attract new enterprises, and support the system of accumulation.

Incinerators and landfills are not the only way of enticing companies to locate in a given state in order to strengthen its economy. In what amounts to a public "bribe," states across the country have put together attractive financial packages to lure large corporations and industries (Goodman, 1979). Large companies offering hundreds of jobs find themselves in an excellent negotiating position with states. Since profits are the bottom line, and since companies want the best deal possible for plant location, they have become very astute at playing one state off against another. For instance, Georgia is a "right-to-work" state, meaning that it is harder to unionize in that state than in northern industrial ones. Wages in Georgia are generally low, with little history of strikes, high worker absenteeism, or labor-management conflict. Georgia, in fact, boasts about its deplorable working conditions. To compete with right-to-work states, other states spend millions of state and local monies to subsidize industry through tax abatements and urban renewal projects. These urban renewal projects include building railway and highway corridors so industry can transport their goods, lending money to companies at lower interest rates, and instituting tax-supported worker training programs. States have even used pension funds to finance training programs for industry and have lowered worker compensation costs to industry as means of luring them. Hard-earned gains by labor have been eroded as states compete with one another, boasting about the worst possible labor conditions in order to attract industry (Goodman, 1979). State and local governments pass regressive legislation to put together financial packages that erode health, workplace safety, and environmental protection.

Chambers of Commerce at the local level do projection studies and work closely with local mayors and city councils to enhance the city as a growth machine. Zoning laws are changed and tax abatements are given to encourage growth and development of new roads, sewer, and water lines. New parking structures at tax payers' expense are another form of subsidy to attract industry. Undesirable industries, incinerators, and commercial landfills are often located in minority and low-income neighborhoods—neighborhoods that are already confounded by a number of environmental insults. Also, older city dwellings are left to the new influx of young black families whose children often become victims of lead poisoning from eating flakes of lead-based paint or from drinking water from eroded solder-joint water pipes. Needleman, cited in Truax (1990), stated that lead poisoning not only results in school failure, disordered thinking, impaired muscle control, and reduced verbal skills, but it causes children to adopt anti-social responses and thus end up in the criminal justice system. These antisocial behaviors are increasingly met with more state control and oppression. The federal Centers for Disease Control state that lead poisoning endangers the health of nearly eight million inner-city, mostly black and Hispanic, children. Countless more live with crumbling asbestos in housing projects (cited in Russell, 1989).

An increase in deaths from asthma may be attributed to air pollution in inner-city neighborhoods. Deaths from asthma have increased by one-third nationally in the past decade. There may be a relationship between victims and where they live in that asthma kills blacks at three times the rate it kills their white counterparts. McCaull (1977) stated that if a person was black, had a low income, and lived in an impoverished area, the chances were far above average that he or she would be exposed to toxins that were more intense and more injurious to health than experienced by their more affluent white counterparts. Kruvant's (1975) study in Washington, D.C., stated that when taking the entire population of the poor into consideration, the probability was much greater that the poor would live in a higher pollution area.

Using hazardous waste disposal facilities to attract and maintain industries means jobs and prosperity. To keep the ones it already has from fleeing to less regulated states or Third World countries, Detroit must build cheap disposal facilities for industry. A 1985 report by Southeast Michigan Council of Governments (SEMCOG) prepared for the Metropolitan Affairs Corporation stated that the scarcity of hazardous waste disposal sites prevents expansion of industry and capital investments, and could drive business away. The questions become: should the state sacrifice long-term health of its citizens by building commercial hazardous waste facilities to attract polluting industries for short-term economic gain? What mitigation measures seem appropriate for the compensation of risks? What compensation measures would be appropriate for a fair redistribution between predicted winners and losers? How do we define equity when siting a hazardous waste facility in a given neighborhood? What are the costs and risks involved with people living near such facilities? These are questions that must be evaluated on an ongoing basis. As more and more products are placed on the market, there will be an increasing need to dispose of them and/or their by-products safely. More often than not, these by-products of "goods" and "services" may be hazardous and life-threatening. In a given year thousands of new chemicals will appear on the market; we seldom know the singular or combined impact these chemicals will have on our lives.

The Michigan Department of Environmental Quality's (MDEQ)[2] interest is to manage the state's waste safely so as to protect the public health and environment and at the same time to ensure that profits can be made. If MDEQ denies permits or applies excessive fines to force polluting industries to adhere to strict environmental regulations, this would discourage companies from doing business in Michigan and this would certainly fail to serve the long term interest of the State. Because Michigan already finds itself needing to convince industry to remain in the state, it has a dire need for safe and clean hazardous waste disposal facilities. Although environmental regulations are viewed by industry to be the culprit, industries will shut their doors and close shop rather than replace inefficient and outdated equipment.

The power or the weakness of the MDEQ is manifested by the small number of staff at its disposal. Even at its peak staffing levels, the state did not have enough qualified people for monitoring purposes. The Berlin-Farro controversy near Flint showed what can happen when lower level and untrained bureaucrats in legal or administrative positions are in charge of regulating hazardous waste facilities. The state regulatory agency found itself in somewhat of a permissive role and allowed hazardous waste facility owners like Chuck Berlin of Berlin-Farro to take advantage of the situation (Truchan, 1986). Due to its lack of qualified personnel, the state often has to accept what companies say at face value. In addition, over the years corporations have offered employment to professionals from the Michigan Department of Natural Resources (MDNR), creating a revolving door between "Aid to Dependent Corporations" and MDNR. It is to the companies' advantage to have former employees of the regulatory agencies on their payroll because such staff understand the operating procedures of government agencies and are familiar with appropriate channels

---

[2] The Department of Environmental Quality was created by Executive Order No. 1995-18, which transferred environmental regulatory programs from the Department of Natural Resources to the newly created Department. Subsequently, the following executive orders transferred additional responsibilities to the Department.

to work through to make things easier when dealing with the state. Former employees of regulatory agencies are good at cutting through the "red tape," allowing for a much smoother permitting process. And to make the permitting process easier, the state amended Act 64. The amended act was a response to the state's frustration with local communities and their ability to thwart siting proposals. Act 64 (Michigan Hazardous Waste Management Act) as amended, prohibited local governments from passing or implementing ordinances for the sole purpose of preventing the siting of hazardous waste facilities.

Race, Income, and Equity Discussion

The issue of whether income or race is the better predictor will dominate the debate on the siting of commercial hazardous waste facilities in this country for some time to come. There is indeed an income effect: poor white communities are indeed affected, but objective data, particularly from the 1987 United Church of Christ Report and the 1990 Detroit Area Study and many others as noted before, clearly indicate that the race effect is more important than the income effect in the location of commercial hazardous waste facilities. Interviews of a township official and several black people who lived near a landfill in Sumpter Township in Wayne County are instructive. Ms. P, a black woman responding to a question as to whether class or race was important in locating such facilities, responded with "class yes and race yes, and in that order." Yet, Freddie, a black man, felt that racial factors have a lot to do with the siting of a hazardous waste facility and that a black community would be chosen before a white one. Wanda, a black woman, stated that if it came down to a choice between a white community and a black one, the black one would be chosen before the white one. A white Sumpter Township official, when asked the same question, stated: "It's not so much race, but income and class that dictate where landfills are sited. I think race is an issue, but only after income and class" (DeGannes et al., 1991). It is interesting to note that while two of the three black people interviewed indicated that race was more important in the location of the landfill, the white official reported that income or class dictated where landfills are sited. The debate over race vs. social class can become divisive: white Americans will tenaciously cling to social class as the explanation because historically and even today it has been difficult for them to view racism as a potent force that is operating to disenfranchise people of color.

Issues of Trust, Anger, and Fear

Uncertainty about the health impacts of toxic wastes has concerned citizens across the nation. Some of that concern has turned to activism as people protest and challenge both government and corporate siting decisions that affect their communities. People are determined to fight to make their neighborhoods safe or keep them free of life-threatening poisons. In Los Angeles, a group of citizens prevented the California Waste Management Board from building five incinerators; in Warren County, North Carolina, blacks and whites banded together to prevent the landfill in their county from becoming a permanent site for the burial of PCBs. People fought to keep the Detroit incinerator from being brought on line, even though they ultimately lost. A coalition of environmental and community groups succeeded in closing down the Henry Ford Medical Waste Incinerator. Only one out of 159 medical waste incinerators still exists in the state, a testimony to the critical role that community activists and environmentalists have played over the years (Garfield, 2000).

People who feel they are at risk organize out of anger and out of fear for their health and the health of their children and loved ones. Public health, natural resource and agricultural officials often fail to heed their complaints. However, to operate from the assumption that scientific information is too complex for lay people to understand, or that they are too emotional or irrational, only breeds contempt and distrust of governmental officials. While governmental offices define "risk communication" as getting people to respond appropriately to protect themselves from environmental threats, risk communication is now taking on new meaning for community activists. In order to be taken seriously community activists are using their anger to organize large numbers of people to empower themselves to confront and to communicate effectively personal health risk to professional decision-makers. They often combine both science and the mobilization of a variety of resources to gain the attention of policymakers. When activists use science and threats of militant action, the relationship between them and professionals becomes more symmetrical in character, and where there is mutual respect conditions for communication improve.

To avoid or lessen moral outrage, governmental officials must change their widely held assumptions about community activists and integrally involve them in the decision-making that affects their communities. Even without advanced degrees in science, community activists are generally well-informed. This is supported by Freudenberg (1984), who stated that the vast majority of activist groups interact regularly and effectively with scientists (89%) and health professionals (73%). Freudenberg also stated that experts were identified as the groups' most important valued source of information, indicating a sophisticated understanding of toxic and hazardous waste issues. With such understanding, it would be a mistake to prevent activist groups from being a part of the decision-making process or to keep information away from them. Freudenberg further stated that if citizens feel they are victims of a cover-up or that an agency has not been forthright with them, they will form an adversarial relationship with professionals in order to get what they want.

To withhold information only breeds more distrust and suspicion, increasing the level of hostility and anger toward officialdom. Wanda, a resident of Sumpter Township, was interviewed about the landfill in the Township and said: "We didn't even know it was going to be a landfill until it was too late to do anything about it because it happened so fast." Can we as citizens trust our government, which is supposed to protect us? Can we trust corporations? Jay of Sumpter Township said that all governmental officials are crooked and that he trusts none of them. Gladys of Augusta Township raised the issue of trust in talking about a landfill near her house. She said, "We've been lied to many times. I used to trust the government when I was younger and did not know any better." (DeGannes et al., 1991). We feel it does not have to be this way. People should be able to trust their government because the government is supposed to work for them. Freudenberg (1984) found that activist groups, if involved in the information flow and decision-making process, were cooperative and understood the broader issues and complexity of environmental problems and worked cooperatively to solve them.

Although regulatory officials and community people may not always agree on what constitutes risks, they should address the issue of trust and perception. Perceptions may not always be based on fact, but they are real to people and people often operate as if they are facts. A failure to address both the perceptual and factual issues may lead to or exacerbate distrust or conflict. Another factor that gives rise to distrust in government is the lack of interagency coordination and lack of trained professionals. Because of the variety of new wastes and new technologies, government agencies are often uncertain about their impact; they are uncertain about how to test for safety or to formulate acceptable risks. For example, in 1985 almost a year after MDNR had issued a permit to operate the incinerator in Detroit, Gerald Avery, director of the Permit Section in the Michigan Department of Natural Resources, discovered an engineering calculation error. What was thought to be relatively safe (1 in 1,000,000 chances of getting cancer in one's lifetime) was now cited to be unsafe (1 in 1,000), 19 times greater than any risks the state had approved. This led to a war of statistics in which the Department of Public Health came up with a different figure and Weston Consultants, hired by the company that ran the incinerator, came up with yet another set of figures. Who was right? Who could be trusted? Although it was important that MDNR owned up to the fact that it had made a mistake, such mistakes and contradictory information cost both the public and private institutions the trust and confidence of citizens and increased the anger and frustration of community groups.

The above example is not only of an agency attempting to correct its mistake, but also of what Rogers and Whetten (1982) called "fragmented services," that is, of the incompatible jurisdictional boundaries and contradictory program standards that prevent governmental agencies from putting together a comprehensive program of services. In the 1970s at different periods of the Berlin-Farro crisis the Michigan Department of Environmental Quality, Air Pollution Control Commission, and the Toxic Substance Control Commission were all involved and each had its own policy on how to handle the situation. Various agencies and commissions confused not only local citizens but state agency and other government workers as well. Different agencies were filing suit against Berlin-Ferro and often gave Berlin-Farro contradictory information. The confusion, the complexity of the bureaucracy, the lack of communication and coordination among government agencies, and their failure to respond within a reasonable amount of time contributed to citizens' anger and distrust of government bureaucracies at all levels. Undoubtedly this predicament also frustrated governmental officials who failed to respond adequately to the need of citizens who depended upon them for protection. Interagency coordination if perfected can help reduce redundancy and extend the size of the technical resource pool. Often there are just not enough trained people to monitor hazardous waste disposal facilities or polluting industries. Interagency coordination can help economize monitoring efforts by sharing costs of programs. It can also reduce the cost of innovation since multiple agencies will each contribute a portion of the venture capital as we move into an era of shrinking resources (Rogers and Whetten, 1982). While the concept of interagency is fine on paper, it will not work unless the agencies can overcome organizational inertia. Even though the Toxic Substance Control Commission (no longer in existence) played this coordinating role, we found in the Berlin-Farro Case Study that Verna Courtemanche who lived in proximity to the landfill had to go to numerous government agencies and hearings to seek help. Her anger and alienation at what she experienced is clear when she said:

> I have been patronized, scoffed at, and belittled, called names such as hysterical housewife, paranoid citizen, meddling gray panther, and a few other names I do not care to mention. I have been put off, given the runaround, lied to, and put "on hold." I have become doubtful and suspicious, not only with the government and its representatives, but I find that this same suspicious attitude is spilling over into my personal relationships. *I don't like this!*

Case studies that are presented here could be also told by people from communities across the country. These case studies do not represent a random sample but a purposive sample of how both incinerators and landfills are impacting people's lives. Low-income and minority communities already experience a disproportionate amount of life-and health-threatening environmental stressors;

they are the most vulnerable and least likely to resist and protect themselves from the siting of commercial hazardous waste facilities; they are often least able to afford health insurance or hospitalization. In a rapid growth-oriented society, we can expect the by-products of production or environmental hazards to increase, thus creating problems of safe disposals. We are running out of land space for commercial hazardous waste facilities. We are not only producing more toxins and hazards but an additional problem is the temporal and spatial relations that result from the by-products of new technology: we are polluting larger and larger areas, and it takes the Earth more and more time to heal itself. Even though hazardous wastes may be buried "safely," their potential danger like nuclear waste may linger for hundreds and in some cases thousands of years and threaten precious underground water supplies and our existence on planet earth. Calculations of the cost of production fail to take into account subsidies that people must pay with their health and even their lives, so that others can live a life-style of affluence. We must reverse this perilous trend and provide environmental protection and quality of life for all regardless of income, race, or where they may live.

———————————

ENVIRONMENTAL AWARENESS, HAZARDOUS WASTE, AND THE DISPROPORTIONATE IMPACT ON LOW-INCOME COMMUNITIES AND COMMUNITIES OF COLOR

Bunyan Bryant and Paul Mohai

While we anticipated that blacks' answers to these quality of life ques-tions would be qualitatively different from those of their white counter-parts, we were surprised to find that there were more similarities than differences between the two groups on more abstract environmental issues. Taken together, blacks may demonstrate a greater environmental concern than whites in the Detroit area.

Today the growing concern is not only about the importance of clean and pristine wilderness areas or wetlands, but there is a growing concern about the quality of life in local neighborhoods. People of color have always been concerned about high levels of crime, decent schools for their children, accessible neighborhood recreation facilities, the number of boarded up homes in their community, and a whole host of problems that impinge upon their life. They are becoming equally concerned about the disproportionate numbers of locally undesirable land uses (LULUs), such as incinerators, landfills, and polluting industries, sited or to be sited in their com-munities. Although they expressed dissatisfaction with large numbers of LULUs in their neighborhoods, they also criticized the slow response of government to ameliorate environmental conditions in their communities as compared to more affluent white neighborhoods. Both the overburden of LULUs and differential response to environmental cleanups in people of color communities have been defined as "environmental racism."

The Detroit Area

For almost 50 years, the Detroit Area Study has collected data from Ma-comb, Oakland, and Wayne Counties—the three counties surrounding Detroit and known collectively as the Tri-County Area. Each year the study, under different University of Michigan faculty investigators, chooses a different area of inquiry. In 1990, the area of inquiry was the environment. The Detroit area, as defined by the study, is a part of the industrial heartland of the Great Lakes

Region. It is strategically located near an international corridor of waterways for the shipping of raw materials and manufactured goods. In 1987, the total value contributed by manufacturing to the state amounted to sixty billion dollars. The leading industrial groups ranked by employment were transportation and equipment, industrial machines and equipment, fabricated metal production, and primary metal industries. These accounted for about 55% of the state's 1987 employment. Ranked by employment, Wayne, Oakland, Macomb, and Kent counties lead the state. Together they accounted for approximately 54% of the state's 1987 manufacturing employment.

It is clear that the southeastern part of Michigan is the hub not only of in-dustrial growth, but also of commercial hazardous waste facilities and industrial pollution. To allow industrial growth without having adequate hazardous waste disposal facilities has the potential for creating considerable problems for any manufacturing sector and the people who live there. Production cannot continue unless the problem of waste disposal is dealt with, or it may ultimately curtail economic growth, thus disrupting the social fabric and well-being of people in the surrounding area. Therefore, having places to store, treat, and dispose of hazardous waste is of political and economic significance. Of the 21 commercial hazardous waste facilities in Michigan, 16 (76%) are located in the Tri-County Area, and of the 16 sites, half are located in Detroit. The census data indicated that Wayne County is 57% white and 40% black, with 3% other. This is in sharp contrast to the surrounding counties: Macomb 97% white, 1% black, and 2% other; Oakland 90% white, 7% black, and 3% other. As a whole, whites make up 74% of the Tri-County Area, blacks 25%, and other 1%. The city of Detroit, however, is 80% black and less than 20% white.

Given the impact of economic growth upon the environment in the Tri-County Area and given the location of the commercial hazardous waste facilities we pose the following questions. Are there differences and similarities between environmental awareness, attitudes, opinions, and concerns of blacks and whites? Are blacks too concerned about their daily survival to be concerned about the environment? We were particularly interested in the latter question, one raised repeatedly by white environmentalists. We were interested not only in the black and white awareness of the differential siting and cleanups of hazardous waste facilities and sites, but also in their similarities and differences of opinion about more abstract environmental issues. To test this notion of black disinterest in the environment, we decided to assess the Detroit area residents' awareness and perceptions of both abstract and specific neighborhood environmental issues. To answer these questions, we used the data from the University of Michigan 1990 Detroit Area Study—a study of 793 face-to-face interviews of residents 18 years or older in the area. Respondents were identified from households that

Table 3.1: Percent of Whites and Blacks in the Detroit Area Who "Strongly Agree" on a Wide Range of Opinions About Environmental Issues

Environmental Issues	Blacks	Whites	Differences
Humans must live in harmony with nature to survive.	58%	67%	-9%
There are limits to growth beyond which our society cannot expand.	26	30	-4
Humans have the right to change the natural environment to suit their needs.	23	9	14*
When humans interfere with nature, it often produces disastrous consequences.	54	56	-2

*p < .001

were selected with equal probability using a stratified two-stage area probability sampling design.

In order to assess the awareness and concerns of blacks and whites in the Detroit area, we asked the residents to rate their level of agreement with a range of abstract environmental statements, such as: "humans must live in harmony," "there are limits to growth," "humans have the right to change the natural environment," and "when humans interfere with nature, it often produces disastrous consequences." With the exception of one question, "humans have the right to change their natural environment to suit their needs," we found no significant differences between blacks and whites (Table 3.1). "Humans have the right to change the natural environment to suit their needs" was an issue with which blacks were more likely than whites to be in strong agreement.

We next asked the Detroit residents to rate the level of seriousness of a number of issues (Table 3.2) that were more specific and less philosophical in character — issues whose direct effects are somewhat removed from everyday life and consciousness. We asked them to rate the seriousness of the loss of natural scenic areas, the depletion of the ozone layer, oil spills, global warming or the greenhouse effect, the loss of natural places for fish and wildlife to live, and acid rain. Two exceptions were noted where blacks and whites reported statistically significant differences. These were questions that dealt with depletion of the ozone layer and the loss of natural places for fish and wildlife to

Table 3.2: Percent of Whites and Blacks in the Detroit Area Who Rate Environmental Issues as "Very Serious"

Environmental Issues	Blacks	Whites	Differences
Loss of scenic areas	34%	33%	1%
Depletion of the ozone layer	43	69	-26*
Oil spills	75	79	-4
Global warming or the greenhouse effect	40	44	-4
The loss of natural places for fish and wildlife to live	60	64	-4**
Acid rain	49	47	2

*p <.01; **p < .001

live. The depletion of the ozone layer and the loss of natural places for fish and wildlife to live were problems that whites more so than blacks were likely to rate as very serious.

At least a couple of important facts emerged from tables 3.1 and 3.2 that refutes the notion that major differences exist between blacks and whites regarding a whole range of abstract environmental problems. First in only three out of ten instances did blacks and whites differ significantly (humans have the right to change the natural environment to suit their needs, depletion of the ozone layer, and the loss of place for fish and wildlife to live). Regarding the first issue, blacks, often living in racially segregated and impoverished conditions, may after years of struggle feel they have little control over their environment or the natural environment to suit their needs and may want to reserve the right to change their natural environment in order to better their social and economic condition. Second, although whites more so than blacks were more likely to rate the depletion of the ozone layer and the loss of natural places for fish and wildlife to live as very serious problems, this difference may disappear over time as blacks better their social and economic condition.

We next examined the extent of the difference between blacks and whites with respect to environmental issues relevant to quality of life (Table 3.3). More specifically, we asked the Detroit residents to rate the seriousness of a variety of neighborhood environmental problems such as traffic congestion, noise level, new construction, boarded-up houses, litter or garbage, rats, mice or roaches,

Table 3.3: Percent of Blacks and Whites in the Detroit Area Who Rate Neighborhood Environmental Issues as "Very Serious" or "Somewhat Serious" Problems

Neighborhood Issues	Blacks	Whites	Differences
Traffic Congestion	43%	49%	-6%
Noise level	53	28	25**
Abandoned or boarded-up houses	42	7	35*
Problems with litter or garbage	55	14	41**
Rats, mice or roaches	43	5	38*
Exposure to lead	21	4	17**
Crime and drugs	72	39	33**

*p < .01; **p < .001

exposure to lead, and crime and drugs. Six out of seven answers were statistically significant. Blacks were more likely than whites to rate these as problems, were more likely to report that neighborhood environmental problems were very serious or somewhat serious more so than whites. This may be due to the fact that a larger percentage of blacks may be more exposed to poorer neighborhoods where multiple environmental problems abound. Neighborhood environmental problems may force blacks to take note and express concern because these problems may be a matter of life and death for them. Noteworthy also is that 43% of the blacks and almost 50% of the whites rated traffic congestion as a very serious to somewhat serious problem, a large proportion for both groups. The transportation corridors from the suburban areas to downtown Detroit may account for large amounts of traffic, affecting blacks and whites unequally as people from the suburbs commute to and from work by car, adding to the already over polluted inner city. Yet automobile traffic was perceived to be a problem regardless of one's race, income, or place of residence. But this may change for many blacks if the intermodal transportation system is built in Detroit significantly increasing the flow of traffic.

Taking all three tables into consideration, we find that for the abstract environmental problems there are more similarities than differences, between blacks and whites, in Tri-county area. Yet, when compared to the quality of life environmental issues, there are more differences than similarities. Blacks are more concerned about neighborhood quality of life environmental issues than are whites. We anticipated the answers of blacks to quality of life questions would be qualitatively different from those of their white counterparts, yet we were surprised to find that there were more similarities than differences between the two groups on the more abstract environmental issues. Taken together, blacks because of their living conditions may demonstrate a greater environmental concern than whites in the Detroit area. As mentioned before, the spatial location of blacks may account for this difference.

Hazardous Waste Facilities: Opportunities for Grassroots Environmental Organizing

Until recently, people of color and low-income groups from across the country have seldom used environmental concepts to protest against institutionalized and cultural forms of racism. They are now developing a whole new language to bring currency to their age-old struggle. By using environmental concepts, they are making important connections between environmental degradation and the quality of life in their neighborhoods, between environmental rights and civil rights. The use of terms such as environmental racism, solid waste, acid rain, underground water aquifers, dissolved oxygen, ecosystems, endangered species, sustainable development, non-biodegradable point-source pollution, habitat, and names and classes of different chemicals, such as PCBs, carcinogens, dioxins, pesticides, herbicides, cadmium, carbon monoxide, mercury, and zinc, that threaten their lives are becoming more commonplace in the language of environmental justice activists. While acid rain, depletion of the ozone layer, global warming, and preservation of wildlife habitat were just as much a concern to blacks as to whites, blacks were undeniably more concerned about quality of life issues than were whites when it came to expressing concern about the environment and health hazards associated with rodents, litter, garbage, crime, drugs, boarded-up homes, noise, and lead poisoning.

To find out how much weight community opposition and lobbying have in decisions about siting or cleanups and to find out whether respondents felt that more weight was given to scientific guidelines, to political opposition, to lobbying or to government's weighing of health risks in the siting of a hazardous waste facility, we asked the following questions:

> "Some people think that when selecting a piece of land for a new facility, decision-makers give more weight to scientific guidelines about how suitable a certain location is. Other people think that more weight is given to the level of opposition from that community. Which best describes your opinion of how these decisions are made?"

> "Some people think that when selecting sites for cleanup, decision-makers give more weight to the amount of lobbying for cleanup a community does.

Other people think that more weight is given to the government's rating of a site's risk to people's health. Which best describes your opinion of how these decisions are made?"

The responses of blacks and whites are given in Table 3.4, indicating no clear differences between them; both groups felt that more weight was given to community opposition and lobbying for cleanups than to scientific guidelines or to government's weighing of health risks. Although no differences were noted between the two groups in their response to this question, the more affluent white groups, however, can more readily mobilize political power to act upon their perception: they can make real their opposition to the selection of their communities for LULUs or make real lobbying efforts for community cleanups. Such efforts have been much more difficult for people of color and low-income communities, because historically they have often lacked the political power and the technical know-how.

In many places across the country, communities of color have been put on hold for environmental cleanup. In the meantime people suffer from toxic induced and aggravated diseases. History suggests that we cannot wait to refine our research paradigm in order to show cause and effect. We cannot afford to wait to show causality while millions of people suffer or die. In some cases we must jettison the cause and effect paradigm and evoke the precautionary principle: we must clean up our communities to a point that when adverse health effects disappear, then we know we have dealt with the cause, even though we may never know the specific nature of the cause. But won't this be expensive? Yes, it will be expensive, and yes, we must evoke the precautionary principle of avoiding harm when there is not absolute scientific certainty. We must err on the side of environmental protection and social well-being, regardless of costs. Furthermore, if we fail to pay the price now, a much larger price tag will haunt us in the future. We can ill afford to become involved in esoteric debates as to whether we have enough data, while people cry out for help.

Although social and environmental impact studies are part of the siting process, the siting of these hazardous waste facilities may have little to do with scientific data. It may have more to do with finding the avenues of least political resistance, as exemplified by a study done by Cerrel Associates. This 1984 study, prepared for the California Waste Management Board, carefully delineates the demographics of where opposition to the siting of a network of three 1,600-ton garbage incinerators would most likely come from if such facilities were actually sited. While the results of this study showed that most resistance to such facilities would come from liberal, college-educated, young or middle-aged, middle-to high-income groups in large urban areas, the least resistance would come from communities that conformed to some kind of eco-

Table 3.4: Percent of Blacks and Whites in the Detroit Area Who Perceive That the Selection of a Piece of Land for a New Hazardous Waste Facility Is by Scientific Weight or Community Opposition, Lobbying or Government's Weighing of Health Risks.

The Perception	Blacks	Whites
More Weight Given to Scientific Guidelines	36%	36%
More Weight Given to Community Opposition	57	58
Both Given Equal Weight	7	6
Chi-square=.09724; d.f.=2; p<.9514		
More Weight Given to Lobbying for Cleanup	56%	63%
More Weight Given to Government's Weighing of Health Risks	41	36
Both Given Equal Weight	3	2
Chi-square=4.97843; d.f.=2; p<.08		

nomic need criterion, such as a lower economic neighborhood that was also in a heavy industrial area with little, if any, commercial activity (forwarded from Russell, 1989). Communities of color, by virtue of racial discrimination in housing, education, and jobs, are often prime candidates for an economic need criterion, and as such they become prime candidates for the siting of noxious industries and hazardous waste facilities. Because they often perceive economic benefits as flowing from the siting of such waste facilities in their communities, they may in some cases sacrifice their long-term health for short-term economic gain. Local and state governmental officials in desperate need to find jobs to stem the tide of growing unemployment are quick to say "yes" to these facilities, without first thinking through the potential long-term environmental and social consequences. (Although recycling is a worthy concept and often championed by environmentalists as an alternative to landfills and incinerators, it fails to address issues of environmental justice in that most recycling jobs pay minimal wages. If we are serious about recycling, we must pay the appropriate price for it.) The Cerrel study in this instance confirms the speculation that the location of hazardous waste facilities in communities of color and low-income communities is not by accident, but a conscious policy decision, often backed by sophisticated research.

Yet there are instances where people would resist these landfills if they knew from the beginning exactly what was being built in their neighborhoods. Below is a quote from a black woman living in the Detroit area, indicating her feelings regarding a landfill near her home:

> We didn't know it was going to be a landfill until it was too late to do any-thing about it, because it happened so fast. You don't know what you're inhaling. They dump illegal stuff over there because they do what they want. (DeGannes, et al. 1991).

Because landfills are often sited in areas where there is the least political resistance, the people who live near them may feel powerless to do anything about them. They are not a part of the decision-making of county or city govern-ment, nor do they have access to the decision-making process. They are often politically weak and live in areas where the land is relatively inexpensive and in places where transportation corridors make it convenient to transport waste. Because they are not informed and are often the last to find out, they feel even more helpless in the face of powerful corporate interests. Although people are told that the most advanced liners and technology are used in landfill construc-tion to prevent the downward migration of waste into the underground water table, there is no guarantee the liners won't leak in the future.

As available land runs out, local governments will become more desperate to find solutions for hazardous waste disposal. While incineration has been championed as an alternative to landfills, it merely produces another kind of problem for communities of color. Even with state-of-the-art incinerators, heavy metals, unburned waste, and products of incomplete combustion often form new chemicals during the incineration process. And even though incin-erators may achieve 99.99 percent destructive and removal efficiency, there will be approximately 7,000 pounds of unburned chemical released into the air annually from just an average-sized incinerator (Costner and Thornton, 1990). Some products of incomplete combustion formed during incineration are far more dangerous to health than are others. While we know that low exposures to many metals, organochlorines, and other pollutants cause cancers, birth defects, reproductive dysfunctions, neurological damages, and respiratory ailments, we continue to build a disproportionate number of incinerators in communities of color, as if they were not harmful. Incinerators reduce waste to 60 to 90 percent of its weight, yet they still produce something like 342 million pounds of ash residues each year in the U.S. These highly toxic ashes are buried in landfills even though they contain products of incomplete combustion, PCBs, and other hazardous waste (Costner and Thornton, 1990).

Because of the stated 99.99 percent destructive and removal efficiency of incinerators, they sound safe. Nothing could be further from the truth, particularly with respect to certain fugitive emissions. As mentioned before, we find that fugitive fat-soluble and persistent chemicals will bio-accumulate and/or amplify and move up the food chain in more concentrated forms to be consumed by humans, thus potentially resulting in major health problems. It has been found throughout the nation that chemicals have accumulated and persisted in the body, particularly chlorinated aromatics such as PCBs and pesticides, DDT, chlordane, dieldrin, and hexachlorobenzene. While the levels of these chemicals in the body may vary regionally, they undoubtedly are of much concern to people throughout the nation. People of color and low-income groups who live near these incinerators and commercial hazardous waste facilities are often exposed to noxious pollutants and may suffer more from stress and physical illness based on where they live. Even though they may not show physical signs of ill health they nonetheless may experience anger and stress: people overexposed to toxins become health risks and preoccupied with the thought that they or their children may succumb to cancer or some other life-threatening, toxic-induced or aggravated disease. This preoccupation with health weighs heavily on the minds of people of color who are often forced to live in segregated communities near polluting industries that are dangerous to their health (Unger, et al., 1992).

How do people cope with the anger and stress that come from living near a hazardous waste facility? How do they cope with such stress on a daily basis? It has been documented that potential risks from hazardous waste facilities may result in feelings of depression, feelings of helplessness, a lack of control over their environment, more family quarrels, worries about health and the health of children, and recurrent guilt about raising children in such situations (Unger, et al., 1992). In their attempt to cope with the uncertainty or the lack of immedi-ate solutions some families have split apart: husband and wife have had bitter arguments on the nature of the problem, mother and daughter have vehemently disagreed on the solution to the problem, and this discord can run wide and deep. People who live near a hazardous waste facility may often experience isolation from friends and relatives who have chosen not to visit them in fear of being exposed to environmental pollutants or contaminated drinking water or food. Homeowners who live near polluting or hazardous waste facilities may experience financial loss from the depreciation of property values and an inability to sell their homes.

Not only are communities of color more often sites for commercial hazard-ous waste facilities and noxious polluting industries, but they are often low on the national priority list for toxic cleanups as compared to their white counterparts. Although this may be news to some, people of color have always known that their communities were the last on the priority list. This was something that they have witnessed. A cursory glance at the amount of pollution found in most communities of color would lead one to draw the same conclusion. Lavelle and Coyle (1992) reported that the average penalties under the hazardous waste laws for sites having the greatest number of white people nearby were six times higher than the average penalties of sites having the greatest number of people of color nearby. These objective data were compared to the perception of Detroit area residents in order to examine the extent of perceived environmental inequities. We specifically asked:

"Some people feel that decisions made by the government about who should receive priority in the cleanup of abandoned hazardous waste sites are also unfair to certain communities. Other people feel these decisions are fair. I would like to know your opinion."

"First, do you think a wealthy community or a poor community is more likely to get priority for cleanup?"

"Do you think a black community or a white community is more likely to get priority cleanup?"

The responses of Detroit area blacks and whites are given in Table 3.5. Well over 90 % of blacks and 85 % of whites report that wealthy communities are more likely to get priority cleanups--a significant difference between the two groups. More blacks than whites report that white communities are more likely to get priority for cleanup, indicating a perception of both a racial and class bias with respect to the government's priority in cleaning up communities with hazardous waste sites. Also, while 91% of blacks report that white communities are more likely to get priority cleanups, only 66% of the whites report that white communities are more likely to get priority cleanups; 3% of blacks report that black communities are more likely and 9% of the whites report that black communities are more likely. The perception of blacks and whites of the hazardous waste cleanup priority were consistent with the data reported by Lavelle and Coyle (1992) in that it takes 20% longer for an abandoned hazardous waste site to be placed on the national priority action list under the Superfund cleanup program in communities of color than in white communities. Different penalties and response efforts to enforce hazardous waste cleanups in people of color communities were obvious. White communities—not black communities—are given first priority for environmental cleanup. Because the fines on polluters are so low in people of color communities, corporations can write off such low penalties as the "cost of doing business," without seriously cutting into their profit margins. That is to say, that if the government levied legitimate fines against polluting industries in people of color communities or fined these polluting industries to the fullest extent of the law, these communities would have potentially cleaner and safer air, water, and land. They would probably be environmentally and socially healthier places to live. We assert

Table 3.5: Percent of Blacks and Whites in the Detroit Area Who Perceive Government Inequities in Priority of Cleanups of Abandoned Hazardous Waste Sites in Certain Communities

The Perception	Blacks	Whites
Black Communities More Likely to Get Priority	3%	9%
White Communities More Likely to Get Priority	91	66
Neither Community More Likely to Get Priority	6	25
Chi-square=33.17708; d.f.=2; p<.001		
Wealthy Communities More Likely to Get Priority	92%	85%
Poor Communities More Likely to Get Priority	6	8
Neither Community More Likely to Get Priority	2	8
Chi-square=6.78480; d.f.=2; p<.05		

that there are more than 40 million people in this country without health insurance protection and a sizeable percentage of that 40 million are people of color and people of low-income living near hazardous waste facilities or in polluted areas. Those who need health insurance protection the most are the least able to afford it and live in communities that are the least likely to get priority cleanup. Even though the EPA attempts to be race neutral, the fact remains as shown by Lavelle and Coyle (1992) that its policies are racially biased. While greater cleanup priority may be unintentionally given to white communities, the fact remains that EPA is still as much a culprit as is industry.

We also examined the extent of awareness of Detroit area residents about environmental injustice in the site selection for hazardous waste facilities (Table 3.6). Since a number of studies have documented that black communities are more likely than white communities to be locations for hazardous waste facilities, we thought we would ask the residents in the Detroit area a question regarding this issue:

"Some people don't like the way decisions are made about where to place new facilities that treat or store hazardous waste because they feel that these decisions are unfair to certain communities. Other people feel that the selection process *is* fair. I would like to know *your* opinion."

"Do you think a black community or a white community is more likely to be chosen as the site of a new hazardous waste treatment or storage facility?"

"Do you think a wealthy community or a poor community is more likely to
be chosen as the site of a new hazardous waste treatment or storage facility?"

Blacks and whites alike overwhelmingly stated that a poor community is
more likely to be chosen for the site of a hazardous waste facility. Furthermore,
58% of the blacks and 34% of the whites felt that a black community is more
likely to be chosen for a hazardous waste treatment or storage facility. It is
clear that the perceptions fall along racial lines in that significantly more blacks
than whites felt that way.

Some policymakers prefer not to look at the issue of race. Most are willing
to look at the issue of social class as the major culprit in the inequitable siting
of hazardous waste treatment facilities. They may feel that poor people are
differentially burdened by toxic exposures more so than the more affluent ones,
regardless of racial characteristics. Therefore, the issue from a policymaker's
standpoint may be poverty—not race. This thinking is only partially true. If
one makes an objective observation of the underpinnings of the legacy of racism
in America, one may draw different conclusions: Value neutral policies often
result in a discriminatory effect which is an integral part of the institutional form
of racism that relegates people of color to a marginal existence in this country.
Most policymakers find it difficult to concede this point. Nowhere has this been
more visible than in the Detroit area. For many years the discriminatory policies
of the Federal Housing Administration (FHA) programs prevented people of
color from obtaining federally guaranteed housing loans in order to move out
into the Tri-County Area. As a result Detroit became overwhelmingly black.

Black students in Detroit are often forced to attend inferior and economically poor schools. Blacks also earn significantly fewer dollars than their white
counterparts at all income levels. These are all forms of institutional racism. In
other instances, welfare policies that required fathers to be continually absent
from the home in order for the family to be eligible for welfare was not that
much different from slavery, an institution that structurally broke up families for
the economic benefit of the slave owner. Although the modern welfare policy
may not have been meant to be racist in character, the net effect was that it had
a greater impact upon black than white families in this country. These policies
tended to break up black families, not to hold them together. Such policies kept
blacks in a state of economic weakness, and that weakness was transmitted
down through the generations with each succeeding generation unable to escape
their impoverished condition and their detestable environmental surroundings.
As mentioned before, the government's uneven response to toxic cleanups in
neighborhoods is a form of discrimination, particularly when it takes 20 percent
longer to place a hazardous waste facility located in the black community on the
national priority list, and when RCRA fines are approximately six times more

Table 3.6: Percent of Blacks and Whites in the Detroit Area Who Perceive Inequities in the Selection of Sites for a New Hazardous Waste Treatment or Storage Facility

The Perception	Blacks	Whites
A Wealthy Community Is More Likely to Be Chosen	15%	3%
A Poor Community Is More Likely to Be Chosen	80	87
Neither Community Is More Likely to Be Chosen	4	10
Chi-square=32.03606; d.f.=2; p<.001		
A Black Community Is More Likely to Be Chosen	58	34
A White Community Is More Likely to Be Chosen	25	28
Neither Community Is More Likely to Be Chosen	16	38
Chi-square =33.17708; d.f.=2; p<.001		

for white communities than for black communities.

If racism were not a factor, hazardous waste facilities would be more randomly distributed spatially throughout the various income levels within the Detroit area. Is the government doing enough, given community awareness and the increased number of hazardous sites throughout the country? In recent years, the awareness of communities of color of the harmful effects of hazardous waste has increased significantly. Thousands of groups throughout the nation are resisting the siting of hazardous waste facilities in their communities or are pressuring the government to cleanup abandoned hazardous waste facilities and Superfund sites. Complaints continue to mount about government inaction and, given the limited resources of governmental agencies responsible for such cleanups, they are forced to make priority choices. As we have seen from our previous discussion, it is the white and wealthy communities that are more likely to be placed on the national priority list for hazardous waste cleanup. Thus, we asked the following question:

> "Sometimes people or businesses leave hazardous waste on a site that was not designed for it. In general, do you think the government is doing enough to make sure these sites are cleaned up properly, or do you think government is not doing enough?"

While 94% of blacks felt that the government was not doing enough,

Table 3.7: Government Doing Enough to Cleanup Unauthorized HWS?

	Blacks	**Whites**
Yes, the Government Is Doing Enough	6%	14%
No, the Government Is Not Doing Enough	94	86

Chi-square=5.44582; d.f.=1; p<.02

86% of the whites felt that the government was not doing enough. Although both groups overwhelmingly felt that the government was not doing enough, significantly more blacks than whites felt this to be true. This, however, is not unusual, in that we have shown that black communities are more often sited for hazardous waste disposal than white communities. Black communities are often neglected for environmental cleanup.

In response to the requirement set forth in the Comprehensive Environmental Response Compensation Liability Act of 1980 (PL96-510), also known as CERCLA or the "Superfund Law," EPA identified and ranked as a part of its national priority list hundreds of hazardous waste sites across the country to be significant threats to the environment or public health. Clearly, many of them failed to make the priority list, and new ones are appearing on the scene every day—i.e., the ones not on the priority list could also be dangerous to one's health. With so many sites needing to be cleaned up, and with environmental protection lagging behind, and given the financial resources of local governments, it is clear that the federal government should do more. The question is whether we should underwrite the cost of cleanup of post-production waste with our health, with our tax dollars, with our private dollars, or some combination of them all. But in any case there is no such thing as a free lunch. While we are morally outraged about welfare recipients getting subsidies for survival, we are seldom outraged about the captains of industry getting subsidies for increased profits.

Because racism is so entrenched in the fabric of American society, it is almost impossible for individual acts of fairness to make a significant difference in the structural inequalities that affect people's lives. Equal protection of environmental laws in an unequal society that has evolved over the centuries only perpetuates the system of unfairness. We must move well beyond equal protection and individual acts of fairness to a system of environmental justice, where people can live in a society free of racial and income discrimination and where they are free to interact with an environment that is nurturing, productive and safe, and where distributive justice prevails, regardless of race, color, creed, or sexual preferences.

Conclusion

In conclusion, the findings of the Detroit Area Study, along with supporting research, unequivocally demonstrate that blacks in most instances are just as concerned as whites about more abstract environmental issues and more concerned than whites about quality of life neighborhood issues. While the former finding was surprising, the latter was not. Blacks often live in polluted and dangerous neighborhoods. Therefore, it stands to reason that they would be more concerned about quality of life issues. Not only is the average black concerned about these issues, but black leaders and scholars alike have played a major role in championing the cause of the environment and environmental justice. They have been concerned not only about the disproportionate impact of environmental burdens on communities of color, but also about the disparate treatment of communities of color in the government's cleanup efforts. And as we run out of space for landfills or ways to deal with our waste, more pressure will be placed upon black communities for hazardous waste disposal. Inability to deal effectively with the waste problem could have a profound effect upon our production, our economy, and our most vulnerable populations.

Therefore, blacks must question growth and development, because the relative position of blacks have not improved significantly in this country since slavery. The metaphor used is a bus with blacks seated in the rear. While the bus is making fast progress, the relative position of blacks to whites on the bus has not changed. During the 1980s the transfer of wealth away from the middle and working classes to the wealthy through tax breaks and other incentives benefited the rich and not the poor or the middle class. Those who were already rich increased their wealth, while those who were not wealthy increased their poverty. While growth and development increase wealth, they also increase the number of hazardous waste facilities, making people of color communities vulnerable to siting decisions. Should we grow and develop at any cost? In what direction should we develop? How can we develop sustainable communities where economic, racial, and environmental justice will be served?

Even if growth and development were more equally distributed throughout society, we would have to ask the question: What impact is this growth having upon the planet? TV fantasies of owning multi-million dollar homes and $50,000 cars, and living a life of affluence, are part of the American dream. Yet the other side of the coin is the American nightmare of poverty and a struggle to keep hazardous waste facilities out of black communities as it struggles to keep from starving. We need to think about a different kind of growth—one that embraces environmental justice. We need to think of growth and development that do not produce large amounts of pollutants and toxic and solid waste for disposal purposes. Status and recognition should not be anchored in the accumulation of material wealth, but in growth and development of the mind and spirit. Growth and development should not only reaffirm our connectedness with each other as human beings, but growth and development should reaffirm our connectedness with non-human life forms. Growth and development should be rooted in environmental justice if we are to survive on planet earth.

4
METHODS AND ISSUES

Elaine Hockman, Bunyan Bryant, and Charles Morris

It is difficult enough to create the laboratory conditions necessary to prove beyond scientific doubt that a certain chemical causes a certain ailment, let alone to show these causal relations in the real world. Even though industry understands the difference between "no proof of harm" and "no harm," it still uses the scientific language of "no proof" to imply "no harm" (Bruno, et al. 1999).

Environmental justice is a very serious, controversial concept, and, as with most such concepts, both subjective and objective arguments are proposed and defended on both sides of the issue. Chapters five to nine of this book focus on attempts at objectivity by looking at the facts of hazardous waste sitings and population characteristics in the State of Michigan. Each of these five chapters uses the same database for its analyses. The history of this database, which we call the "Michigan Environmental Database," is presented in this chapter along with issues of concern for any study employing such a database. Chapter 5 by Bryant and Hockman analyzes information in the earliest version of the database. Later, their students in the School of Natural Resources and Environment at the University of Michigan used the growing database as a foundation for empirical research they would conduct in conjunction with a seminar on environmental justice. Three of these student papers form chapters 6 to 8, while a fourth student paper is quoted in the "issues" portion of the present chapter. The tenth chapter, by Morris and Hockman, draws on further expansion of the database.

The original manuscripts for each of these five chapters described the development and content of the database, sections that would be necessary for individually published papers. However, to avoid unnecessary repetition in this book, the database development section of this chapter should be considered as a preamble to each of the five chapters that follow.

Developing the Michigan Environmental Database

In 1990, we (Bryant and Hockman) began to think seriously about building a database to study environmental justice issues. We asked ourselves two guiding questions:

- What objective data would illustrate environmental justice/injustice?

- What analyses of these data would confirm or disconfirm the existence of environmental justice in Michigan?

We thus set ourselves the task of pulling together demographic and environmental information pertaining to Michigan to answer these questions. First, we needed to locate reliable sources of data on environmental hazards; second, we needed to locate reliable sources of demographic information; third, we needed to join these data sets; and, finally, we could begin analyses to describe objectively the condition of environmental justice in Michigan.

Our starting point in 1990 was to link pollution data with race and income data for Michigan to ascertain their relative contributions to the incidence of pollution sites in our state. The Michigan Department of Natural Resources would serve as the source of pollution data, and the U. S. Census would serve as the source of race and income data. Later, with the Michigan Department of Public Health as the source, we would add public health data to the database. The one variable in common across all data sources was zip code, thus zip code became our linking agent to join the various data sets into one ever larger, usable computerized database. As new data sources became available over the years, any zip code changes reflected in the new data were retrofitted to the corresponding 1990 census zip codes to maintain consistency and accuracy in the database.

The Pollution Variables

Data on six different environmental pollution sources have been made available to us over the past ten years: the Toxic Release Inventory (TRI); the Michigan Environmental Response Act (MERA), known as Act 307; Leaking Underground Storage Tanks (LUST); hazardous waste management facilities; incinerator emissions; and landfills.

Toxic Release Inventory, 1989 and 1993

Under section 313 of the Emergency Planning and Community Right-to-Know Act of 1986, manufacturing facilities are required to compile and report information to the Environmental Protection Agency (EPA) on over 320 toxic chemicals released directly to air, water, or land or that are transported to off-site facilities. The law requires EPA to compile these reports into an annual inventory of releases and transfers, known as the Toxic Release Inventory (TRI), in order to make such data available to the public in a computerized format. The TRI requirement covers all manufacturing facilities in the 50 states, the District of Columbia, and territories that meet the following conditions: 1) they produced, imported, or processed 25,000 or more pounds of TRI chemicals, or they used in any other manner 10,000 pounds or more of a TRI chemical, 2) they are engaged in general manufacturing activities, and 3) they employed the equivalent of ten or more employees full time. TRI chemicals vary widely in toxicity, frequency, amounts, and in industrial processes used. Except for those industries able to justify a need to protect trade secrets, those with fewer than ten full-time employees, and those involving amounts below designated threshold levels, this Act covers essentially all releases by manufacturing firms. The information requested in the TRI form includes facility addresses, off-site locations to which TRI chemicals are transferred, specific chemical release information, and off-site transfers and treatment. Penalties of $25,000/day per chemical for each violation may be levied.

The Michigan Department of Natural Resources (MDNR) supplied the 1989 Michigan TRI data. The Department of Environmental Quality (DEQ), one of two departments resulting from the 1995 reorganization of the MDNR, supplied the 1993 Michigan TRI data. In both years, the data consisted of a computer record for each chemical release citation, giving among other information, the chemical being released; the type of release into the air, water, or land; the amount of release; the name of the site and its address, including zip code. Thus a manufacturing facility that released more than one chemical would be in the data set from the MDNR as many times as there were chemicals that it released. For each of the two years, the data were aggregated by zip code, first by counting the number of records for a zip code. These variables we call "TRI citations." The next set of aggregations represented the sums, within the year, of the emissions in each reported category. The "TRI citation" variable for each year provides greater quantitative information about the extent of environmental hazard in a zip code than merely a dichotomy of presence or absence of a TRI site.

Act 307 Sites, 1990, 1995, and 1996

The Michigan Environmental Response Act (MERA), known as Act 307, P.A. 19823, as amended, was passed to respond to citizen and government concern about environmental contamination that threatened drinking and water supplies, the environment, and communities or personal property. Sources of contamination may be an old landfill, the corner gas station, abandoned dry cleaners, or unknown sources. MERA was designed to provide an objective process for evaluating sites of contamination to be ranked, reduced, or eliminated or to prevent the release of contaminants that may cause risks to human health and the environment.

The federal Comprehensive Environmental Response Compensation Liability Act (CERCLA), commonly known as Superfund, established site evaluation ranking and response programs at the national level. Although this program is administered by EPA, the DEQ plays a major role in the managing and cleanup of sites, and in providing assistance to EPA on the remaining sites funded under the CERCLA program. Although the MERA program is similar to Superfund, it differs in that MERA addresses more sites than can be addressed by the federal program alone. Sites eligible for money under the Superfund program may also be eligible for MERA funds to cover activities excluded by the federal program to supplement site response actions or to carry out short-term interim responses that would not otherwise receive federal funds. The two programs are both overlapping and similar.

The 1990, Act 307 data were provided on computer disk by the MDNR; the 1995 and 1996 data, by the DEQ. Each record in Act 307 files identifies a pollution location and includes the names of the chemicals in question, a score reflecting the severity of the problem imposed by that site ("SAM" score), the status of action on cleanup of the site at the time of entry into the computer record, and the address of the site, including zip code. For each year, the records were aggregated by zip code. The two major variables per zip code per year were: the number of Act 307 sites and the average SAM score. In addition, the total number of chemicals recorded for a zip code was computed for the 1990 data set. Cleanup statuses were coded for the 1995 and 1996 data.

Leaking Underground Storage Tanks (LUST), 1990

The 1990 LUST computer data file was supplied by the MDNR and contained the addresses, including zip code, of all sites in Michigan. The State Department of Natural Resources collected these data so that corrective action could be taken to minimize, eliminate, or clean up a release or its effects in order to protect the health, welfare, and safety of individuals and the environment. A number of specific actions are used in the remediation of these sites. They include: 1) release investigations, 2) mitigation of fire and safety hazards, 3) tank repair or removal, 4) soil remediation or hydrogeological investigations, 5) removal of regulated substances in liquid phase—not dissolved in water that has been released into the environment, 6) monitoring, 7) exposure assessments, 8) temporary or permanent relocations of results, and 9) the provision of alternative water supplies. A civil fine of not more than $10,000 for noncompliance of each underground storage tank system may be levied or a civil fine of $25,000 for noncompliance for each day may be levied against violators.

Records were aggregated by zip code, resulting in a measure that represents the total number of LUST sites in the zip. This variable is called "LUST."

Hazardous Waste Management Facilities, 1996

The DEQ supplied the 1996 list of hazardous waste management facilities. This list included the address of each facility and the type of facility at each site. The facility types are disposal, in-surface impoundment, landfill, waste pile, land treatment, incinerator, storage in tanks or containers, and chemical, physical, or biological treatment. These data needed to be recorded into computer-readable form. Each site formed a record; these records were then aggregated by zip code. The total number of hazardous waste management facilities in a zip code is called "Hazfac."

Incinerators, 1996

The DEQ provided a computer file of incinerators that contained addresses with zip code, type of incinerator and emission amounts of ten different chemicals (Cl, CO, Fl, Mercury, NO_2, Lead, PM_{10}, Particulate Matter, SO, and Volatile Organic Compounds). These data were aggregated by zip code, resulting in variables corresponding to the total number of chemicals emitted by incinerator(s) in a zip code. The total number of emissions by chemical in a zip code are also included in the database, although the studies in the following chapters focus only on the number of "incinerations" for analytic purposes.

Landfills, 1996

The DEQ gave us a list of recognized landfills, including zip code, in the State of Michigan, which we entered into a computerized data set. These records were then aggregated by zip code, giving as a variable for the database the number of landfills in the zip code. Our studies to date have scratched only the surface of this extensive pollution database. Individual chemicals, amounts of emissions, and types of facilities have yet to be looked at. Change over the years is still another expected line of investigation and will be accompanied by more current measures of these sources.

The Demographics of Michigan

Because the linking variable among the environmental hazards data sets was zip code, we used the 1990 U.S. Census of Population and Housing, Summary Tape File 3B, the zip code data file, for the State of Michigan. This file contains information from both the long and short forms of the 1990 census for the 873 Michigan zip codes with population.

Race

According to the 1990 U. S. Census, the total population of Michigan was 9,295,297. Of this population, 16.5% were minorities. Blacks accounted for the largest segment of the minority population (84% of the minorities; 14% of the total Michigan population). These figures represent individuals. When the population count is sorted into its respective zip codes, which is our unit of analysis, we find that the percentages of minorities range from 0 to 99%, with an average of 7.2% minorities per zip code. The average number of individuals living in a Michigan zip code is 10,647, but the majority of the population lives in zip codes classified by the Census as "inside urban." The population within a Michigan zip code is, on the average, 92% white. Although the values of "percentage white" cover the full range from 1% to 100%, the distribution is negatively skewed: zip codes with a small proportion of whites are relatively rare. Within a Michigan zip code, the population is, on the average 5% black. However, the percentages per zip code range from 0% to 99%, showing a strong positive skew in the distribution: few zip codes have large percentages of blacks. The average percentage of Hispanics per zip code is 1.5%. For Native Americans and Asians, the average proportions are .6% and 1%, respectively.

Income

The average household income, recorded as median household income for a zip code, was $28,962, with a standard deviation of $10,822 and a slight positive skew. Household income was selected as the major income variable, as opposed to per capita or family income, because of its greater reliability.

The 1990 census data reported grouped frequency distributions of median household income for blacks and whites separately. Dividing household income into low, middle, and high categories, the average breakdown by race is shown in Table 5.4 on page 72. The data for blacks were available for only 475 zip codes as 398 zip codes reported no black households. Black households were more heavily represented in the lowest category of income; white households, in the middle category of income. Disparity in income becomes an important issue in discussing disproportional environmental burden.

The number of households on public assistance was reported in the 1990 Census. This figure, converted to a proportion or percent in each zip code, serves as an additional indicator of socio-economic status. The average percent of households on public assistance within a zip code in 1990 was 8.7. The public assistance index ranged from 0 to 46% and showed a positive skew.

The 1990 Zip Code Census File offered a large selection of variables to describe the socio-economic characteristics of Michigan for use in answering questions about the state of environmental justice. Many of these variables were added to the database. Descriptions of these additional indicators appear in the chapters that analyzed them.

Public Health

The Michigan Department of Public Health (MDPH) provided us at different times with computer files for cancer incidence and birth weight by zip code as well as printed lists, by zip code, of asthma-related hospital discharges.

The cancer data files provided the numbers of new cancers diagnosed in 1987, 1990, and 1993 in each of six age categories. The age groupings were less than 15 years of age, 15-29, 30-44, 45-64, 65-74, and greater than 74 years of age. The birth weight data covered the years from 1989, 1990, and (1991). The asthma hospital discharges for primary and secondary diagnoses were for the years 1989 to 1993 for Michigan children and youth from 1 to 18 years of age. The zip codes included in these data files—cancer, birth weight, and asthma—were only those with a population of at least 5,000. This cut-off is due to a Department of Public Health policy designed to protect individual privacy. These data were aggregated by zip code for the database and used in various ways by the authors of the next five chapters in this book.

The merging of data sets required a common linking element. The link universally available was zip code. Although the U. S. Postal Service had changed zip codes for several communities around the time of the 1990 Census, it was possible to update/revert data records as necessary to maintain consistency in zip codes so that both pollution siting information and public health measures correspond to the Michigan zip codes recorded in the 1990 U. S. Census data.

ISSUES

Unit of Analysis and the Ecological Fallacy

The Detroit Area Study, presented in the previous chapter, used individual persons as the unit of analysis. In any serious research concerning the health and well-being of people, the response of the public is often, "But what does this mean for me?" Attempts to answer this question may lead to the ecological fallacy, when the unit of analysis is an aggregation of persons rather than the individual. In short, the ecological fallacy is attributing to individuals the results from studies that do not employ the individual as the unit of analysis.

The studies in chapters 5 to 9 were based on our Michigan Environmental Database and therefore used zip code as the unit of analysis. Inferences regarding the impact upon individual persons are therefore not warranted. However, inferences about geographical aggregates are. The choice of unit of analysis was not merely that of convenience. While there is controversy about what unit should be employed in studies of environmental justice, zip code provides a reasonable and meaningful compromise

The concept of zip code, a U. S. Postal Service administrative unit, is a geographical area familiar to most people even though it may not reflect a political or census statistical area. A huge variety of information is available at the zip code level. The two most frequently cited alternatives to zip code for environmental justice studies are census tract–smaller than a zip code but only in urban areas– and county–much larger than a zip code.

The major unit of analysis for the groundbreaking United Church of Christ study was zip code (UCC, 1987). This study showed a strong relationship between race and the locations of environmental hazards. The study most often cited as showing no relationship between race and siting, the Anderton et al. study (1994), used census tract as the major unit of analysis. Bowen et al. (1993) used county as the unit of analysis and showed a relationship between siting and race. The question is, "To what extent does unit of analysis determine valid and reliable inferences?" Proponents of census tract claim that zip codes are too large for meaningful results, subjecting researchers to "ecological fallacies." But the ecological fallacy is that of applying aggregate results to the individual. Any analysis that uses an aggregate rather than the individual is prone to the ecological fallacy. The proponents of zip code claim that census tracts are too small for meaningful results because of spatial homogeneity. Correlation is curtailed by homogeneity. Indeed, when Anderton, et al. combined TSDF tracts with their surrounding-area tracts for comparison with the remaining tracts of the SMSA, their study found that the larger unit of comparison in fact produced findings similar to the Toxic Waste and Race Report by the UCC. Because census tracts are much smaller than zip codes, the dependent variable–pollution siting–generally becomes a dichotomy, especially when only one siting source is included for analysis. Zip codes afford a greater range of environmental hazards per unit of analysis. Furthermore, when one considers the impact of airborne contaminants, such as incinerator emissions, census tracts represent too small an area when measuring pollution impact. Census tracts relate to SMSAs and are not found in rural areas. Using census tract as the unit of analysis would limit the geographical areas for analysis in a study of the State of Michigan. Zip code allows inclusion of the entire state. The influence of aggregation on correlation has been in the literature from long before the U. S. Postal Service introduced the 5-digit zip code. Croxton and Cowden (1955) state, "The correlation of state averages will ordinarily be higher than that of the county values." By extension and in practice, we find that the correlations among variables at the zip code level are stronger than at the census tract level.

The effect of unit of analysis is limited not just to size of geographical area represented in the aggregation. The correlational structure of the variables included in analysis, especially when that analysis employs regression techniques, must be considered. Are the correlations between the two major predictors of siting—income and race—consistent across different levels of aggregation? Colinearity of predictor variables, when present, needs to be addressed in the analysis. One way of handling this is to study indirect effects, a topic that will be explored later in this chapter. The correlation structure may be very different for a selected geographical area than for the state as a whole. This correlation structure, in turn, affects the regression coefficients used to characterize the differing influences of race and income. Indeed, when considering all 873 zip codes in Michigan, our study population, we find a correlation of only -.22 between proportion minority and median household income. In the 206 zip codes that make up Southeastern Michigan, the part of the state that includes the metropolitan Detroit area, the correlation between proportion minority and median household income is -.59; for the 667 zip codes in the rest of the state, the correlation is only -.18. For just Wayne County zip codes, which include Detroit, the correlation is even stronger, -.76. Any regression studies employing zip codes, or census tracts, from just Southeastern Michigan run into the problem of colinearity. Indeed, at the tract level (1267 census tracts in Southeast Michigan), the correlation between proportion minority and median household income is equally strong as for zip codes, -.56.

Measurement Issues

A major problem faced in using aggregate data is how to form indices to measure the variables of interest. For example, how should racial composition of each zip code be represented in studies of environmental justice? In chapters 5 to 9, several different methods have been used. One procedure is to express the number of minorities in the zip code as a proportion or percentage of all minorities in the state. Closely related to this method is the index of dissimilarity recommended by one of our students, Steven Wise. The following from Wise's paper for the Environmental Justice seminar explains the rationale and importance of this index.

The last point directly raises the main concern of environmental justice: whether communities of color are consistently exposed to greater environmental risks, and whether this exposure leads to adverse consequences in health and other areas.

Although the index of dissimilarity provides a very useful description of the extent of segregation in a zip code, its importance as an index for use in correlational studies is hampered because of its direct correlation with the number of residents in a zip code. The larger a zip code, the more likely the greater number of environmental hazards. Minority status, measured by the number of minorities in the zip code taken as a proportion or percentage of all minorities in

Index of Dissimilarity and Environmental Justice
By Steve Wise

The environmental justice movement and the movement against racial segregation in the United States share common contexts and goals, but the two have not been extensively or explicitly combined. Both movements examine the distribution of people by race, especially the distribution of African Americans, and both seek to resolve inequities associated with the distribution of population by race or associated demographic factors.

The concept of environmental justice is based on the notion that people of color are disproportionately affected by environmental hazards. Confirming that notion requires first establishing the distribution of sources of environmental hazard and second examining the relative exposure to that hazard of people of color compared with other populations. The first question is answered, at least in an aggregate sense, by evaluating available statistics of toxic chemical sources by geographic unit. Segregation studies begin with the second question, where populations are divided on a racial basis. They then examine corollary social differences exhibited between populations. So far, the segregation studies have not generally addressed environmental hazards as an associated factor.

Yet segregation studies have the advantage of a relatively long and established record compared with environmental justice research. Segregation is also an issue that has a history of social, political, and legal responses. Applying the methods of segregation analysis to environmental justice can relate the concerns about environmental hazard to the scientific and social institutions of desegregation, and can suggest avenues of redress to the environmental justice movement.

One segregation measure, the index of dissimilarity, can be used to study the distribution of potential environmental hazard in Michigan.

The modern history of addressing segregation in the United States begins in 1954 with the famous Brown versus Board of Education Supreme Court ruling. The court ruled against the doctrine of "separate but equal" that had been in place since the 1896 Supreme Court ruling in Plessy v. Ferguson. In denying the legality of segregation in schools, the ruling said of minority students:

To separate them from others of similar age and qualifications solely because of their race generates a feeling of inferiority as to their status in the community that may affect their hearts and minds in a way unlikely ever to be undone. (Brown v. Board of Education of Topeka, 1954)

That ruling was followed by a series of others on education and was one step in the development of civil rights legislation that today makes segregation and discrimination illegal in schools, housing, employment, and other areas

(McDonald and Powell, 1993). The ruling also suggests that indirect effects of segregation, in this case on children's emotional development, are relevant grounds on which to mandate its elimination.

The measure of segregation suggested here, the index of dissimilarity, has its roots a year after Brown v. Board of Education in an article by Duncan and Duncan (1955). Although White (1988) criticizes the index for various reasons in a review of segregation indices, the index is suggested here because of its prevalence in previous studies and its simplicity. "The index of dissimilarity has been the workhorse of segregation measurements for decades.... It is very easily interpreted as the percentage of one group that would have to change residences (from those parcels where it was over- represented) in order to produce an even distribution." ("Parcel" is the generic term used for a geographical or administrative unit for which population statistics are measured.)

The impact of segregation has been the focus of research in a number of areas, notably education, housing, employment, social opportunity, and civil rights. Recent examples include Santiago's paper (1991) on general influences of spatial stratification by race, Orfield, Monfort, and George's examination (1987) of persistent desegregation in education, Denton and Massey's study of residential segregation (1988) and Frey's assessment of "white flight" (1992), Jencks and Mayer's study (1990) of employment opportunities and Massey, Gross, and Eggers' study (1991) of "life chances" affected by segregation.

Health impact is one area of segregation studies that begins to overlap directly with the issues of environmental justice. LaVeist (1993) suggests that segregation is one factor associated with differences between black and white urban populations in relation to general poverty and health. Without directly employing the language of segregation, Harding and Greer (1993) provide a bridge between these areas by examining the health impacts of hazardous waste sites. They suggest that recent evidence indicates "increased risk of disease and disability for all populations living in proximity to hazardous waste sites..." and "mounting empirical evidence that minority and low income communities are disproportionately burdened with hazardous waste sites and facilities in their neighborhoods... Although existing scientific evidence cannot conclusively link socio-economic and ethnic variables to environmentally induced disease, it is postulated that health risks are likely to occur with increasing exposure to hazardous substances."

the state, suffers from the same problem. Indeed, these two indices, the index of dissimilarity and the proportion of minorities in the state that are in the zip code, are highly correlated as they share common elements as well as a strong relationship to size of zip code.

A viable alternative to either the index of dissimilarity or proportion of the state's minorities in the zip code is the proportion of the zip code population that are minorities. This is the procedure used by some of our authors as the measure of minority status. This index has a direct, easily understandable meaning, the number of minorities per hundred residents in the zip code. The major drawback of this index is its distribution, which is badly skewed to the right. The majority of the zip codes have few minorities; a smaller number of zip codes have ever increasing numbers of minorities. Regression analysis argues against the use of badly skewed distributions. The bulk of the proportions or percentages pile up near zero. The values of this index are limited to the range from 0 to 1. Log transformations, giving zip codes with no minorities a token miniscule proportion, have been employed by some of our authors to normalize the distribution of the proportion/percent minorities in the zip codes.

Yet another index used in some of our studies is the ratio of the number of minorities to the number of whites. The advantage of this ratio as an index of minority presence is that its range is not limited to 0 to 1. Instead, it is readily interpreted as the number of minorities expressed as a proportion (or percentage) of the number of whites, and can thus range from 0 upwards. When the index is less than 1, there are fewer minorities in the zip code than whites; when the index is equal to 1, there are just as many minorities in the zip code as there are whites; when the index is greater than 1, there are more minorities in the zip code than there are whites. One of our students has published independently an article based on our database in which he computed the ratio of whites to blacks (Downey, 1998).

Causality

Aside from the arguments about unit of analysis and the ecological fallacy problem, the major criticism, or come-back, or complaint we hear with respect to studies of environmental justice is, "But you can't show causality." We are not trying to show that race causes siting; instead, we are showing the correlates of siting, and race tends to be a major correlate. Everyone who has studied statistics knows that correlation does not prove causality. Social, political, and economic phenomena such as siting industrial and waste management facilities are the result of multiple considerations. However, when it is shown over and over again that minorities tend to live in areas with greater exposure to toxic and hazardous waste, and exposure to toxic and hazardous waste may have negative effects on health, there is a problem that needs remediation. The rejoinder that "it's income, not race" that influences siting is naive.

The major analytic technique used in environmental justice research has been multiple regression. The results are usually summarized as standardized regression coefficients (beta weights) that indicate the amount of change in the outcome variable per unit change in the predictor variable, holding the other predictor variables constant. The process of standardization puts all variables on the same unit of measurement, one with a mean of 0 and a standard deviation of 1, a necessary conversion when employing measures of such disparate units as median household income and proportion minorities. The larger the absolute value of the regression coefficient, the greater importance attributed to that variable as a contributor to the outcome variable. This direct interpretation is fine as long as the predictor variables are not strongly related to each other. How to deal with the confounding relationship between predictors is to identify a model that takes this relationship into effect. This modeling is often referred to as path analysis, causal modeling, or structural equation modeling (Blalock, et al., 1964). The basic model for environmental justice research is diagrammed in Figure 4.1.

The arrow from "proportion of minority" to "siting" represents the direct, independent influence of minority concentration on the frequency of environmentally hazardous sites. A positive regression coefficient is expected here, indicating that siting increases as minority concentration increases. The arrow from "household income" to "siting" represents the direct, independent influence of income level on the frequency of environmentally hazardous sites. A negative regression coefficient is expected here, indicating that siting increases as income decreases. These two arrows are the emphasis of most environmental justice research. The arrow from "minority" to "income" represents our assumption that minority status influences income, more specifically, that overall income decreases as minority concentration increases. This model shows that we expect

Figure 4.1: Basic model for environmental justice.

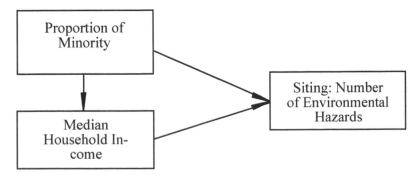

minority concentration to influence siting in two ways, first in a direct path, and second, indirectly through the mediation of income. When income is a (negative) correlate of race, this is yet another manifestation of racism.

To illustrate the evaluation of this model, consider the figures in Table 4.1. Proportion of minority and median household income are used to predict an overall environmental hazard index, the number of pollution sources in a zip code per square mile. The first row of results represents all 873 Michigan zip codes. The next two rows separate the Michigan zip codes into Southeast Michigan (206 zip codes from seven counties) and the rest of the state (667 zip codes from 76 counties). The last row includes just the 64 zip codes in Wayne County.

In Southeast Michigan and in Wayne County–a part of Southeast Michigan–income and race are highly correlated (-.59 for Southeast Michigan and -.76 for Wayne County), thus an indirect effect of race on siting is observed. In all of Michigan and in the zip codes beyond the southeast portion of the state, income and race are weakly correlated (-.22 for all Michigan zip codes and -.18 for the rest of the state beyond the Southeast). Here, indirect effects are at a minimum, but so also are the effects of income on siting. When race and income are essentially independent of each other, race is the dominant predictor. When race affects income, race has both direct and indirect effects on siting. Although statistical effect and cause are not synonymous, the relationships are of a magnitude that cannot be ignored.

Causality: Beyond Statistics to Where Effects Count:

Table 4.1: Direct and Indirect Effects (regression coefficients) of Race and Income on Siting of Environmental Hazards

Sample	Direct Effects		Indirect Effect of Race on Hazard	Total Variance Accounted for
	Income Hazards	Race Hazards	Race Income Hazards	R^2
All of MI	.012	.614	-.003	.374
Southeast MI	-.318	.461	.189	.488
Rest of MI	-.005	.482	.001	.233
Wayne County	-.527	.151	.398	.421

A causal relationship should meet three conditions. 1) The cause precedes the effect in time. 2) The two variables are empirically correlated with one another. 3) The observed empirical correlation cannot be explained away as being due to the influence of a third causal variable (Babbie, 1989). The sitings of industrial and waste management facilities are the result of multiple economic, political, and social considerations. It bears repeating that minorities tend to live in areas with greater exposure to toxic and hazardous waste, and because exposure to toxic and hazardous waste may have negative effects on health, there is a problem that needs remediation.

Cause and effect relations are more complex than what is described above. At this point, we want to take a few minutes to set the context and briefly describe some of that complexity. One of the basic goals of the social scientist is to explain human behavior, to show why things are the way they are. To gain a greater appreciation of causality, we must view it within the context of determinism and free will. Although determinism and free will have been debated by philosophers for centuries, we do not offer a resolution, but we do raise the issue for greater appreciation of its complexity. The fundamental issue is this: Is a person's behavior the product of that person's personal will power or the behavioral outcome of forces and factors in the world that one cannot control or may not even recognize? What factors determine certain outcomes? Whenever we undertake explanatory social science research, i.e., when we set out to discuss the cause of prejudice, for example, we adopt a model of human behavior and assume that people are without freedom of choice. Because of free will, social scientists do not believe that all human actions, thoughts, and feelings are determined. Also the deterministic model does not assume that causal relations are simple ones, nor does it assume that we are all controlled by the same factors or forces. Social science is on much firmer ground when it operates mainly from a probabilistic causal model or model of association. However, the deterministic model is at the base of explanatory social science and suggests that we do not know all there is to know about causes or that we ever will. We look for reasons why people behave the way they do. We look for reasons why people of color are overburdened with toxins or live in poverty or experience a disproportionate amount of toxic-induced and aggravated disease. We implicitly assume that these characteristics are determined by forces and factors that operate on them. Even though the behavior of human beings is not totally determined, we must use the deterministic model for explanations when we engage in social science research.

This brings us to the questions that have troubled researchers, policymakers, and lay people alike. Was the polluting facility there first and the people then moved to the nuisance? Or, were the people there first and the nuisance moved to where the people lived?[1] With respect to the first question, it looks as though free will was involved in that people made a deliberate choice of moving to where the facility was located. Yet people may have moved to these nuisances because of racial discrimination in housing patterns or because of cheaper housing stock. But the choices that people make about where to live may not be based on the fact that they are black but because their ancestors were black and faced gross forms of racial discrimination in employment, housing, and education. Said another way, when whites take over from where their parents left off, they are in much better economic condition than when blacks take over from where their parents left off. People of color have fewer resources to work with because of past wrongs, and because of their economic condition they make decisions to move to areas where housing stock is cheaper and often closer to an environmental nuisance. Even though some blacks can afford to move to environmentally safe and productive neighborhoods if they choose to, the legacy of racism has played a deterministic role in limiting where most blacks live and are able to live today. If policy makers fail to take historical factors of racial discrimination into account, then value-neutral siting policies will most often end in a discriminatory effect. But no matter whether the choice was based upon free will or determinism or whether the sites or people were there first, the problem of the disproportionate environmental burden must be dealt with.

The second part of the question, were the people there first and the nuisance moved to where the people lived, raises another issue, that of intent. Is free will at the base of intent? Did policy makers intend to locate facilities in neighborhoods of people of color? Were these decisions socially determined, based upon the effect of racism that shaped certain patterns of behavior? To what extent is free will or intent influenced by broader deterministic factors that created the racial context in which decisions are made? While economic

---

[1] One such study was by Been (1994) where she states that the evidence of locally undesirable land uses (LULUs) are disproportionately located in communities of color and communities of low income. Been claims that her research does not establish that host communities were disproportionately minority at the time the sites were selected. She raises the question of whether the disproportionate burdens of LULUs were due to siting decisions or whether they were due to discrimination in the housing market. For example, if the neighborhood was disproportionately populated by people of color or people of low income at the time of the LULU siting, then a reasonable inference would be to change the siting policy. On the other hand if people moved into an area after the LULUs were built and the area became increasingly poor or increasingly populated by people of color, then the solution becomes more complex, because the distribution of LULUs then looks more like the age old problems of housing discrimination and poverty. Been speculates that communities surrounding LULUs may have become poorer and inhabited by more people of color because of poverty, housing discrimination, job location, and lack of transportation and public services. These forces may have led the poor and racial minorities to gravitate toward the nuisance because neighborhoods near the LULUs offered the cheapest housing.

arguments are advanced as reasons for siting environmental nuisances in certain areas, perhaps we must view the problem as historical rather then ahistorical. The overwhelming majority of blacks are poor because of historical circumstances as mentioned above. The historical patterns of racism that have helped to shape where people of color live, i.e., in poor neighborhoods, makes them vulnerable to policy decisions when cheap land values become the primary target for siting decisions. Although it is difficult to prove intent, i. e., whether decisions were based upon free will or determinism, we should look for patterns of disproportionate impact of toxins on communities of color and communities of low-income and find remedies for the lack of environmental protection. Although a considerable amount of this book takes a cross section view of the problems in Michigan, we urge the reader to keep historical factors in mind. The analyses and profiles of Michigan and its cities that follow show the overburden endured by people of color and low income.

Issues of Denial, Defense, Delay, Distraction and Division

Companies or governments, when confronted with the probability that they may be responsible for environmental harm or the biophysical ill-health of people and communities, often respond in the following, overlapping ways.

The first response is to deny the charge of wrongdoing by emphatically stating that "there is no harm to human health." More specifically, companies have denied the link between asbestos and cancer, and between smoking and lung cancer, and have denied in many cases the ill effects of chlorine and the evidence of global climate change.

The second response is to defend one's position. To bolster their denials of harm, industry uses scientific sounding phrases such as "no proof of harm has been shown." The use of scientific sounding language such as "no proof of harm" as a defense can be misleading. "No proof of harm" may sound like "no harm" to the undiscriminating ear. In a scientific laboratory situation, a scientist works to prove cause and effect and to replicate results. But in the laboratory, the scientist has control over conditions, and assures the reliability of statements such as "all things being equal" when results are presented. It is difficult enough to create the laboratory conditions necessary to prove beyond scientific doubt that a certain chemical causes a certain ailment, let alone to show these causal relations in the real world. Even though industry understands the difference between "no proof of harm" and "no harm," it still uses the scientific language of "no proof" to imply "no harm" (Bruno, et al. 1999)

The third response is delay (Bruno, et al. 1999). The cause and effect argument raises a moral dilemma. By definition, the proof of a cause-effect relation comes after the damage has been done. To prove cause and effect relations or to claim no proof of harm takes us down the road of the "paralysis of analysis" or arguments that stifle action and creativity. The no proof of harm cited by the cigarette industry lasted more than 30 years and proved to be a rather effective delaying action. In the meantime thousands of people suffered from cancer or died from it. To imply no harm in the face of people who suffer from toxic-induced or aggravated disease is insensitive and ineffective. People know something is wrong, and when their demands for certainty and immediate solution result in the paralysis of analysis, their feelings of anger and distrust of corporate and government policymakers are reinforced (Bryant, 1995).

When we can show association between two events, or probable causality or strong connections between two events, or a strong possibility of a problem, then we should use the precautionary principle of avoiding harm even when there is no absolute scientific certainty. We should err on the side of health and not on the side of harm.

The fourth response is to divide opinion through delaying and distracting tactics. In addition to the causality arguments that delay action, other arguments center on the value to society of the product in question. If a product is discontinued, the downside arguments would be inconvenience, increased prices for substitutes, and loss of jobs. It is interesting to note that any time there are attempts to regulate industry to protect communities against environmental harm, it has fought back by claiming that regulations put industry in unfair competition with international competitors—competitors who are not subject to stringent environmental regulations. Industry claims such regulations cut deeply into profits and that workers must choose between environmental protection and jobs. Forcing a choice between jobs and environmental protection is called "Environmental blackmail," as workers are pitted against environmentalists by industry. Industry has made large financial contributions to legislators, and even unions and churches, for public relations purposes in exchange for political support. Industry attempts to gain political support by controlling the environmental debate, by co-opting and distorting environmental language, by forming environmental departments and giving speeches about the importance of the environment to business, by creating corporate-sponsored environmental groups, by allying themselves with mainstream non-governmental organizations, by investing in small-scale projects that are environmentally friendly and distract from their destruction of nature, and by posing as friends of the environment and leaders of the movement. On the surface these seem to be laudatory endeavors, but in fact they are a Trojan horse. In some cases industry may be sincere, but in other cases actions like those mentioned above are only a green scam, a bold attempt to appear green when they are not.

Attempts to divide the ranks of environmentalists are manifested in other ways, too. The community becomes split in that some want to invoke the pre-cautionary principle and others do not in fear that to admit there is a possible health problem will erode property values, the source of their life-savings. People are put in the position of choosing between the safety of their community and the protection of life savings. If the burden of proof were on industry, the com-munity would be relieved from fighting an uphill battle. The burden of proof must be borne by industry, not by the community.

Conclusion

Our Michigan Environmental Database continues to grow. For example, educational achievement data and lead counts for young children have recently been added, as well as an additional year of cancer data. There are plans to continue adding updates to the environmental hazards portion of the file, as well as aggregating data on specific chemicals, emission types, and facilities types by zip code.

The Michigan Environmental Database is not, and never will be, complete. We must continue to add variables as more information becomes available in order to further our work of analyzing the condition of environmental injustice in Michigan.

5

HAZARDOUS WASTE AND SPATIAL RELATIONS ACCORDING TO RACE AND INCOME IN THE STATE OF MICHIGAN

Bunyan Bryant and Elaine Hockman

While some feel that it will be too expensive to clean up our communities, we disagree. The long-term costs of pollution-related illness will most likely be greater than the short-term costs of cleanup. Although it was not possible to prove causality, the results indicate quite strongly that minorities tend to live in areas with greater exposure to toxic and hazardous waste, and exposure to toxic and hazardous waste may have negative effects on health.

Purpose of the Study

Because a considerable amount of the current debate centers upon disagreements over the extent of the relationship between locations of hazardous waste sites and where people of color and people of low-income live, this chapter has two objectives. First, we will assess the extent to which knowledge of the racial and economic status predicts the incidence of TRI, Act 307, and LUST sites in the state of Michigan. Second, we wish to clarify the understanding of environmental injustice by comparing defined geographical areas in the state of Michigan with respect to the incidence of hazardous waste sites and socio-economic characteristics.

The first objective focuses on exposure to environmental pollution that comes as a by-product of manufacturing and commercial endeavors, while the second objective focuses on exposure to sites that were deliberately built to handle environmentally hazardous waste. Each objective has a different implication for the issue of environmental justice. Because pollution sites may have predated population trends, significant results with respect to the first objective will have tremendous implications for clean-up measures. Significant results with respect to the second objective have tremendous implications for the existence of racism because of the planned decisions for siting these facilities.

To accomplish the first objective, multiple regression analysis was used to weigh the relative strengths of race and income with respect to the distribution of TRI, LUST, and Act 307 sites. The sample for this analysis was the 873

Michigan zip codes. Zip codes, rather than census tracts, were used as the unit of analysis because they were a common linking variable from one data source to another.

To address the second objective, multivariate analysis of variance was used to compare six groupings of Michigan zip codes with respect to exposure to environmental hazards and socio-economic characteristics. The 873 Michigan zip codes were divided into six categories on the basis of incidence of two other types of hazardous facilities and geographic distance. The first group, with average size of 34,680 people, consisted of nine zip codes that were known to house incinerators. The second group, with average size of 33,846 people, consisted of the 26 zip codes that surround the nine incinerator zips. The third group, with average size of 35,268 people, consisted of 9 more zip codes that were known to house commercial hazardous waste facilities in the greater-Detroit area. The fourth group, with average size of 34,233 people, consisted of the 24 zip codes that surround the nine hazardous waste facilities. The fifth group consisted of 30 zip codes that represent other Michigan geographical areas of approximately the same size, in terms of population, to those already identified. This group of zip codes, with average size of 28,388 people, serves as "comparison cities." The last group consisted of the remaining 775 Michigan zip codes, with average size of 7,887 people. In contrast to the first five zip code categories, which were mostly in the "inside urban" category, this last group of remaining Michigan zip codes was classified mostly as "rural, non-farm." Using multivariate analysis of variance, these six zip code classifications were compared with respect to incidence of TRI, LUST, and Act 307 sites as well as socio-economic indicators.

Research Questions

1. Do race and income predict incidence of TRI, Act 307 and LUST sites? The dependent variables for analysis associated with the first study question were, for each zip code, a) the number of Act 307 sites, b) the number of chemicals cited in the Act 307 sites, c) the number of TRI sites, d) the log of the total number of pounds of emissions, from all sources, from the TRI sites, e) the number of LUST sites, and f) presence/absence of an incinerator or commercial hazardous waste site. The two independent, or predictor, variables were a) race distribution taken as the log of the ratio of the number of blacks to the number of whites, and b) median household income. Thus in the several analyses linked to the first objective, multiple regression was used to predict the incidence of pollution sites from knowledge of race and income.

2. Do zip codes that a) house incinerators, and b) house hazardous waste facilities differ from a) zip codes in their immediate geographical area, b) zip codes from the rest of the state of similar population size, and c) remaining Michigan zip codes with respect to incidence of pollution sites, racial distribution, income, education level, and birth weight? Analysis of variance was used to address the second research question.

Results

Population Characteristics: A Portrait of the 873 Michigan Zip Codes Taken from the 1990 U. S. Census

Although the average number of individuals living in a Michigan zip code was 10,647, the majority of the population lived in zip codes classified by the Census as "inside urban."

The population within a Michigan zip code is, on the average, 92% white. Although the values of "proportion white" cover the full range from .01 to 1.00, the distribution was negatively skewed: zip codes with a small proportion of whites were relatively rare.

Within the Michigan zip codes, the population is, on the average 5% black. While the proportions per zip code ranged from .00 to .99, the distribution showed a positive skew, indicating few zip codes with a large proportion of blacks. The average proportion of Hispanics per zip code was .015. For Native Americans and Asians, the average proportions were .010 and .006, respectively.

Taken as a whole, the average proportion of minorities—where minority-proportion was defined as total number of persons in the zip code minus the number of whites in the zip code, divided by the total number of persons in the zip codes—was .08 and ranged from .00 to .99. The distribution was positively skewed. Few zip codes have large proportions of minorities.

A variable that may indicate crowded living quarters was the proportion of households with seven or more people. While this category was relatively rare, with an average proportion of .013 per zip code, it has a strong positive skew, indicating, on the average, few large households.

The census data reported a grouped frequency distribution for highest level of education obtained. Two sets of indices were computed from these frequency distributions. Within each set, the education categories were classified as high, mid, and low, using the following definitions:

Table 5.1: Highest Level of Education Attained: Average Proportion.

Highest Level of Education Attained	Proportion of All Persons in Zip Code	Proportion of Adults Reporting Education Level in Zip Code
Low	.160	.249
Mid	.395	.618
High	.086	.133
Sum	.641	1.000

Low: less than a high school diploma or GED.

Mid: high school diploma, some college, or Associate's degree.

High: bachelor's degree or graduate/professional degree.

The first set of indices used the total persons in the zip code as the base for computing the proportion of persons achieving a low, mid, or high education level. The second set of indices used the number of persons in the zip code for whom education level was reported as the base. The second set was based upon the adult population in the zip code. The average proportions per zip are:

On the average, 36% of the population in a zip code were younger than the age for which highest education level was reported. Some zip codes had no black population. Zip codes with a black population had fewer adult black persons responding (57%) than whites (65%).

The census data reported the grouped frequency distribution for highest level of education obtained separately for blacks and whites. The two sets of education indices were computed for the two races.

Birth weight was included in the study as an indicator of possible physiologi-

Table 5.2: Highest Level of Education Attained by Blacks and Whites: Average Proportion of Total Zip Code Population

Highest Level of Education Attained	Proportion of All Black Persons In 575 Zip Codes	Proportion of White Persons in 873 Zip Codes
Low	.171	.160
Mid	.313	.401
High	.082	.089
Sum	.566	.650

cal effects of exposure to pollution. These data were supplied by the Michigan Department of Public Health for 425 zip codes with populations over 5,000. Zip codes with small populations were excluded in order to protect anonymity. For the purposes of this paper, the definitions of low, mid, and high birth weights are:

Low: less than 3,000 grams (less than 5.48 pounds).

Mid: 3000 grams – 3,999 grams (5.49 - 8.77 pounds).

High: 4,000 grams and higher (greater than 8.77 pounds.

The average proportion in the low category was .102; in the mid category, .752; and in the high category, .144.

The number of households on public assistance was included in the study as an indicator of socio-economic status. The average proportion of households on public assistance within a zip code was .087. This index ranged from .00 to .46 and showed a positive skew.

The average household income, recorded as median household income by zip code, was $28,961.66, with a standard deviation of $10,822.47 and a slight positive skew.

The census data reported a grouped frequency distribution for median household income for blacks and whites separately. Indices representing the proportion of households with high, mid, and low incomes were computed. For this study the definitions of high, mid, and low are:

Low: less than $14,999

Mid: $15,000 - $49,999

High: greater than $50,000

There were no black households in 398 zip codes.

Table 5.3: Highest Level of Education Attained by Blacks and Whites: Average Proportion of Adult Zip Code Population

Highest Level of Education Attained	Proportion of Black Adults in 524 Zip Codes	Proportion of White Adults in 873 Zip Codes
Low	.284	.245
Mid	.560	.619
High	.157	.136

Information was available for the number of Act 307, LUST and TRI sites in each zip code from the year (1989). The mean number of each of these sites per zip code is: 5.8 for Act 307, 6.2 for TRI, and 12.5 for LUST.

Do Race and Income Predict Incidence of Toxic Variables?
Regression Analyses

To determine the extent to which population characteristics predict the incidence of toxic sites, a series of multiple regression analyses were computed in which the log of the ratio of blacks to whites and median household income were used as predictors of toxic site incidence. The log of the black to white ratio was used to normalize the distribution. The resulting seven equations gave very similar results. No matter which toxic site variable served as the dependent variable, the ratio of blacks to whites was a significant predictor; as the number of blacks in the zip code increased relative to the number of whites in the zip code, so did the incidence of toxic sites. In only one instance (number of LUST sites) did median household income make a significant contribution to the equation. The results of these multiple regressions are summarized in Table 5.6, which presents the beta weights and the corresponding t tests as well as the multiple correlations. The multiple correlations, ranging from .18 to .43, show that racial distribution and income account for 3% to 18% of the variation in toxic waste variables.

Table 5.4: Average Proportions of Blacks and Whites in Three Household Income Levels.

Household Income Level	Blacks from 475 Zip Codes	Whites from 873 Zip codes
Low	.307	.262
Mi	.464	.534
High	.230	.204

Table 5.5: Number of Toxic Sites per Zip Code

Toxic Site Type	Mean Number of Sites per Zip Code	Standard Deviation
Act 307	3.5	6.10
Lust	6.8	9.96
TRI	3.1	8.10

Do areas with incinerators or commercial hazardous waste sites differ from their neighbors and the rest of the state with respect to incidence of other toxic sites and socio-economic indicators?

Multivariate Analyses of Variance.

The first analysis to answer this question used as dependent variables six toxic incidence variables used in the regression analyses reported above. The purpose of this analysis was to determine if there was a differential incidence of other toxic sites, given that the zip did or did not house incinerators or hazardous waste sites. In order to maintain a favorable ratio of number of variables to number of cases in this multivariate analysis, the nine zip codes with incinerators were combined with the nine zip codes with hazardous waste sites to form one group; the two sets of surrounding zip codes were also combined into one group. The omnibus F was 19.125, which was significant beyond the .001 level; all univariate F's were significant beyond the .001 level. The mean number of toxic incidence variables for the four zip code categories is presented in Table 5.7.

Table 5.6: Ratio of Blacks to Whites and Median Household Income as Predictors of Toxic Sites.

Toxic Site Variable	Log Ratio of Blacks to Whites		Median Household Income		
	Beta	t	Beta	t	R
Total Number of Sites	.386	12.301*	.048	1.520	.385*
Incinerator and/or Hazardous waste Sites	.211	6.357*	-.030	.911	.216*
TRI Sites	.318	9.852*	.013	.403	.317*
Log TRI Emissions	.310	9.585*	.038	1.163	.309*
Act 307 Sites	.168	5.027*	-.046	1.376	.178*
Number of Chemicals in Act 307 Sites	.201	6.054*	-.031	.921	.206*
LUST Sites	.420	13.669*	.114	3.715*	.427*

*$p < .001$

The second analysis used the proportion of minorities in the zip code and median household income as dependent variables. Thus this analysis of variance was parallel to the regression analyses reported above. The omnibus F of 22.183 was significant beyond the .001 level; only the univariate F for minority-proportion was significant. Locations containing and locations near incinerator/hazardous waste sites were more heavily populated with minorities than were locations at a distance from these sites. Income distribution was not significant. The means for the six zip code categories are presented in Table 5.8.

The next analysis in this series used proportion whites, proportion blacks, proportion of births in the highest weight category and proportion of births in the lowest weight category. Both the multivariate F of 7.71 and each of the univariate F's were significant beyond the .001 level. The highest proportion of whites was found in the zip codes beyond the areas housing and neighboring especially dangerous waste sites. These same distant zip codes have the largest proportion high-birth-weight babies and the lowest proportion low-birth-weight babies. The mean proportions for the six zip code categories are presented in Table 5.9.

The proportion of households with seven or more people, the proportion on public assistance, and the proportion of Hispanics were used as the dependent variables in the next analysis. The overall F was 11.977, which was signifi-

Table 5.7: Mean Toxic Incidence for Zip Codes With Especially Hazardous Sites and Control Zip Codes

Toxic Incidence Variables	F	Incinerator / Hazardous waste	Surrounding Zip Codes	Comparison Cities	Rest of Michigan
Total Number of Sites	92.10	50.2	36.3	42.8	10.0
TRI Sites	61.72	16.4	13.2	8.1	2.0
Log TRI Emissions	38.98	4.3	3.5	2.7	1.1
Act 307 Sites	25.39	9.4	5.1	10.9	3.0
Number of Chemicals in Act 307 Sites	28.54	22.9	13.3	26.5	6.6
LUST Sites	104.16	24.3	17.9	23.9	5.0

Table 5.8: Mean "Proportion Minority" and Mean "Median Household Income" for Zip Codes With Hazardous Sites and Control Zip Codes.

Zip Code Group	Proportion Minority	Median Household Income
Incinerators	.304	$24,093
Surrounding Incinerators	.314	$27,159
Hazardous waste Facilities	.430	$26,847
Surrounding Hazardous Facilities	.265	$31,531
Comparison Cities	.230	$25,524
Rest of Michigan	.054	$29,157
F	48.193	1.508

cant beyond the .001 level. The univariate F's for proportion of Hispanics and proportion on public assistance were also significant beyond the .001 level; the F for proportion of large households, a variable with very little variation and small values, was significant at the .03 level. The means and F ratios for these three variables are presented in Table 5.10. Although there were relatively few Hispanics in Michigan, the largest proportions were found, on the average, in zip codes housing incinerators and in the comparison cities. Zip codes with incinerators and zip codes with hazardous waste facilities have the largest proportions on public assistance. The one zip code category with a higher incidence of large households was the one including hazardous waste sites.

The last multivariate analysis of variance looked at the proportions of adult whites and blacks in the lowest and highest levels of education and income. From this analysis, we observed to what extent blacks and whites within zip codes differed from each other as well as how they differed across zip code categories. The overall F was 3.64, which was significant beyond the .001 level. Significant univariate F's were found a) for both education levels among the whites and b) for the lowest income levels for both whites and blacks. The means for this analysis were presented in Table 5.11 for education and Table 5.12 for income.

Limitations of the Study

Our analysis reflects a single "snapshot in time" of data collected in 1989 and 1990 and as such do not provide insight into the processes that have resulted in the current socio-economic landscape. A more detailed study of the process

Table 5.9: Means for "Proportion Whites," "Proportion Blacks," "Proportion High-Birth-Weight," and "Proportion Low-Birth-Weight" for Zip Codes with Hazardous Sites and Control Zip Codes.

Zip Code Category	Proportion Whites	Proportion Blacks	Proportion High Birth Weight	Proportion Low Birth Weight
Incinerators	.696	.239	.126	.150
Surrounding Incinerators	.693	.258	.123	.146
Hazardous waste Facilities	.570	.407	.116	.166
Surrounding Hazardous Facilities	.735	.235	.133	.140
Comparison Cities	.797	.139	.139	.113
Rest of Michigan	.922	.046	.149	.091
F	17.81	16.51	9.71	25.05

Table 5.10: Means for Proportion Hispanic, Proportion in Households of 7 or More, and Proportion on Public Assistance for Zip Codes With Hazardous Sites and Control Zip Codes.

Zip Code Category	Proportion Hispanic	Proportion in Large Households	Proportion on Public Assistance
Incinerators	.052	.019	.188
Surrounding Incinerators	.035	.016	.142
Hazardous waste Facilities	.013	.026	.157
Surrounding Hazardous Facilities	.019	.016	.117
Comparison Cities	.046	.012	.128
Rest of Michigan	.013	.012	.081
F	24.29	2.48	18.94

Table 5.11: Mean Education Levels for Adult Whites and Blacks: Proportion in Each Category of Education.

Zip Code Category	White Lowest Educ. Level	White Highest Educ. Level	Black Lowest Educ. Level	Black Highest Educ. Level
Incinerators	.332	.134	.409	.103
Surrounding Incinerators	.253	.204	.295	.156
Hazardous waste Facilities	.353	.126	.286	.149
Surrounding Hazardous Facilities	.291	.112	.225	.103
Comparison Cities	.207	.224	.328	.162
Rest of Michigan	.219	.163	.265	.173
F	9.90, $p < .001$	3.16, $p=.008$	<1	<1

that gave rise to the racial disparities as reflected in this paper needs to be done. The use of zip code as the unit of analysis has limitations because of varying size, in terms of both number of people in a zip code and geographic territory covered. Using proportions and other ratios provided a means of control for unequal population sizes. It was unknown how people distribute themselves within a zip code. The actual distance of residence from pollution site was also not known. Further research using more refined measures of proximity is needed.

Conclusions and Discussion

The statistical results of this research confirmed findings from other studies: race—not income—has significant impact on disproportionate incidence of exposure to toxic and hazardous waste. Using a variety of minority and socio-economic indicators, this study decisively and consistently demonstrated that minorities in the state of Michigan, regardless of income and education, were disproportionately burdened by environmental pollution. Whether predicting incidence of exposure to environmental pollutants in the form of TRI, LUST, or Act 307 sites, or assessing differences in socio-economic composition of Michigan zip codes with respect to presence or absence of incinerator and/or

Table 5.12: Mean Income Levels for Whites and Blacks: Proportion in Each Category of Income.

Zip Code Category	White Lowest Income	White Highest Income	Black Lowest Income	Black Highest Income
Incinerators	.340	.191	.423	.144
Surrounding Incinerators	.271	.219	.402	.161
Hazardous waste Facilities	.310	.219	.439	.160
Surrounding Hazardous Facilities	.252	.244	.216	.191
Comparison Cities	.289	.195	.456	.133
Rest of Michigan	.225	.249	.290	.248
F	4.33, p=.001	1.21, p=.301	2.98, p=.012	1.43, p=.213

commercial hazardous waste sites, the study results were clear:

- As the number of blacks relative to the number of whites increased so did incidence of TRI, LUST, and ACT 307 sites, their emissions, and number of chemicals released.

- Income did not predict incidence of TRI and ACT 307 sites or their emissions. There was a small positive but significant predictive relationship between income and number of LUST sites.

- The largest proportions of minorities live in zip codes that housed commercial hazardous waste facilities, zip codes surrounding incinerator sites, and zip codes with incinerators.

- Zip codes with incinerators and/or commercial hazardous waste facilities also have the greatest exposure to environmental pollution from TRI and LUST sites. Exposure to Act 307 sites and their chemicals were equally as great as for comparison zip codes.

- Income was not significantly related to the six zip code categories identified in this study.

- The highest proportion of low birth weight babies was found in zip codes housing incinerators and/or commercial hazardous waste facilities.

• Zip codes that house incinerators have the largest proportion of people on public assistance.

In view of the findings from this study, the need for action to correct the disparities in exposure is clearly evident. The fact that race predicted the incidence of pollution sites that may predate population trends indicate the need for strong clean-up efforts. When these efforts are not forthcoming, it will be easy to attribute this inertia to racism. While some feel that it will be too expensive to clean up our communities, we disagree. The long-term costs of pollution-related illness will most likely be greater than the short-term costs of cleanup. Although it was not possible to prove causality, the results indicate quite strongly that minorities tend to live in areas with greater exposure to toxic and hazardous waste, and exposure to toxic and hazardous waste may have negative effects on health. The birth weight results presented above—that lower birth weight was found in pollution sites—supported the validity of the claim that toxic waste exposure has a negative impact on health. One of many health effects may come from the residential proximity of a waste site during pregnancy, thus increasing the maternal risk of bearing a child of low birth weight. Such babies, because of their low weight, may be more susceptible to multiple disease and developmental problems. In addition to other toxic and aggravated disease, little information is known about the psychological and economic stress that comes from living near such facilities. The constant preoccupation with personal and family safety often spill over into anger or despair; in some instances the depreciation of homes or the loss of life savings, perhaps due to health expenses, make it impossible for them to sell their homes in order to move to cleaner neighborhoods. Would people have moved into pollution areas if they knew the potential risks involved? Would they have done so if they could afford to move to cleaner environments? The more insidious forms of racism often keep people of color in the low wage category and seriously limit their housing options or places to live. While environmental racism exists, the question of whether people lived in these areas first or moved in later should not be a significant part of the discourse for cleanup.

The question becomes one of who will pay for cleanup. Should the cost be distributed between citizen taxpayers and industry, or should industry by itself be held accountable? It can be argued that those who live near the major pollution sites were already paying more than their share in terms of probable ill effects on their health.

Cleanup is not the only action that needs to be taken. There is the question of how to provide for continued disposal needs. The results of this study clearly indicate that areas with large proportions of minorities have already suffered more than their share of pollution sites, while areas of the state with few or no minorities have enjoyed few or no toxic or hazardous waste sites. Areas with large minority populations were already supersaturated with pollution sites. If decisions to locate additional facilities in these same geographic areas continue to be made, the case for the existence of environmental racism is made stronger.

In view of the findings from this study, the need for action to correct the disparities in exposure is evident. We need a short-term, an intermediate, and a long-term strategy for cleaning up our communities.

Short-range Strategy

We must call a moratorium on the siting of new hazardous and non-hazardous waste facilities in low income and minority communities until EPA and state governments develop equitable siting policies. Any siting strategies should include people from high-risk populations as an integral part of any decision regarding siting. In addition, local community groups should also be involved in any decisions regarding environmental cleanup. This is to suggest that every community must find a way to pull its weight. Is it justice when one group of people can share in society's waste disposal, but because of racial discrimination cannot share in society's rewards?

Intermediate to Long-Range Strategies

One of the best ways to deal with pollution is not to produce it in the first place. If we do not use toxic materials at the front end of production, we will not have to dispose of it at the back end of production. Although we will never be able to live in a toxic-free environment, we can do a lot to reduce the amount of exposures. Pollution prevention, although expensive, is a viable alternative. Clearly the $200 billion chemical industry will have the most to lose if we embarked upon a serious pollution prevention program. We must reward industry to research and produce products that are relatively free of toxins.

The government must also be willing to help industries through tough transitions. We cannot afford to continue business as usual nor can we afford to seriously disrupt the economy.

The social costs of pollution are real. The data of this study help foster our belief that racism and its correlate, poverty, may be more of a determinant of illness than any microbe or chemical. We feel that in order for environmental justice to occur, we not only must cleanup our neighborhoods but we must provide people with decent paying and safe jobs. We need to provide educational opportunities for students to realize their highest potential. We feel it is only when we provide opportunities for people to grow and develop that they will have greater options of where to live and more chances of improving their health. Indeed, the exposure to pollutants already suffered by minorities may be keeping them from their highest growth potential.

When the Kerner Commission (1968) reported that America was rapidly moving toward two unequal societies, one black and one white, little did it know that soon the black society would not only be overburdened with poverty, but also with life-threatening toxins.

Because the cleanup of communities of people of color has been neglected for years, we must take up the challenge of restoring these communities. We can clean them up to make our communities sustainable, safe, nurturing, and productive. Equal protection of the law and building safe and productive communities must be applied, regardless of race or income.

6

ENVIRONMENTAL JUSTICE AND THE LATINO COMMUNITY

Amy Holmes-Chavez

It seems that Latino communities in Michigan that are exposed to disproportionate levels of environmental hazards are of at least two types: Mixed Latino/Black communities located in large urban centers, and Latino communities located in smaller cities where the population is largely white and Mexican American. In the second case, qualitative evidence from interviews suggests that Mexican American communities in these small cities are often geographically segregated from the white population.

The term "Latinos" encompasses all people with family roots in Latin America. People of various national origins, people who ar-rived under a variety of circumstances in what we now know as the United States, immigrant and internally colonized groups, people of varying socio-economic backgrounds, and people with a great variety of ethnic and racial backgrounds and identities are designated as "Latino." Some Chicano/Mexican-American Latinos, for instance, became part of the United States as a result of military conquest when the U.S. annexed half of Mexico in 1848. Other Mexican Americans trace their family history to immigration from Mexico. Mexico and the United States have, since the establishment of the two modern nation-states, engaged in a series of formal agreements that have brought Mexican people to the United States under labor contracts, and have depended economically on informal (and often undocumented) labor migration (Acuña, 1988). Puerto Ricans have a long history as part of the United States. After the Spanish-American War (1898) Puerto Rico was transferred from colonial status under Spain to territorial status under the United States as part of the war settlement. It was not until the mid-1950s, however, that Puerto Ricans both on the mainland and in Puerto Rico were given U.S. citizenship. During the 1980s and 1990s, many people from Central American countries, particularly working class people and impoverished people from rural areas, have come to the United States to escape political repression and wars. The United States has played both a direct and indirect role in recent Central American wars. The United States has a complex relationship with Latin America, part of which has always been migration between Latin American countries and the United

States. People continue to immigrate to the U.S. from all over Latin America. This immigration has often been a result of political turmoil, but has also been motivated by economic factors, family ties, and personal motivations (Aguirre-Molina and Molina, 1994; Marin and Marin, 1991).

Fundamental to studying disproportionate exposure of Latino communities to environmental hazards is an understanding that Latinos have experienced discrimination and structural oppression in the United States. This oppression is part of a complex combination of racial, ethnic, class, and nativist discrimination in the United States rooted in the history of the United States' relationship with Latin America. One student at the University of Michigan, who self identifies as "*Mexicano*," explained oppression of Mexican American communities in this way:

> Mexicans were viewed by Anglos as beaners, greasers, wetbacks, and lazy.

> (Ceasar- March, 1995)[1]

Ceasar's comment about Anglo treatment of Mexican Americans reflects the complex nature of discrimination against Latinos in the United States. The derogatory ethnic slurs and stereotypes he refers to carry implications related to the type of work that many Mexican people have done in the United States, historical circumstances of U.S. conquest of northern Mexico, and subsequent labor migration between Mexico and the United States (Acuña, 1988).

Purpose of the Study

In undertaking this study, I felt it was important to examine the exposure of Michigan Latino communities to environmental hazards. Studies undertaken by Bryant and Hockman (see Chapter 5) and Mohai and Bryant (1992) examined the ability of the variables "percent minority" or "ratio of blacks to whites" in a community to predict prevalence of environmental hazards. Latinos make up only a small percentage of these variables if they are included at all. To better understand the exposure of Latino communities to environmental hazards, other methods than just census count must be used to locate Latino communities. Very little has been recorded about Michigan Latino communities in the social science literature. Thus results of this study can contribute to a growing body of information that can help present and future generations to understand better the experience of Latino communities in Michigan. For Latino communities, this can contribute to recognition in academia of what has been, for a long time,

---

[1]   Holmes interviewed several Latino students at the University of Michigan in preparation for this study. Names of the people interviewed have been changed where direct quotes from these interviews are presented.

a significant presence in the state.

Concern is growing about the health effects of environmental hazards on Michigan's Latino communities. One young woman from Southwest Detroit commented to me:

> Yes, it's really bad. My cousin used to play with a couple of friends down in the river [in Southwest Detroit.] She had a lot of trouble getting pregnant later in life, and none of the friends who used to play with her down there have been able to get pregnant.

> (Anita - March 1995)

This kind of story alarms me. I hope that this study can contribute to efforts to improve environmental conditions in Latino neighborhoods in Michigan, and can reduce threats to people's health associated with these hazards.

I have four goals for this study:

1. Better understand patterns of Latino settlement and residential segregation in Michigan. This includes levels of segregation in the state, and location of Latino neighborhoods in the state.

2. Determine whether Latino communities are disproportionately exposed to environmental hazards in comparison to both the overall population and to non-Hispanic whites.

3. Determine whether the presence of Latinos in a community is a significant predictor of presence of environmental hazards. Determine if this is true when the percent of African-American and median household income are taken into account.

4. Better understand the relationship of the percent Latino and percent African-American in neighborhoods in predicting prevalence of environmental hazards.

This study does not seek to determine the causes of inequity in distribution of environmental hazards. While determining why and how environmental hazards become distributed unevenly throughout the state is important, this study seeks simply to examine associations between the variables examined as a means to determine whether inequity exists.

Latinos and Environmental Justice Nationally

Information on the exposure of Latino communities to environmental hazards is available in a number of forms. Two national studies give us an indication of how environmental inequity affects Latino communities. First, the national study conducted by the United Church of Christ examined the disproportionate exposure of African-American and Latino communities to environmental hazards (Lee, 1992). Because information was reported for African-Americans and Latinos together, we can only guess that the findings of this report apply in a similar way to Latinos alone as they do to African-Americans and Latinos together. While this may not be true for isolated local cases, it is likely true nationwide, as African-Americans and Latinos often live either in the same or adjoining communities, or in separate communities, under similar environmental and economic circumstances. The second national study that is useful in determining the disproportionate exposure of Latino communities to environmental hazards is a nationwide examination of air pollution conducted by Wernette and Nieves (1992). Researchers found that, for data aggregated nationwide, Latinos are more likely to live in areas in which air pollution exceeds national standards than poor people (all ethnicities included), whites, or African-Americans. Wernette and Nieves found that 80% of Latinos, 65% of African-Americans, and 57% of whites live in areas with substandard air quality. For Latinos, 15% live in seven counties in the country where air pollution exceeds national standards for four or more pollutants (Wernette and Nieves, 1992).

Some work has been done on documenting local environmental problems and community struggles against environmental pollution in Latino communities. Peña and Gallegos (1993) have recorded events in the struggle of rural Chicano communities in northern New Mexico and southern Colorado to protect local water and land resources from contamination due to strip mining activities of the Battle Mountain Gold Company. Community members were particularly concerned over rising levels of lethal cyanide in water resources. Peña and Gallegos (1993) point out that this environmental struggle is fundamentally linked to an ongoing conflict in the area over land control and use which dates back to the mid-1800s when land in the Southwest was first transferred from Mexico to the United States as a result of a war settlement (the Treaty of Guadalupe Hidalgo). Land grant issues, they say, involve the environment, the law, economics, and culture. Rural Chicano communities that were granted rights to the land in contention in the 1800s have long practiced communal ownership and farming. Ethnic conflict over land grants and land control in southern Colorado and northern New Mexico gained national attention during the 1960s and 1970s when struggles became physical and involved armed occupations. Now, Chicano struggles over land in the area have evolved as environmental and health concerns (Peña and Gallegos, 1993).

In another example of Latino community activism around environmental problems, Latino and African-American youth in Williamsburg, Brooklyn, have led efforts to rid their neighborhoods of hazardous materials and block further contamination by local corporations. High school and college students in Williamsburg, where a majority of residents are Latino from the Caribbean and Central America, have engaged in community organizing and education activities, documented environmental hazards, brought about cleanup of illegal toxic waste dumps, and started a community recycling program. Currently, they are concerned about the proximity to a public school playground of the Radiac Research Corporation, which stores and transports toxic waste and low-level radioactive and flammable materials. The "Toxic Avengers," as the group calls itself, contend that cases such as this in their neighborhood are examples of environmental racism (Prout, 1992).

National attention has been drawn to two environmental problems affecting populations that are overwhelmingly Latino, and largely Mexican-American/ Chicano. The United Farm Workers (UFW), led by the late César Chávez, brought national attention to the way in which use of pesticides in U.S. agriculture affects the health of migrant farm workers through a national grape boycott. The UFW grape boycott, started in the 1960s as a way to establish union contracts with California grape growers, was revitalized in early 1980s to combat pesticide use after children in a predominantly Chicano community located near grape fields in a California county were found to have childhood cancer levels grossly exceeding national averages (AFL-CIO, 1993; Shavelson, 1988). The Farm Labor Organizing Committee in Toledo, Ohio, as well as other organizations, have also contributed to ongoing struggles to make agriculture safe for farm workers, of whom a majority in the United States are Mexican-American (Perfecto and Velásquez, 1992).

A second environmental problem whose consequences affect an almost entirely Mexican and Mexican-American population caught brief national attention in the late 1980s and early 1990s. Along the U.S.-Mexico border, unusually high rates of cancer and birth defects were linked to use of hazardous chemicals in U.S.-owned assembly operations located just south of the U.S.-Mexico border in northern Mexico. Communities on both sides of the border have been affected by hazardous chemicals released into rivers and ground water through unsafe disposal practices that often violate Mexican and U.S. laws, and international agreements (Gershman, 1991; Hansen-Kuhn and Hellinger, no date). In addition, factory workers in the assembly plants face workplace hazards related to poor air quality and exposure to toxic chemicals (U.S. News and World Report, 1991). While the North American Free Trade Agreement (NAFTA) was being debated by United States and Mexican congresses, environmental groups from both the U.S. and Mexico protested potential intensification of border pollution under NAFTA and gained some commitment from both governments to devote resources and attention to border cleanup.

Latino Settlement in Michigan

While little work has been done on how environmental hazards affect Latinos in Michigan, some historians have begun work on documenting settlement patterns of Latinos in the state. This information is useful in understanding potential environmental inequity, as environmental justice issues are closely linked to where people live.

Prof. Dennis Valdes of the University of Minnesota established the first presence of Mexican people in Michigan in trading patterns between indigenous (Native American) people of central Mexico and Native American tribes in the Upper Peninsula of Michigan long before Spanish and British arrival to what is now the U.S. and Mexico. Modern migration and settlement patterns of Mexican and Mexican-American people seem to be related mostly to the development of jobs in agriculture and industry in Michigan. During the economic boom of World War I and the 1920s, Mexican immigrants to Texas were recruited to work in sugar beet fields in Michigan. As other labor-intensive agriculture developed in the state, a pattern of labor migration was established between Texas and Michigan. Many people were recruited to work in Michigan during the summer months. Some returned to Texas each winter, and others settled in Michigan. During both World War I and World War II, many Mexican-Americans immigrated to the state and moved into jobs in booming heavy industries in such cities as Detroit, Saginaw, and Lansing. Temporary labor contracts in Michigan agriculture have continued to make migration patterns between Texas and Michigan an important part not only of Michigan's economy, but also of its social and cultural history (Rochin, Santiago, and Dickey, 1989; Valdes, 1992).

Valdes (1992), Rochin, Santiago, and Dickey (1989) have also documented the roots of a significant Puerto Rican community in Southwest Detroit. In 1950, 5,000 people from rural areas of Puerto Rico were recruited by the Michigan Sugar Company to work in the sugar beet industry. The workers were treated terribly, and after a tragic airplane accident in which many people being transported from Puerto Rico to Michigan sugar beet fields died, workers literally walked away from farms around Bay City, Saginaw, Pinconning, and Freeland to Detroit. There, they were received by priests from the Most Holy Trinity parish in the heart of Detroit's Mexican neighborhood, who helped them find housing and jobs in the area. Since then, immigration of Latinos from Mexico, the Caribbean, and Central America to Southwest Detroit has made it one of the most diverse and established Latino neighborhoods in the state (Rochin, Santiago, and Dickey, 1989; Valdes, 1992).

Demographic Profile of Latinos in State of Michigan

In the 1990 census, Latinos made up 2.2% of the Michigan population. Among Latinos, respondents to the long form of the U.S. Census reported the following national origins:

68.6%   Mexican

9.2%   Puerto Rican

2.6%   Cuban

19.2%   Other Hispanic

Presence of Latinos in the state is probably more significant than is reflected by census data for two reasons. First, migrant workers are only partially counted by the census as Michigan residents, though during the summer months they are a significant presence in the state. Second, undocumented residents of the state, many of whom are of Mexican and Central American origin, are unlikely to have answered the short or long form of the census (Aponte, 1994).

Latinos in Michigan are relatively young; the average age for the group is 23.1 years as opposed to the overall state average of 32.6 years. Educational attainment of Latinos is increasing but continues to lag behind non-Latinos. In 1990, 61% of Latinos over the age of 25 had completed high school, while 75% of the state's adults as a whole hold high school diplomas. This figure is somewhat affected by recent immigration from Mexico, where schooling is organized differently, and many students complete only six years of public education. Attainment of at least four years of college education among Latinos has also improved, at a current 12% of the Latino population. Statewide, 18% of adults have completed at least four years of college (Aponte, 1994).

Latinos are more likely to be in the labor force than non-Latinos as a whole. Labor force participation among Latino men is 75.1%, higher than the state average of 73.4%, and labor force participation for Latinas is 58.4%, over the state's 55.7% average for women (U.S. Census data 1990, as reported by Aponte, 1994). Nevertheless, Latinos in Michigan face high unemployment rates—13.4% for men and 12.4% for women. Aponte's analysis of U.S. Census measures of type of employment shows that most Latinos in Michigan work in manufacturing (20% of all Latinos), services (20%), and retail trade (13%). Aponte points out that Census data show only 2.7 percent of Latinos in Michigan working in agriculture, however migrant workers are not fully represented in these statistics. In 1989, median household income for Latinos in Michigan was approximately $26,900, while the overall median household income for the state was about $31,000. Median household income for Latinos was above medians for African-American and American Indian, and Eskimo and Aleut families, but below whites, and Asian and Pacific Islanders, who have the highest median household income in the state. Between 1979 and 1989, median household income in real dollar terms declined for every ethnic and racial group in Michigan. Declines in real income were more severe for Latinos than for whites, but less severe than for African-Americans, American Indian, Eskimo and Aleut, and Asian & Pacific Islanders (Aponte, 1994).

1990 U.S. Census Classification

Researchers have often used racial categories in their attempts to understand the consequences of the United States' troubled history of racial and ethnic relations. For most of its history, the U.S. Census used a single question regarding race as the primary method for respondents to express ethnic, cultural, and racial self-identification. Of course, racial categorization also has a long history in the United States, dating back to European colonization and to slavery. Attempts to understand the experience of Latino communities through use of racial categories is nearly impossible. In Latin America, European invasion of indigenous (Native American) groups, colonialism, slavery of Native American and African people, indentured servitude of people from Asian countries, and later immigration from all corners of the globe, has made Latin America a place of a great racial and ethnic mix. While some people may have preserved a racial, ethnic, and language identity that ties them closely to a particular indigenous group, or may identify closely with African, European, or Asian roots, many consider themselves part of a mixed racial group, or a mixed racial, cultural, and ethnic identity. Indeed, many national governments in Latin America express pride in "mixed" national identities (Aguirre-Molina and Molina, 1994; Marin and Marin, 1991).

For the purposes of this study "number Hispanic" and "percent Hispanic" will be used to identify Latino communities. This is a decision largely of convenience, since these are the only U.S. Census measures currently available. In addition, for Michigan the census measure "Hispanic" probably comes close to measuring Latino populations. It seems that most people in Michigan with family roots from Latin America are likely to have answered, "yes" to the U.S. Census question regarding "Hispanic Origin." Since the Spanish population of the state is quite low, most people answering "yes" to the "Hispanic origin" Census question in Michigan will, in fact, be of Latin American descent. The 1990 census probed for a further breakdown of type of Hispanic: white, black, Asian, Native American, or Other. The official U.S. federal government definition of "Hispanic" is not provided on the U.S. Census, so the question is left up to individuals to interpret.

When I asked University of Michigan students who were involved in Latino student campus organizations how they would answer the "Hispanic Origin" question on the Census, most said that they would check "yes." Many commented that they did not like the term as a way to identify themselves, but that, given the question, they would respond "yes." Though this information is anecdotal, it supports the idea that the census category "Hispanic," though problematic, is the most appropriate U.S. Census measure of Latino populations available at this time. We should remember that when we discuss "Latinos" in Michigan, we are largely talking about people of Mexican descent, though the Puerto Rican population is also substantial in some communities.

Until 1980, the primary way that the United States Census identified racial and ethnic groups was through a question about race that asked people to choose one of the following racial categories:

Census Question P9: RACE

__White

__Black

__American Indian, Eskimo, or Aleut (Tribal Affiliation_____)

__Asian or Pacific Islander

__Other race_____

Many Latinos have found this question impossible to answer, and inadequate as a way of expressing ethnic, racial, and cultural identity. This problem has been well documented by researchers in many areas of the social sciences (Aguirre-Molina and Molina, 1994; Marin and Marin, 1991). In informal interviews, I asked 12 Michigan-raised students at the University of Michigan (of mostly Mexican heritage) how they would answer the U.S. Census question about race. Most answered that they would check "Other race" and then write in "Mexican," "Mexican-American," or "Latino." One Chicana student who is originally from Detroit commented:

> After so many years of a mestisaje [mixing of indigenous and Spanish people and culture in Mexico and other Latin American countries], how can you ask someone Latino to identify their "race"? (Anita - March 1995).

She went on to comment:

> would put "other - Mexican-American," but that's because I'm here [at college.] If you ask people in Detroit, including my parents, lots of people would say, "white," because that's what their birth certificates say.

Historically, many people of Mexican and other Latin American descent have been classified on birth certificates as "white." While working at a health care clinic serving migrant farm workers, I observed hospital workers classifying the newborn children of indigenous (Native American) women from Guatemala as "white." People from Latin American countries where African descendency has been a significant historical factor may answer "black" on the U.S. Census form. One University of Michigan student from Puerto Rico commented to me:

> I'm Puerto Rican, so therefore I consider myself to be of African descent
>
> (José - March 1995).

One student originally from the Dominican Republic commented to me:

> I don't know how I would answer that form [U.S. Census short form.] I'm black, but I'm not a black American, if that's what they are asking.
>
> (Antonio - March 1995).

Because the U.S. Census question regarding "race" cannot identify Latino communities, the 1980 and 1990 Censuses included a question about ethnic heritage. Census respondents were asked to put "yes" or "no" in answer to a question about "Hispanic Origin." People of "Hispanic Origin" are officially defined by the U.S. federal government as those who live in the United States and trace their family history to Spanish-speaking Latin American countries or to Spain. Many Latinos have objected to use of the term "Hispanic" as a way to identify Latino communities. Some have commented that "Hispanic" emphasizes Spanish descent while Latinos actually trace their roots to countries where indigenous, African, Asian, and other European roots, or a mixed identity, may be equally or more important. Others have objected to the idea of lumping together people with different national origins, different ethnic/cultural identities, and different experiences with migration to the United States, particularly in terms of sectors of the economy entered on arrival. Many people have questioned the rationale for including people with family origins in Spain with those from Latin America, as the circumstances of Spanish and Latin American history, racial and ethnic identity in these places, and circumstances of Spanish and Latin American immigration to the United States are quite different. For research purposes, "Hispanic" presents some other definitional problems in identifying people of Latin American descent. People from Brazil may very well consider themselves Latin American or Latino, though Brazil is not a Spanish speaking country. People from Nicaragua, Bolivia, Guatemala and other multilingual countries may find an identification based on Spanish language to be disquieting (Aguirre-Molina and Molina, 1994; Marin and Marin, 1991).

1. *How are Latino populations distributed in Michigan? Where are significant Latino communities located?*

To get some sense of where significant Latino communities live in Michigan, I first examined historical work done on Latinos in the state and then interviewed Michigan-raised Latino students at the University of Michigan about their perceptions of where significant Latino communities are located in Michigan. Data from interviews with students are purely anecdotal, but in the absence of much current demographic documentation of Latinos in Michigan, it may help orient us in locating these Latino communities. I asked students both to identify where they thought Latino communities were located in the state, and to point out any identifiable Latino neighborhoods in the cities where they live.

Next, I examined U.S. Census data to determine where zip codes with the largest number of Latinos are located. When a number of zip codes from the same city appeared among those zip codes with high numbers of Latinos, I examined zip code maps of those cities to see whether the zip codes were adjoining. I considered these multiple-zip cases to signify especially large Latino communities.

Last, I examined census data to look at demographic characteristics of zip codes with large Latino communities. I looked at percent African-American, percent white, percent Latino, median income, and size of city or town to get some sense of racial, ethnic, and income dynamics in these zip codes.

Students I interviewed at the University of Michigan identified a number of cities and towns as places with significant Latino communities. The students also made comments about whether Latinos were distributed throughout the city or concentrated in specific neighborhoods. Thus the data in Table 6.1 are purely anecdotal data from informal interviews.

Historian Valdes (1992) has collected information and documented the historical development of Latino communities in a number of Michigan cities and towns during the past 100 years. These are listed in Table 6.2 and includes all the cities identified by students except for Kalamazoo and Pullman/Grant.

U.S. Census data provide demographic information for individual zip codes throughout the state. In order to use census data to locate Latino communities, I first aggregated zip codes by range of percent Latino to demonstrate the level of concentration of Latinos into particular zip codes throughout the state. These data are in Table 6.3 and indicate that there is significant residential segregation of Latinos in Michigan. If no residential segregation existed, we would expect to see approximately 2.2% Latino for each zip code, since this is the overall rate of Latinos in the state. The overwhelming majority of Michigan zip codes

Table 6.1: Cities and Towns in Michigan With Significant Latino Communities Identified in Interviews with Latino Students at the University of Michigan.

City or Town Identified	Students' Comments
Detroit	The [Detroit] Latino community is in Southwest Detroit
Saginaw	No comments made
Bay City	There are two neighborhoods that are Mexican and Black
Lansing	The North Side of Lansing is the Mexican part of town. There is also another neighborhood sort of central south where a lot of Mexican families live.
Flint	No comments made
Grand Rapids	The Southwest side of town is Mexican and poor white. African-Americans tend to live on the East Side.
Kalamazoo	There are quite a few Latinos, but I'm not sure if I would say there is a Latino neighborhood. There are two areas where a lot of Mexican and Black families live.
Adrian	When you see all of the industry sort of in the center of town, that is where Mexicans live. A lot of white people live in beautiful areas on the outskirts of town. That's sort of a rural area—a lot of white people are farmers.
Holland	There is a Mexican community in Holland, because a lot of people came as migrant workers and then settled.
Pullman and Grant	You wouldn't imagine this, but there are Mexicans in some little towns over on the west side of the state. It's because of the agriculture over there.

currently have below the state percent Latino, while some zip codes have a much higher concentration of Latinos—up to 32%.

In order to locate significant Latino communities using census data, I listed the 25 zip codes in Michigan with the largest number of Latinos. For these zip codes, I show in Table 6.4 the number Latino, percent Latino, percent African-American, percent white, median household income, and size of city/town.

These zip code data demonstrate a number of important issues. First, there is residential segregation of Latinos in Michigan. Second, there are particular zip codes and cities in Michigan that are significantly Latino in their ethnic composition. Census data support qualitative data from interviews with students at the University of Michigan, and historical documentation by Valdes,

Table 6.2: Cities and Towns Discussed by Dennis Valdes (listed in alphabetical order)

Adrian	Lansing
Bay City	Muskegon
Dearborn	Oil City
Detroit	Pontiac
Ecorse	Port Huron
Flint	Saginaw
Grand Rapids	Shepard
Grand Traverse (county)	Winn
Holland	Wyandotte

suggesting that significant Latino communities and popularly identified "Latino neighborhoods" exist in particular cities and towns in Michigan. Because Census data are aggregated here by zip code, rather than aggregated by city or town, it is difficult to draw direct comparisons between census data, Valdes's work, and interviews with students. In addition, Valdes's work documents the development of Latino communities over the past 100 years, whereas Census data measure communities in (1989). Nevertheless, most of the cities identified by students and by Valdes as having clearly identifiable Latino neighborhoods or communities appear in the Census data among those with zip codes with high numbers of Latinos.

2. *Are Latino communities in Michigan disproportionately exposed to environmental hazards in comparison with both the overall population, and to non-Hispanic whites?*

To determine whether Latino communities in Michigan are disproportionately exposed to environmental hazards, the distributions of the six environmental hazards defined in Chapter 4 (TRI citations, Act 307 sites, LUST sites, incinerator reports, hazardous waste facilities, and landfills) were examined for zip codes grouped to reflect Latino presence.[2] The zip code groupings were based upon the best descriptor of the minority representation and population density. The sizes and descriptions of these groupings are given in Table 6.5.

---

[2] When Holmes first wrote this paper, zip code area was not yet available and the only environmental hazards in the database were Act 307, TRI, and LUST. The analyses that follow maintain Holmes's intent, but a) use a different method to characterize the Latino distribution by zip code and b) use all six environmental hazards from the augmented database.

Table 6.3: Residential Segregation Patterns: Concentration of Latinos Throughout the State.

	Zip Codes With Below State % Latino			Zip Codes With Above State % Latino		
Range	0 %-2.2	< 1%	1% -< 2.2	2.2%- < 4	4 %- < 10	10 %- < 32
Number of Zip Codes	N = 97	N = 345	N = 281	N = 95	N = 45	N = 10

Number of Zip Codes in Michigan = 873

Average % Latino for the State of Michigan overall = 2.2 %

The mean numbers of the six environmental pollution sources were compared across these five zip code groupings using multivariate analysis of variance. The overall F ratio (10.512) was significant beyond the .001 level. For
the univariate Fs, both for differences among the means and for linearity of
the means, only that for landfills was not significant. The average number of
problems increases significantly with minority concentration. The means are
presented in Table 6.6.

Clearly, in the aggregate, zip codes with large Latino communities or a high
concentration of Latinos (in comparison with the general population and with
non-Hispanic whites) are exposed to higher levels of toxic releases.

3. a) Is the variable "proportion Hispanic per zip code"[3] a significant pre-
    dictor of environmental hazards and b) do these relationships hold when
    the percent of the population that is African American, and the median
    household income, are taken into account?

Multiple regression was used to answer these questions. The predictors
included proportion Hispanic, proportion non-Hispanic black, the product of
these two proportions (an interaction variable, as the joint distribution of black
and Latino is an important consideration), and median household income.
The prediction equation was significant for each environmental hazard except
landfills. The overall density index was also significant. In every instance, the
regression coefficient for proportion Hispanic was significant, indicating an
increase in the extent of environmental problems as the minority representation
increased. Proportion black was a significant predictor of TRI, LUST, incinerators, and hazardous waste facilities. Income was significant for only LUST.
The interaction variable was significant for only incinerators where proportion
black is by far the strongest predictor. The results of the multiple regression
analysis are presented in Table 6.7.

---
[3]   Proportion Hispanic is used as the level in stead of % Latino to reflect the source of data, the
      U.S. Census.

Table 6.4: Twenty Five Zip Codes With the Largest Number of Latinos, and Demographic Characteristics of These Zip Codes.

Zip Code	City	Number Latino	% Latino	% African-American	% White	Median House-hold Income	City or Town Size (By Category*)
48209	Detroit	11,923	31 %	10 %	58 %	$ 11,923	Metropolis
48601	Saginaw	6,426	12 %	55 %	33 %	$ 17,374	Medium City
48210	Detroit	4,840	12 %	42 %	45 %	$ 13,634	Metropolis
49423	Holland	4,825	12 %	1 %	84 %	$ 32,830	Small City
49221	Adrian	3,699	11 %	3 %	85 %	$ 28,505	Small City
48906	Lansing	3,065	11 %	11 %	75 %	$ 26,139	Large City
49507	Grand Rapids	2,974	8 %	42 %	48 %	$ 30,346	Large City
48911	Lansing	2,621	7 %	22 %	69 %	$ 30,089	Large City
48342	Pontiac	2,313	9 %	54 %	34 %	$ 17,900	Detroit Suburb
49509	Grand Rapids	2,308	4 %	2%	92 %	$ 35,713	Large City
48216	Detroit	2,273	27 %	39 %	32 %	$ 12,816	Metropolis
48602	Saginaw	2,182	6 %	4 %	88 %	$ 24,703	Medium City
48910	Lansing	2,179	6 %	10 %	83 %	$ 28,292	Large City
48340	Pontiac	2,024	9 %	16 %	73 %	$24,501	Detroit Suburb
49503	Grand Rapids	1,996	6 %	23 %	69 %	$ 21,008	Large City
48180	Taylor	1,957	3 %	4 %	91 %	$ 32,659	Detroit Suburb
49424	Hart	1,843	7 %	0 %	90 %	$ 38,622	Town
48228	Detroit	1,762	3 %	57 %	39 %	$ 23,119	Metropolis
49504	Grand Rapids	1,724	3 %	1 %	95 %	$ 29,364	Large City
48912	Lansing	1,700	9 %	12 %	76 %	$ 24,057	Large City
48506	Flint	1,645	5 %	2 %	92 %	$ 25,122	Large City
48708	Bay City	1,565	5 %	3 %	91 %	$ 22,243	Small City
48146	Lincoln Park	1,525	4 %	1 %	95 %	$ 30,640	Detroit Suburb
48603	Saginaw	1,452	3 %	2 %	93 %	$ 36,422	Medium City
48126	Dearborn	1,442	4 %	0 %	94 %	$ 27,219	Detroit Suburb
Averages for These 25 Zip Codes		**2,890.52**	**9 %**	**17 %**	**73 %**	**$ 25,536**	

*Scale and Indicators For Size of City/Town:
Metropolis = Over 1,000,000 ; Large City = 100,000 - 200,000 ; Medium City = 50,000 - 99,999 ; Small City = 10,000 - 49,999 ; Town = Under 10,000 ; Detroit Suburb = Identified as Ranally Metro Area of Detroit by Rand McNally. Data on size of city provided for 1990 by the Rand McNally Commercial Atlas and Marketing Guide.

Table 6.5:

Identifier	Number of Zip Codes	Average Proportion Hispanic	Average Proportion Black, Non-Hispanic	Description
White	32	.005	.001	White, Non-Hispanic
Hispanic White	138	.019	.001	Minority population is predominantly Hispanic white
Hispanic Minority	65	.038	.004	Minority population is predominantly Hispanic-nonwhite
Mixed	604	.012	.029	Minority population is predominantly non-Hispanic
Black	34	.027	.740	Non-Hispanic Black is the majority with Hispanic concentration as well

It is interesting to note that the six zip codes in the state of Michigan with over 3,000 Latinos are quite different for a number of characteristics, yet generally are all severely impacted by toxic releases and Act 307 sites. Among highly polluted zip codes with over 3,000 Latinos, those in Detroit and Saginaw are significantly African-American, located in cities with a history of intense heavy industry, and located in large urban centers. Other highly polluted zip codes with over 3,000 Latinos, those in Adrian and Holland, are located in smaller urban areas with histories of agriculture and light industry, and are largely made up of Latinos and whites. (Adrian and Holland both have a history of Mexican American settlement related to migrant farm labor streams, and the development of jobs in light industry (Valdes, 1992; Rochin, Santiago, and Dickey, 1989).) Yet in all of these cases, numbers of TRI citations are severe. Among the six zip codes with over 3000 Latinos, zips which are especially polluted with Act 307 sites are those in Adrian, Holland, Saginaw, and Lansing. Again, these cities are quite different both in racial make-up and industrial history. It seems that Latino communities in Michigan that are exposed to disproportionate levels of environmental hazards are of at least two types: Mixed Latino/black communities located in large urban centers, and Latino communities located

Table 6.6:

Zip Group	Mean Act 307	Mean TRI	Mean LUST	Mean HazFac	Mean Incins.	Mean Landfills
White	1.88	.03	.78	.00	.19	.03
Hispanic White	3.80	1.28	3.20	.07	1.38	.18
Hispanic Minority	6.35	3.03	4.75	.28	3.17	.20
Mixed	9.18	3.40	7.67	.27	3.82	.34
Black	12.24	9.32	15.76	.91	28.50	.29
All zips	7.97	3.14	6.81	.26	4.21	.29
F ratio	6.127	8.386	17.377	9.699	59.930	2.170

in smaller cities where the population is largely white and Mexican American. In the second case, qualitative evidence from interviews suggests that Mexican American communities in these small cities are often geographically segregated from the white population. More research is called for in this area.

Issues for Consideration

A number of issues should be taken into account when considering these results.

- Zip code analysis is only partially adequate in locating Latino neighborhoods in the state. Zip code analysis allows us to determine zip codes with large numbers of Latinos or a high concentration of Latinos. Communities with Latino neighborhoods that are divided between zip codes may not appear among my list of zips with largest number Latino, but, when adjacent zips are taken together, may constitute a significant neighborhood. Likewise, when Latino communities are part of a large zip code, they may not appear among those with high concentration of Latinos, even if there is in fact a high concentration of Latinos in part of the zip code. For instance, the towns of Grant and Pullman were identified by a student as having Mexican American neighborhoods. Although they did not appear among my list of zips with large numbers or high concentration of Latinos, in the context of small towns in Michigan, and in certain parts of the zips in which Grant and Pullman are located, there may, in fact, be areas that are largely Mexican-American.

- Further analysis is called for in cases like Adrian where the whole city is located within one zip code. A next step might be to consider location of facilities that release toxins to see how close Latino neighborhoods within the Adrian zip are to polluting facilities.

- The level of environmental pollution of some locations may be underestimated. Manufacturing facilities with fewer than ten full time employees are not required to report toxic releases, reporting is not required for some chemicals, and some manufacturers may avoid reporting, even if this is in violation of the law. Act 307 sites include those sites eligible for Michigan Environmental Response Act (MERA) dollars. This includes many Superfund sites and additional Michigan-designated sites. It may, however, exclude some sites that are already being cleaned up under Superfund and are not eligible for MERA dollars. Some of these sites may actually be the worst in the state. In addition, no requirements exist for reporting Act 307 sites. They are identified voluntarily through citizens groups and industry.

- A resident of an especially polluted Michigan zip code commented to me, "Well, this area has a lot of Latinos, but just because my neighbor is Arab, black, or white doesn't mean that they aren't affected by the pollution." (Antonia, April 1995) This is an important concept to keep in mind. The analysis in this paper was conducted to examine the question of environmental inequity towards Latino communities. However, in looking for solutions to local problems, it is important to keep in mind that pollution and environmental degradation are problems affecting geographical communities, including all those living in exposed areas. All residents of communities where environmental hazards exist can have their health severely affected, and all residents are potential allies in struggles to reduce and prevent pollution. This is an important political consideration to keep in mind.

- Separation of African-American and Latino variables in the analysis in this paper is not meant to create competitions over "who is worse off." This, again, would be a foolhardy political position to take, and could be detrimental to organizing efforts. It is, however, important to examine the experience of Latino communities in isolation from other ethnic groups. Though many places where Latinos live in Michigan are neighborhoods that are largely black and Latino, or black and Mexican, this analysis has demonstrated that many Latinos also live in mid-size cities where demographic ethnic dynamics are largely white and Mexican-American or white and Latino. Qualitative anecdotal and historical evidence suggests that in these cases Latinos often live quite segregated from whites. In both cases— mixed "minority" neighborhoods, and Latino neighborhoods in largely white cities—Latinos are disproportionately affected by environmental hazards.

Table 6.7:

Predicted Pollution Factor	Standardized Regression Coefficients for Predictors				R2
	p Hispanic	p Black	Hispanic X Black	Income	
Act 307	.124*	.078	.001	-.023	.026*
TRI	.224*	.246*	-.049	.045	.100*
LUST	.231*	.258*	.004	.149*	.140*
Incins	.269*	.597*	-.209*	.036	.321*
HazFac	.232*	.226*	-.003	.060	.114*
Landfills	.100*	.075	-.079	.040	.010
Pollution Density	.126*	.543*	.083*	.013	.389*

*$p < .05$

Analysis of the experience of Latino communities is important, for it may help us discover this type of information, which has implications both for policy decisions and community organizing tactics. There is another rationale for looking at the particular experience of Latino communities. As Valdes points out, very little has been written about the history of Latinos in the state of Michigan. Any information that can be recorded about the experience of Michigan Latino communities can help Latinos and others establish and keep records of Latino communities' significant history and presence in the state.

Conclusions[4]

Following models established in earlier research examining "minority" communities, I have determined significant problems faced by Latino communities with regard to environmental degradation and inequity in the state of Michigan. I established that, by and large, as the number of Latinos, percent Latino, and ratio of Latinos to whites in Michigan zip codes increases, so do TRI citations and Act 307 sites. In addition, the percent of the Latino population per zip code in Michigan was found to be a significant predictor of Toxic Release Inventory citations and Act 307 polluted sites. This relationship was found to be true even when the median household income per zip code and percent of the African-American population per zip code were taken into account. Qualitative and quantitative evidence suggested that Latino communities facing unusually high levels of TRI citations and ACT 307 sites are probably of at least two types: 1) zip codes with a significant combined presence of Latino and African-American populations, and 2) Latino (mostly Mexican American) communities located in small, predominantly white cities in Michigan. In this case, qualitative evidence suggests that geographical segregation of Mexican Americans and whites exists in these cities. Last, I demonstrated that zip codes with a moderate or high presence of both Latino and African-American populations have the highest average level of TRI citations and Act 307 sites in the state. Further thinking about the meaning of this finding is called for, as it may have implications for both understanding the phenomenon of unequal distribution of environmental hazards in the United States, and for community organizing efforts. Having established that Michigan's Latino communities face serious problems with exposure to toxic chemicals and other pollutants with the potential to cause tragic health problems, I hope that this information will be helpful in efforts to reduce environmental hazards in Latino communities and prevent future environmental degradation.

---

[4] These are Holmes's original conclusions. The addition of LUST sites, incinerations, hazard-ous waste facilities, and landfills further supports her position.

7

A COMPARATIVE ANALYSIS OF FLINT-AREA ZIP CODES: EVIDENCE OF ONE COMMUNITY'S DISPROPORTIONATE BURDEN OF ENVIRONMENTAL HAZARDS

Kathy Nemsick Rehill

It was interesting to note that the 48505 zip code where the incinerator has been sited has the highest proportion minority, the highest proportion receiving public assistance, and the lowest median household income. It also has the highest proportion of hospital discharges for patients with any mention of asthma, one of the largest amounts of chemicals in Act 307 sites per zip, and a relatively high number of TRI chemical citations.

Brief Introduction to Flint
Bunyan Bryant

Flint, Michigan, has been the site of social decay for many years. Flint grew and evolved around the automobile industry with a considerable number of its of its population consisting of factory or affiliated workers. During and after World War II, African Americans and whites migrated from the South to Flint in search of jobs and a better life. Industrial jobs, on the assembly line of the automobile plants were very attractive to unskilled laborers. Conceivably, both African Americans and poor whites could earn more money than ever before, even if they lacked specific skill or education.

While economic conditions improved, African American migrants were exposed to many other less fortunate conditions, as they continued to face in some cases racial discrimination. Although blacks and whites brought with them the legacy of unhealthy race relations, the racism practiced in Flint was more insidious and had a profound impact upon African Americans. Even though most of schools were desegregated, local communities were highly segregated.

Today, Flint is the third largest city in the state of Michigan. It is about 53 percent African American and 3 percent Hispanic, most of whom are poor. Over the years, the automobile companies have automated and dismissed thousands of workers or shut their doors and moved parts of their production to different cities or foreign countries, leaving an eroded tax base, unemployment, inadequate city services, and a declining population. Parts of the once viable city now looks like a ghost town, with boarded up buildings and homes. The number of the unemployed and welfare recipients is high, and Flint is subject to the whole alphabet soup of social problems. School failures and violence are commonplace. Although Flint has had African American mayors, and a majority black city council, they could not make any discernible difference in the lives of the people who live there. Even though local politicians have supported numerous economic development projects, they seem to make little difference in the lives of the people who live there. Economic failure befalls a city when the industrial sector decides to withdraw its financial and emotional support and the relatively well-to-do whites withdraw their emotional support of the City. Flint is struggling desperately to regain economic stability against all odds in order to improve the quality of life of its citizens.

Even in economic good times, Flint citizens paid a price in their relatively high exposure to pollution. At the height of industrialization, Flint residents were unaware of the manufacturing products that affected their health. Good jobs meant short-term economic gain but also, perhaps, long-term decline in health status.

As a grassroots community group was fighting what would be the largest demolition wood-burning incinerator in the state of Michigan, it was important to look at the demographics of the Flint/Genesee community where the incinerator was located. By looking at census data and environmental data, this study demonstrates that this community of color bears a disproportionate burden of environmental hazards. The methodology was to compare the Flint zip code of 48505 where the incinerator was being built, to the six zip codes surrounding it, as well as to zip codes throughout the state of Michigan. The purpose was to provide a descriptive and statistically significant profile of a residential community that was primarily African American, working class, living on fixed-incomes, and bearing a disproportionate burden of environmental hazards. While statistical analysis of the demographic and environmental data cannot prove causality or intent of environmental racism, it can provide evidence that low-income communities and communities of color often bear a disproportionate burden of environmental hazards.

The community where the incinerator was being sited already hosted an abundance of documented as well as undocumented facilities that emit tons of pollution to the air, land, and water each year. Documented facilities were those required by law to report the chemicals being used and their associated levels of emissions. Undocumented facilities included junkyards, tire heaps, and abandoned dumps.

Background Information

The Incinerator Proposal

In 1991, a proposal was submitted to the Michigan Department of Natural Resources to build a 35 megawatt wood-burning incinerator that would run 24 hours per day and burn up to 175,000 tons of recycled wood chips per year (Musial, 1995). An assessment of available fuel sources estimated that the future fuel for the proposed incinerator will be demolition wood as well as virgin wood. Because a number of toxic chemicals such as wood sealants, paints, and stains were on demolition wood, the burning of demolition wood would lead to the release of many toxic chemicals according to the Genesee County Medical Society (Stobbe, 1992c). While plant engineer Fred Phelps claimed that only 25 percent of the wood would be from demolished homes and construction debris, and 75 percent would be from tree trimmings (Musial, 1995), the developers were unwilling to put those figures in writing (O'Neal, 1995). The fact that the operating permit did not limit the quantity or proportion of fuel that can be from demolition projects and the fact the permit did not require the incinerator to have Maximum Achievable Control Technology to reduce air pollutants (Stobbe, 1992d), raised considerable opposition to the incinerator from the host community.

Geographical Boundaries

It is important to describe the political and geographical boundaries of the community to understand who benefits and who suffers as a result of the incinerator proposal. The 48505 zip code in which the incinerator was being built consists primarily of the northern section of Flint, Michigan. This zip code was primarily a residential, African American, working class and fixed-income community. The northern most border of Flint was Carpenter Road, which runs East to West dividing Flint from Genesee Township. The 48505 zip code also encompasses the lower portion of Genesee Township. The residents of this part of Genesee Township were primarily African American and retired, lower-income Whites. The majority of Genesee Township's residents lived outside of the 48505 zip code, several miles north of the incinerator in 48458. The incinerator was being built one-half mile north of Carpenter Road (within Genesee Township) across from the Carpenter Elementary School in Flint and a residential neighborhood in Flint. Both Flint and Genesee Township are within Genesee County.

A major highway, Route 475, runs North to South, a few miles West of the incinerator site. Route 75 is a few miles West of 475, running parallel. Route 54 is a few miles East of 475, and is also within a few miles of the incinerator.

The railroad track runs North to South parallel to the highways and within close distance to the incinerator site. Developers of the incinerator argued that the siting decision was based in part on proximity to these major highways and the railroad tracks (Lott, 1994). It should be noted that at least one of these major thoroughfares runs through each of the zip codes being considered in this study. The railroad passes through zip code 48505 and zip code 48458, where the majority of Genesee Township residents live.

Geopolitical Issues

While the residents of Genesee Township would receive the financial benefits of increased tax revenue paid to the township by the company running the incinerator, the City of Flint would receive no financial benefits (Stobbe, 1992b). However, it is the residents of Flint who would be most affected by pollution due to their proximity to the incinerator rather than Genesee Township residents. Since Genesee Township residents would have to bear less of the environmental burden, but would receive financial benefits, Genesee Township Supervisor William C. Ayre who supported the incinerator proposal, had not received strong opposition from voters (Stobbe, 1992b). The incinerator would be the largest single taxpayer in the township. When the incinerator was originally proposed in 1991, developers stated it would bring $1.8 million a year in taxes to Genesee Township (Stobbe, 1992a). Other officials claimed it would add about $200,000 to Genesee Township annually.

Flint elected officials had been asked by their constituents to oppose the incinerator, but the officials had no say over decisions made by Genesee Township. But Flint was represented at the county level with elected officials on the Genesee County Board of Supervisors. The Flint representatives to the County Board had repeatedly voiced their constituents' opposition to the incinerator. But the incinerator would also bring some tax revenue to the county coffers, so it was supported by the Genesee County Economic Development Committee (Stobbe, 1992d). Since Flint's representatives were outnumbered on the County Board, they had had little impact on the decision-making process. The Michigan Department of Natural Resources was another decision-maker in this issue. The MDNR had the ability to deny the permit in response to Flint's opposition, but the MDNR deferred to the local elected officials in Genesee Township (Stobbe, 1992e). The MDNR was unwilling to intervene on Flint's behalf because the Township that would technically house the incinerator was in favor of it being built. The MDNR also asserted that it can approve or disapprove of permits only on their technical feasibility, not on the emotional and political opposition from residents (Stobbe, 1992e; Askari, 1994).

Analysis

In an effort to determine whether the community in zip code 48505 was bearing a disproportionate burden of environmental hazards, a comparative analysis of demographic, pollution, and health factors was conducted. In addition to comparing characteristics in 48505 to the Flint-area averages and the statewide averages for the different indicators, it was interesting to compare zip code 48505 to zip code 48458, its northern neighbor; 48458 was the zip code with a majority of Genesee Township residents who will receive tax benefits from the construction of the incinerator, while 48505 residents will be closer to the pollution sites.

Descriptive Analysis

In our society we often compare ourselves with other groups to measure how we are doing. We compare our height and weight to the average height and weight for our age and gender groups. We compare our grades in school to the rest of the class. For analysis purposes one can see how 48505 compares with each of its neighboring zip codes and the average of those zip codes. One could also compare the 48505 zip code with the average of the zip codes of the rest of the state to see how it ranks against the state.

Community Profile Based on the Data[1]

Table 7.1 provides descriptive information on the means and standard deviations for the average of the six neighboring zip codes and statewide averages for the characteristics being compared with zip code 48505 where the incinerator was being sited. Zip code 48505 had a high proportion of minority and low-income residents and a high proportion of environmental and human health hazards.

Zip code 48505 had the highest proportion minorities in the zip codes in the Flint area and was several times higher than the statewide average across all zip codes in Michigan. In a critique of previous studies that demonstrated an association between race and the incidence of environmental hazards, Been (1994) of New York University's School of Law claimed that other studies inaccurately defined minority communities as those having a higher proportion minority than the national average. Been (1994) further critiqued those studies for not considering the total number of people in a community, but simply ana-

---

[1]   The descriptions and analysis presented in this chapter follow the same methodology used in her original paper. However, her original analysis has been replaced using the expanded database that was not available at the time she conducted her research. Use of the expanded database gives a fuller picture of zip code 48505 and how it compares with its neighbors and the rest of Michigan.

Table 7.1: Zip Code 48505 Compared with Neighboring Flint Zip Codes and the State of Michigan

Descriptor	Target Zip Code: 48505	Six Flint Zips*		State of Michigan	
		Mean	SD	Mean	SD
Proportion minority	.85	.31	.20	.07	.16
Proportion on public assistance	.36	.16	.06	.09	.06
Median household income	$13,321	$24,219	$6,162	$29,012	$10,835
No. of people per zip	42,400	26,351	12,844	10,648	13,736
No. of households per zip	14,984	10,104	4,879	3,922	5,086

*The six zip codes were: 48458, 48502, 48503, 48504, 48506, and 48532.

lyzing the proportion or percentage minority in a community. Clearly that was not the case in this study. Zip code 48505 was 85 percent minority and was one of the most largely populated communities in the Flint area. The 1990 census counted 42,400 people in the zip code compared with a statewide average of 10,648 people per zip code with a standard deviation of 13,736, and a Flint-area average of 26,351 people per zip code with a standard deviation of 12,844. To lay the foundation for this study, 48505 was beyond doubt a minority community where a significant number of people were being impacted by environmental burdens relative to other zip codes in the state and in the Flint area.

The median household income for zip code 48505 was much lower than the median household income for most of the neighboring zip codes and less than half the state average. The proportion of households receiving public assistance in 48505 was more than twice the proportion of the households receiving public assistance for the majority of neighboring zip codes and four times the state average. To put these income figures in context, we can compare them with poverty thresholds as defined by the 1990 U.S. Census. The range of weighted average poverty thresholds in 1989 was $6,310 for one person to $16,921 for a family of six (Bureau of the Census, 1990:B-28, Table A). The average poverty threshold for a family of four persons was $12,674 and $14,990 for a family of five. The median household income of $13,321 for zip code 48505 was very close to the poverty level for households with four people and was in fact below the poverty level for households with more than four people in them. Median household income data and public assistance data demonstrated that zip code

48505 was a low-income community and that its neighboring zip codes have almost double the median household income and half the proportion of households receiving public assistance.

It was not surprising that the zip code with the lowest median household income and highest level of public assistance also had the highest number and proportion of asthma cases. The New England Journal of Medicine (Buist and Vollmer, 1994:1584) reports that:

> ...asthma is especially likely in a setting of poverty. Many components of poverty may contribute to the increased risk, among them poor access to appropriate and high-quality health care and lack of continuity of care, decreased likelihood of treatment with anti-inflammatory drugs, dismal housing with high levels of cockroach and dust-mite antigens and molds, poor systems of social support, and low levels of education.

In a study of asthma among residents of Philadelphia, Lang and Polansky (1994) found that asthma was not only prevalent among the poor, but also among blacks. The asthma data used in this study show that zip code 48505, which has the highest proportion of minorities and the highest levels of poverty, also has the highest incidence of asthma.

Zip code 48505 has relatively high numbers of environmental hazards in the form of toxic chemicals at Act 307 sites. The data showed 48505 as having 38 chemicals present in sites that have been deemed in need of remedial cleanup action by the MDNR. Sites listed on the Act 307 list were in need of cleanup because of their present and potential risk to human health and the environment. On average, the Flint-area zip codes surrounding 48505 have 11 chemicals in Act 307 sites present, and ranged from having 0 chemicals to 39. Zip code 48505 has 38 chemicals present in Act 307 sites, which was the second highest level; more than twice the Flint-area average, and more than three times the state average.

Zip code 48505 has an above average number of environmental hazards in the form of toxic chemicals released under the Toxic Release Inventory. Six TRI chemicals were reported as being emitted in zip code 48505 compared with the state average of three TRI chemical citations per zip code and the Flint-area average of 5.33 TRI citations per zip code. While the 48505 value of six TRI chemical citations was within the range of the Flint-area average for TRI citations, it was twice as large as zip code 48458's number of TRI chemical citations. This comparison was useful because residents in zip code 48458 will receive tax revenue from the incinerator, but residents in 48505 who already have a large number of toxic chemicals emitted into the environment will have to live with the additional pollution from the incinerator.

Figure 7.1. Pollution Sources: Target Zip Code vs Neighboring Zip Codes.

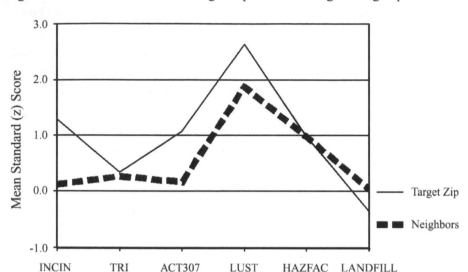

Figure 7.2. Race/Class: Target Zip Code vs Neighboring Zip Codes.

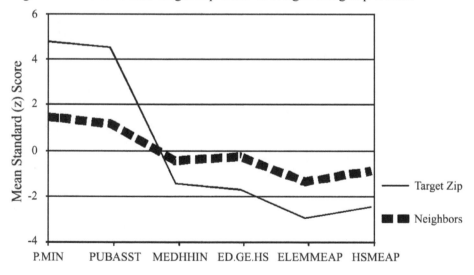

Data regarding treatment, storage, and disposal facilities were available only for the Flint-area zip codes, not statewide. Zip code 48505 was the only zip code with any disposal facilities in the Flint area, and it has two; 48505 has the second highest number of treatment and storage facilities compared to its neighboring zip codes, half of which do not have any treatment and storage facilities. Zip code 48458, the northern neighbor, has no treatment and storage

Figure 7.3. Health Variables: Target Zip Code vs Neighboring Zip Codes.

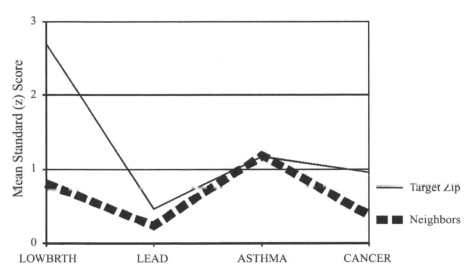

facilities. These data also support the notion that zip code 48505 was currently disproportionately burdened with environmental hazards.

Quantitative Analysis

If there were no disproportionate burdens of environmental hazards in zip code 48505, one would expect the variables representing pollution, race, and income to be evenly distributed among the zip codes. No one zip code would consistently rank highest on each variable. However, the statistical descriptions presented above demonstrate a pattern of a consistently higher incidence of pollution, poverty, and minorities across all of the variables in one zip code: 48505.

To determine if this pattern was statistically significant, an analysis of variance by ranks was computed. Sixteen variables—six indicating pollution sources, six indicating class/race, and four indicating health status—were ranked across the six zip codes. Zip 48502 was not included in the analysis because its small size precluded the availability of health data. Ranks were assigned to the variables so that a rank of "1" indicated the most favorable status, e.g., highest median income or least amount of a pollution source. The results were striking. The chi square for all 16 variables was 39.503 (p < .001). By category of variables, the results were also striking. For the six pollution variables (numbers of Act 307 sites, landfills, hazardous waste management facilities, types of incinerator emissions, LUST sites, and TRI citations), the chi square was 11.667 (p = .0400); for the six class/race variables (proportion minority, median household income, proportion on public assistance, proportion of adults with at least a high school education, the average elementary school achievement level, and the average high school achievement level from the Michigan Educational Assessment Program), the chi square was 22.476 (p < .001); and for the four health variables (asthma rate, cancer rate in the 45 to 65 range, low birth weight, and proportion of children under age 6 from a random sample with significant blood lead levels), the chi square was 17.286 (p = .004). For both the class/race variables and the health variables, the target zip code of 48505 received the worst average ranking. For the pollution variables, the rank for 48505 was second to last, only exceeded by zip code 48506.

To illustrate the results presented above, the 16 variables used in the analysis were converted to standard scores from the distributions for all Michigan zip codes. This standardization process puts each variable on the same scale for the purposes of comparison. The standard score system used, z-scores, sets the state mean at zero with a standard deviation of one. Whether the ranks were assigned according to original values or to the standard scores, the results of the analysis were the same. All that changes was the unit of measurement, similar to translating from Celsius to Fahrenheit. The preceding three graphs—one for the class/race variables, one for the pollution variables, and one for the health variables—show by a solid line the location of the target zip code, 48505 and by a dashed line the location of the average for the other five Flint area zip codes. A value of zero would indicate that the zip, or zips, were average for the State of Michigan. A positive value indicates that the zip, or zips, were above average for the state. Likewise, a negative value indicates below average status. In a normal distribution, a z score of +1.00 is at the 84th percentile.

This analysis of pollution, class/race, and health profiles demonstrated that the zip code of 48505, which has a high proportion of nonwhite residents and a relatively high proportion of low-income households, already has a disproportionate burden of environmental hazards as measured by government databases and census information.

Policy Implications for the Future

Studies of this type, which create a community profile by analyzing de-mographic and pollution data, can be used in future decision-making to ensure that communities that already bear a disproportionate burden of environmental hazards are not continuously dumped upon. By documenting that there was already a disproportionate amount of pollution in a community that does not have the resources to move or to acquire adequate health care, we hope our findings will be used as leverage with local industries and government agencies. Communities need this type of leverage to ensure that they have opportunities for community input in local decision-making processes and in monitoring facilities' emissions. The data can be used to ensure that disproportionately burdened communities receive timely and adequate remedial action funds to clean up present pollution. A community profile can also be used to force industries in their community to install the Maximum Available Control Technology to minimize present and future emissions of toxic chemicals.

Regardless of the cause or events leading up to the conditions that caused low-income communities of color to become polluted, this study and others like it demonstrate that communities of color often bear a disproportionate burden of environmental hazards. By being aware of these trends, policymakers and community residents can try to ensure that these vulnerable communities are at least protected from further environmental degradation through the implementation of pollution-control laws designed to protect the health of residents living under conditions of disproportionate environmental burdens. At best, knowledge of these trends could lead to policies that aim to eliminate environmental contamination in these communities through pollution prevention.

8

A CASE STUDY: THE CONTROVERSY BETWEEN ENVIRONMENTAL DISPOSAL SYSTEMS AND RESIDENTS OF THE CITY OF ROMULUS, MICHIGAN, OVER THE SITING OF A DEEP INJECTION WELL ON WAHRMAN ROAD

Alice Nabalamba

Clearly, communities with low political efficacy and poor economic resources are increasingly being targeted for environmental hazardous waste facilities. Theses communities are the least powerful ones to engage a waste management company in legal or political action. The fewer number of waste sites in non-minority and affluent communities can for the most part be explained not by the availability of cheap land in those areas, but by those communities' political activism against potential environmental hazards.

Purpose of the Study

The purpose of the study is to determine if there are other underlying factors beyond market-related conditions that influence business and/or government decisions to locate environmental waste facilities in any given location. In other words, the idea is to ascertain whether all communities have an equal chance of being selected for siting of a waste or treatment facility and whether they are equally protected against environmental hazards. This study is focused on zip code 48174 of Romulus, Michigan, and the surrounding communities.

Background to the Controversy

Romulus is home to the Detroit Metropolitan International Airport, and it is transected from North to South by Interstate Highway 275 and East to West by Interstate Highway 94. Access to major transportation routes would therefore naturally be taken into consideration by a study involved with siting of industrial and other business facilities, in addition to geological factors in the case of a deep injection well. While this study does not completely ignore the relationship of business to transportation availability, it has looked at other possibilities that may influence the location of specific industrial activities.

The controversy between the residents of Romulus and the commercial waste disposal company Environmental Disposal Systems (EDS) over the first commercial deep injection well in the state of Michigan began in 1993. By the time the community became involved in the debate over the location of the facility, its construction had already begun. The well and its casing were near completion, although the surface storage facilities and other structures had not been completely developed. EDS negotiated the purchase of land for the injection well with one member of the community who agreed to sell one parcel and lease another at a total cost of $300,000.[1] The company received permits to site this facility in Romulus from both the Federal Environmental Protection Agency and the Michigan Department of Natural Resources. However, the company did not apply for land-use or zoning permits from the city of Romulus prior to construction of the well, citing that such a permit was not necessary since the state Department of Natural Resources and the federal EPA were responsible for overseeing projects of this nature. As a result, the injection well, which is categorized as heavy industry, is located on an M1 zoning plot designated for light industrial developments.

Concerns of Romulus Residents

The debate over the injection well has raised a range of questions within the community. First, there is the concern over the vulnerability of communities such as Romulus to big businesses as they expand continuously to new locations as well as into new and environmentally risky ventures. Second, there is the issue of who has an upper hand in the designation of land for projects such as the EDS injection well. Third, there is the issue of whether residents who would be affected by a new development of this nature should be part of the negotiation process. In Romulus, none of the above concerns was addressed prior to the construction of the injection well. Although there are indications that other sites within Romulus were considered, the facility is located within a quarter of a mile from a densely populated residential area. One resident whose entire family has lived in Romulus for the past four to five decades and who owns two parcels of land near the site of the injection well was particularly concerned about his lifelong investments and the potential for property value depreciation. This concern was voiced by many residents of this area, who are primarily homeowners.

As a result, the community residents through Romulus Environmentalists Care About People (RECAP) have asked city officials to oppose the injection

---

[1] This amount is based on both Romulus Environmentalists Care About People (RECAP) records as well as Detroit News coverage of the activities of RECAP.

well. At the moment, the city and the company EDS have been in litigation over the permit to begin operation of the well.

Another concern was the misrepresentation of facts about the well to the people of Romulus and their leaders. Even though the facility is intended to store toxic waste, EDS did not apply for an Act 64 permit. There is already one Act 64 site on the northern side of Romulus, and perhaps it would have been difficult to grant another one within such close distance. However, evidence based on other companies in the waste treatment and management business indicates that once an initial permit has been granted, companies usually request additional permits either to expand the facility or to construct a new one. Evidence also shows that secondary permits take a much shorter time to be approved. A case in point is Chem Waste, an Illinois based company that operates several facilities across the country that it acquired as one category, such as a landfill, and later expanded to include an incinerator or other forms of toxic-waste facilities.[2]

There was an even deeper concern over the future health of the community residents who saw the potential for underground water contamination. Injection wells of this capacity generally share the same environment as the water which over 75% of all urban populations across the country depend on for drinking purposes (US EPA, 1990). What is even more alarming is that over 50% of the entire nation's drinking water and 40-45% of drinking water in the state of Michigan is obtained from the same source. This issue is perhaps the most important element in this controversy, yet little assurance of addressing the problem has been provided by either the operating company (EDS) or the government agencies (EPA and MDEQ). EPA studies indicate that no real guarantee can be provided that underground water or the surface will not be contaminated or affected by the operation of an injection well of this capacity (US EPA, 1990). Injection wells of this type (Class 1) characteristically store toxic liquid waste. The waste is usually trucked in from outside the site of the well. As such, the operators of such a facility would have a storage facility on the premises where the waste can be treated before it is injected into the ground. It is at this stage that there should be increased concern over the possibility of spillage on the surface as well as in the underground water, especially if the process is handled carelessly. Both the EPA and MDEQ assume that the operating company will self-monitor the process.

---

[2] "Environmental Racism: It Could Be a Messy Fight" in Legal Affairs-Business Week, May 20, (1991). This report documents four Chem Waste sites in Chicago South Side, Sauget, IL, Port Arthur, TX and Kettleman City, CA, where the company initially acquired an existing toxic-waste incinerator and later added three on the same site or bought a landfill and later built an incinerator.

Geological Factors

Class 1 injection wells, such as the one under scrutiny in Romulus, have different rules that govern them than other hazardous waste facilities, particularly because they are usually commercial and because of the nature of the waste involved (toxic waste). The EDS facility extends slightly over 4,000 feet deep into the Cambrian rocks and is designed to inject liquid toxic waste beneath the lowermost underground sources of drinking water (USDW) (US EPA, 1990). Generally areas of low or no potential for seismic activity are selected for siting of deep injection wells. Within continental US, such areas are concentrated along the Texas-Louisiana gulf coast and the Great Lakes region. Naturally, therefore, the community of Romulus would be a potential site if all other factors were equal (Mehnert, Gendron, and Brower, 1990). In addition, these two regions offer a combination of suitable injection zones and a large number of waste incinerators (to process the waste that would then be injected into the ground).

Geological data indicate that our drinking water comes from between 100-150 feet below the ground, suggesting that the likelihood of contamination of this resource would be very minimal, since the injection well in this case is over 4,000 feet deep. Yet continuous monitoring of both potential surface spillage and of underground water by the operating company is automatically assumed by the permit granting agencies.

In order to understand completely the opposition to the injection well in Romulus, one would have to look at other environmental and demographic factors that are characteristic of the community. The residents of Romulus are clearly saying that they do not want the well in their community because they are already overburdened with other environmental problems as well as for the reasons cited above.

Statistical Description of Romulus

As previously noted in Chapter 4, the database used in this study has been obtained from a variety of sources including the 1990 Census, the State of Michigan Department of Natural Resources, and the Michigan Department of Public Health. The study examined numerous variables to determine the most influential factors in waste facility siting. The concern was to determine how the Romulus zip code, 48174, differed from its surrounding communities collectively. A statistical profile of Romulus, as well as for the surrounding communities, is presented in Table 8.1.[3] There are clearly major differences between the Romulus zip code, 48174, and its adjacent communities. The most striking differences are found in proportion of minority residents, median family income, and toxic release inventory values.

---

[3]   The zip codes include 48111, 48134, 48164, 48180, 48183, 48184, 48185, 48188 and 48192.

Table 8.1: Comparison of Values for Zip 48174 with Means and Standard Deviations of the Nine Surrounding Zip Codes[a]

Variable	48174 VALUE	9 Wayne Zips: Mean	9 Wayne Zips: STANDARD DEVIATION
Total Population	23,416	37,662.78	26,614.66
Number of Households	8,075	13,962.56	10,195.22
Percent of Minority	25.1%	7.0%	3.0%
Percent on Public Assistance	11.9%	6.8%	2.6%
Median Household Income	$31,993	$36,477	$4,548.91
Median Family Income	$34,772	$41,482	$4,766.13
Percent Black in Poverty	6.3%	0.8%	0.7%
Act 64 Sites	2	0.8	0.7
TRI Citations	32	19.8	23.5
Act 307 Sites	7	5.2	3.1
Number of Chemicals in Act 307	20	15.2	10.1

[a] The zip codes include 48111, 48134, 48164, 48180, 48183, 48184, 48185, 48188 and 48192.

Quantitative Analysis

Romulus consistently falls to the disadvantaged side of the means compared with the communities surrounding it. Using the same 16 characteristics as in the previous chapter on Flint, the Romulus profile was compared with its surrounding zip codes. These 16 variables—six indicating pollution sources, six indicating class/race, and four indicating health status—were ranked across the nine zip codes. One of the surrounding zips in Table 8.1, 48188, was excluded in the analysis because its small size precluded the availability of health data. Ranks were assigned to the variables so that a rank of "1" indicated the most favorable status, e.g., highest median income or least amount of a pollution source. An analysis of variance by ranks was then computed. The results were striking. Across all 16 variables, the chi square was 45.59 (p < .001). Romulus ranked at the bottom. For the six pollution variables (numbers of Act 307 sites, landfills, hazardous waste management facilities, types of incinerator emissions, LUST sites, and TRI citations), the chi square was 21.288 (p = .006); for the six class/race variables (proportion minority in the zip code, median household

Figure 8.1: Race/Class: Target Zip Code vs Neighboring Zip Codes.

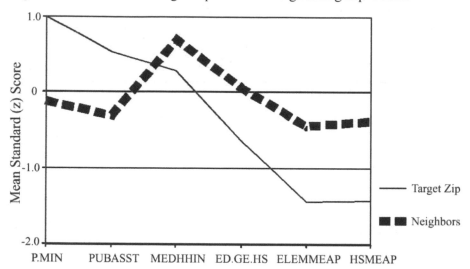

income, proportion on public assistance, proportion of adults with at least a high school education, the average elementary school achievement level and the average high school achievement level from the Michigan Educational Assessment Program), the chi square was 33.822 (p < .001); and for the four health variables (asthma rate, cancer rate in the 45 to 64 age range, low birth weight, and proportion of children under age 6 from a random sample with significant blood lead levels), the chi square was 14.467 (p = .070). For both the class/race variables and the health variables, Romulus received the worst average ranking. For the pollution variables, the Romulus rank was second to last, exceeded only by zip code 48192, a heavily industrial area.

To illustrate these results, the 16 variables used in the analysis were converted to standard scores from the distributions for all Michigan zip codes, as was done in the previous chapter about Flint. This standardization process puts each variable on the same scale for the purposes of comparison. The standard score system used, z-scores, sets the state mean at zero with a standard deviation of one. Whether the ranks are assigned according to original values or to the standard scores, the results of the analysis are the same. All that changes is the unit of measurement, similar to translating from Celsius to Fahrenheit. The following three graphs—one for the class/race variables, one for the pollution variables, and one for the health variables—show by a solid line the location of the Romulus zip code, 48174, and by a dashed line, the profile of the average for the other eight Romulus area zip codes. A value of zero would indicate that the zip, or zips, were average for the state of Michigan. A positive value indicates that the zip, or zips, were above average for the state. Likewise, a negative

Figure 8.2: Pollution Sources: Target Zip Code vs Neighboring Zip Codes.

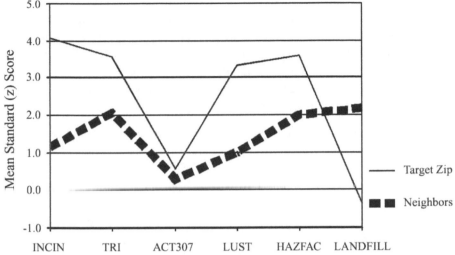

Figure 8.3: Pollution Sources: Target Zip Code vs Neighboring Zip Codes.

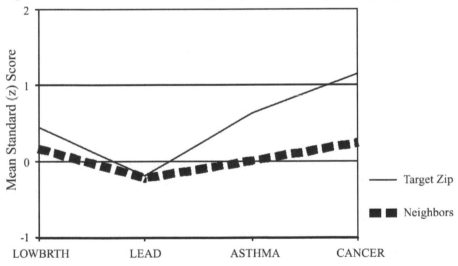

value indicates below average status. In a normal distribution, a z-score of +1.00 is at the 84th percentile, while a z-score of -1.00 is at the 16th percentile.

This analysis of pollution, class/race, and health profiles demonstrates that Romulus zip code 48174 already has a disproportionate burden of environmental hazards as measured by government databases and census information. What is the significance of the data presented on Romulus and the surrounding zip codes and how do we know with certainty that zip code 48174 (Romulus) is being singled out for hazardous waste facility siting? If the zip codes were randomly distributed across a variable, the rank orders of the zip codes across variables should show a random pattern, resulting in essentially equivalent mean ranks across zip codes. The results of the analysis of variance by ranks presented above show that a random pattern was not the case. In fact Romulus stands out as the community with unfavorable conditions, especially evident in the graphic portrayal of the data.

Although this analysis does not explain the siting of environmental hazardous facilities in a given community, it does show the consistencies of variability between communities. In other words, all communities do not have equal chances of being selected for siting of an environmental hazardous waste facility. Some communities are more likely to be selected than others based on their race and socio-economic characteristics. The method of ranking data is powerful because it allows a clear visualization of communities that are more likely to be targeted for environmental hazards. These are generally communities with high proportions of minority populations and high proportions of low-income populations. The ranking clearly shows Romulus as an outstanding community in terms of these conditions.

Implications of This Study to Environmental Justice

The findings in the study of Romulus were not surprising at all. Given the socio-economic characteristics of the zip code 48174, the results of the statistical computation merely strengthen previous studies that have shown a significant correlation between proportion of people of color, level of community affluence, and the incidence of environmental hazards (Mohai and Bryant, 1992). While the results may not necessarily prove intent on the part of the siting agencies, the pattern is conspicuously suspicious. It appears to be much the same in communities of people of color and low income as well as those that are presumed to be of low voting efficacy across the country. Findings like these further energize the new grassroots environmental justice movement that has brought about heightened awareness of issues that have long existed in these communities.

Such conclusions have, however, generated a wide range of public and scholarly criticism. The criticism ranges from the size of the unit of analysis and geographical scope used to arrive at statistical test results that favor race or level of income as the single most important explanatory factors for the high incidence of potential environmental hazards, to the definition of communities of people of color (Boerner and Lambert, 1995). While many studies concur with the significance of race and income as explanatory factors, there are still some that dispute their correlation to incidences of potential environmental hazards arguing that market forces are entirely responsible for the location of hazardous waste facilities (Anderson, Oakes, and Fraser, 1994). Been (1994), for example, argues that cheap land values as well as the dominant land use in a community influence waste management and treatment facility siting. The argument further states that minority populations find themselves living near hazardous waste facilities because they do not have the resources to relocate when their area has been targeted for a new form of land-use such as an industrial or hazardous waste plant.

Such arguments are clearly not convincing. Empirical studies that have attempted to document a historical analysis of land uses in the nation's cities reveal that there is a deliberate policy that encourages massive suburban development, while allowing decay in inner cities where people of color are concentrated. The studies imply that this neglect increases the potential for siting of environmental hazardous facilities in communities of color where land is already degenerated and the likelihood for economic redevelopment is minimal or does not exist. The same studies indicate that people of color find themselves isolated in decayed environments due to growing residential segregation, rather than due to poverty alone (Rusk, 1993; Zubrinsky and Bobo, 1996). In fact, there is evidence that poor whites are more able to escape the inner city than are their minority counterparts.

In addition, given the tradition of the conservationist/environmental movement and its influential "not in my backyard" phenomenon (NIMBY), it is hard to believe that the waste management business would consider only land prices in determining a location for siting a facility. Clearly, communities with low political efficacy and poor economic resources, and therefore least likely to engage a waste management company in legal or political action, are increasingly being targeted for hazardous waste facilities. The fewer number of waste sites in non-minority and affluent communities can for the most part be explained not by the availability of cheap land in those areas, but by those communities' political activism against potential environmental hazards. In addition, such communities have legal and economic resources to confront the hazardous waste management enterprise. Communities of color on the other hand must aggressively utilize voluntary resources within their reach and continuously empower themselves through strong leadership, educational forums on environmental justice issues, and hard facts on the reality of environmental hazards.

Findings and Relationships
After deploying the available data from the various sources including qualitative data, and evaluating previous studies based on Southeast Michigan

and particularly Wayne County, the findings of this study support the following conclusions:

a) Zip code 48174 has the least favorable conditions among its surrounding zip codes and, as such, over the years has experienced increased vulnerability for siting of hazardous waste treatment and storage facilities in addition to increased numbers of contaminated sites and a high incidence of reported Toxic Release Inventory citations.

b) This zip code, which has a total population of 23,416, significantly lower than the mean of the entire region under study, has considerably more environmental hazardous waste facilities per capita.

c) It has a relatively higher proportion of people of color, specifically African Americans, than the rest of Wayne County outside the Detroit metropolitan area.

d) In addition, zip code 48174 has one of the lowest median household incomes. Other zip codes surrounding Romulus with similar characteristics exhibit the same level of vulnerability to siting of hazardous waste facilities (for instance zip code 48184, Wayne).

e) With the exception of zip code 48192 (Riverview), the rest of the zip codes surrounding Romulus fit the general pattern: as proportion of minority composition of the general population increases so does the number of hazardous waste facilities.

f) At the same time, a higher proportion of minority composition corresponds to a lower median household income for the community. Furthermore, recent studies on poverty and race also indicate an increasing level of residential racial segregation in Michigan's large cities. In other words, people of color are more likely to concentrate in the inner city, particularly as their white counterparts leave the city for suburbia.

g) Furthermore, 73% of all the waste treatment and storage facilities, contaminated sites (brown fields) and leaking underground storage tanks (LUSTs) in the area are located in zip codes with a median household income below the area's mean, that is in five out of 10 zip codes.

Limitations of the Study

There are several limitations to this study that might inhibit a conclusive relationship of variables. First, the study did not look at variables such as land use utilization by zip code, thereby limiting the significance of a potential relationship between land-use and number of hazardous waste sites, particularly in the case of zip code 48192. This is one zip code where the high incidence of toxic release inventory citations can be explained by the considerable industrial land use. Secondly, with the exception of Romulus, the study did not look at the racial concentrations or where facilities are located within zip codes. Lack of such data limits a deeper explanation for what is happening in zip code 48111 and 48192. Nevertheless, a concentration of minorities in specific areas within a zip code is assumed in this study, based on the historical development of Wayne County and the Southeast Michigan region in general (Tomboulian et al., 1995). Thirdly, because the study was more focused on the incidence of waste facilities rather than their health effect on human population, it is not possible to determine with certainty the real impact on communities that have significant number of hazardous waste facilities nor if there is a causal relationship between the location of waste plants and the health impact on the surrounding population.

9

THE GREATER DETROIT RESOURCE RECOVERY FACILITY (THE INCINERATOR)

Bunyan Bryant and Elaine Hockman

... sure they say they can discard so many tons of trash and garbage, but we have to inhale that and it kills people, so which way, if you left the trash in the streets or you burn it that way...cause you can't build... nothing next to it; you can't have no schools, no stores, no buildings like that. it's just projects and factories, and so...that's how they change the neighborhood.

Background

Detroit has a history of black workers' organizing for safe working conditions in the local automobile plants. These workers often felt alone and betrayed by both management and often times distrusted the union. Black workers were also at odds with white Appalachians, many of whom migrated to Detroit from Tennessee, Kentucky, and West Virginia at the same time as southern blacks. A third identifiable group in Detroit included Arabs, mostly from Yemen. All three groups tended to cluster in ghettos, and their children most likely attended inferior schools. Appalachian whites tended to be more mobile than blacks or Arabs as they moved back and forth from their home states in the South, particularly during the economic downside of business cycles. Although factory conditions were not good for these groups, racial feelings kept them divided most of the time. The white Appalachians liked the liberal Kennedy brothers, but they also liked George Wallace and the Ku Klux Klan (Georgakas and Surkin, 1998).

Conditions of racism and class exploitation in the Detroit automobile plants and neighborhoods bred a group of black radical intelligentsia committed to revolutionary change. They were committed to changing and using institutions of the City to liberate the black working class (Georgakas and Surkin, 1998). As theoreticians they were second to none in the country. This group of scholar-activists never gained the attention experienced by the mainstream civil rights leaders because many were too far to the left and a part of the Marxist tradition. Mainstream civil rights leaders distanced themselves from these Detroiters because of the communist red baiting potential that could come from such an association. This group of mostly young intellectuals championed the cause of freedom and justice in the factories and community. They increased the community's consciousness of what could be. Their bold attempts to change the city of Detroit and the workplace will never be forgotten.

Racism abounded in the factories, the unions, and the segregated city of Detroit. Although young blacks were sent to die in Vietnam in the name of freedom and democracy, they most likely could not purchase a home in Dearborn, Grosse Pointe, Warren, or any other Detroit suburbs. The 1967, Detroit riot gave birth to one of the most brutal racial confrontations in this country, resulting in a highly racially segregated city, as whites left Detroit for the suburbs.

The world's greatest industrial power not only produced unsafe environmental conditions in the workplace but it also contributed to unsafe environmental conditions in the surrounding communities. Perhaps more than ever, the people in the Detroit area are exposed to a variety of polluting industries and one of the world's largest incinerators that are most likely having a detrimental effect upon their health. In fact, non-attainment ambient air quality may be contributing to the ill health of thousands of people in Detroit. In the 1980s a coalition of environmental groups, most of whom were white, took up the struggle to prevent the world's largest incinerator from opening in the heart of Detroit. Now that the incinerator battle is over, environmentalists still feel the incinerator should never have been built because even the best available control technology is not enough to keep people safe from environmental poisons.

In the late 1990s the "Coalition to Shut Down the Henry Ford Medical Waste Incinerator" was organized. This was a broad-based coalition that included such groups as Detroiters Working for Environmental Justice, Sierra Club Southeast Michigan Chapter, Sierra Club Mackinac Chapter, Ecology Center, Sugar Law Center, ACCESS, Michigan Environmental Justice Coalition, National Wildlife Federation, and the Virginia Park District Council. In February 2000, after a long struggle, Ford Medical Center announced that it would close its medical waste incinerator, an important victory for the Coalition. But the problem of incineration is only one of many environmental problems. Due to the demands of the automobile industry and cross border trade, the trucking industry is emerging as a critical economic booster in Detroit. New road building and road building repair projects will increase as the demand for trucking increases. The Detroit Intermodal Freight Terminal or DIFT, one of many transportation projects, could

---

The Highway Trust Fund that financed the building of expressways for the automobile to travel them, racial discrimination in the Federal Housing Authority, redlining, and discriminatory zoning laws, all allowed whites to migrate to suburban areas, leaving the city of Detroit with a decaying infrastructure, segregated schools and communities and the whole alphabet soup of social problems.

increase the number of trucks going through local neighborhoods of Southwest Detroit and Dearborn from 2,000 per day to a whopping 5,000 per day. Traffic congestion, noise, degraded ambient air quality, increased asthma rates, toxic-induced and aggravated disease, displaced home and business, breakup of communities, and more pedestrian and traffic accidents are all associated with this development (CEHCs, 2009).

Detroit has changed considerably since the 1967 riots. The out-migration of whites and industry to the suburbs and to other parts of the country left a City of mainly black and poor people and one of a lower tax base. The decline of the automobile industry has caused considerable job loss. Industries moved away from the City to other parts of the world to pursue cheaper labor, exacerbating the political and economic situation of Detroit. Also, the incidences of drugs, racial tension, and violence have presented Detroit with serious barriers for improving the quality of life for its residents. The City became unattractive to industry because of high crime rates and high taxes. In addition, the overall disadvantage of locating a business in Michigan had to do with high worker compensation costs, increased energy requirements of a cold climate, and a growing body of environmental laws (Rich, 1989). Growth and development have been uneven in that the majority of the residents are still trying to eke out a living through menial jobs or they are seeking relief from the welfare system even in times of record-breaking prosperity. Many areas of Detroit look war torn with boarded up and partially burnt buildings dotting the landscape. Some parts of the City never fully recovered from the 1967 Detroit riots. Without jobs, Detroit has become vulnerable to an alphabet soup of social and economic problems. Perhaps Detroit would have been in a lot worse shape if it had not been for the political acumen of the late mayor, Coleman Young, who was able to use his influence to save the City from its fiscal crisis, and takeover by the State. Today, Mayor Dave Bing, as with former mayors, is at the helm and is attempting to makeover the City by getting people with resources to invest. The questions to ask are what kinds of investments are being made, and are the investments sustainable and just?

The Case for the Incinerator

Approximately six years following the Detroit riots, the nation experienced a rise in oil prices, which came to be known as the energy crisis. As a result of the Arab oil embargo of 1973, and the rising price of oil, a scramble was on to find alternative and cheaper sources of energy. When the Detroit incinerator was first conceptualized in the 1970s, waste was viewed as a big energy source and incinerator plants that burned trash could generate electricity, save fuel, and cause much less air and water pollution than conventional coal-fired generation plants. At one time Detroit and five other major United States cities considered adapting coal-fired power plants to be trash burning plants. Although the early plans of adapting coal-fired power plants never materialized, the idea of converting trash into energy caught the eye of newly elected Mayor Young.

Incineration was not a new idea for Detroit. In 1967 with the persistent efforts of the Air Pollution Control Division of the Wayne County Health Department, the last of Detroit's four municipal incinerators had closed. Reasons given were simple volume reduction and mass-burn facilities with inadequate control systems (Alter and Pickett, no date B1). Yet, the cost of landfills was increasing rapidly. However, the oil embargo of 1973 provided the impetus for another look at incineration technology as a possible energy source. Further research into this idea showed that the expense of emissions control for incineration was greater than landfilling. However, the federal government promoted the incineration industry through tax incentives. In fact, in 1978 the Public Utility Regulatory Policies Act obliged utilities to buy power from "waste-to-energy" facilities. Even though the cost of incineration was high, it also became more favorable than landfills because of the increasing shortage of suitable space for waste disposal.

In 1974, the representatives of the Detroit City Council discussed building the world's largest incinerator with Wayne County officials. To avert a landfill crisis, the City Council began looking for alternatives to landfills. In 1975, a Resource Recovery Taskforce was formed to consider landfill options. This Taskforce included members from the Department of Public Works, City Lighting, the Building Commission, and others. The goals of this task force included the disposal of solid waste in an environmentally sound manner at a reasonable cost, reclaiming energy in the form of steam, recovering recyclable materials, and minimizing dependence upon existing landfills (Alter and Pickett, no date B1). This Taskforce relied not only upon its own resources but also consulted with experts from the private sector and solicited proposals from industry for the design, construction, and operation of such a facility.

Caught between the prospect of overflowing landfills and a ravaged Detroit economy, the City could ill-afford skyrocketing dumping costs. The City Council, the mayor, and even a few environmentalists supported the construction of the incinerator. Incineration would be an asset in three ways: 1) it would provide an alternative method to overflowing landfills, 2) it would generate electrical power, and 3) its surplus heat energy would be used to produce steam to heat buildings (*Detroit News*, 1986). In addition, such an incinerator would attract industries if they knew there would be a cheap and safe way for waste disposal. With industries come jobs, thus providing an alternative to crime and delinquency. This was a chance for Detroit to bounce back economically and to once again become a world-class city. Mark Richardson of the Oakland County Prosecutor's office speculated that another reason for the incinerator was that Mayor Young did not want to be dependent upon the suburbs for Detroit's waste disposal. Over the objections of environmentalists and local residents the world's largest incinerator is still very much in existence.

The Case Against the Incinerator

Many events fueled the social protests against the Detroit incinerator. First was the uncertainty regarding scientific rationality or risk assessment. The conflict over risk assessment within the scientific and policymaking community failed to instill the confidence of certainty regarding the safety posed by incinerators. For example, in October of 1985, Gerald Avery, director of the Permit Section in the Michigan Department of Natural Resources Air Quality (MDNR), discovered an engineering "calculation error" in calculating the dioxin and furan emissions from the incinerator. While, the permit put the risk at less than 1/1,000,000, it was actually less than 1/1,000. Upon further calculation by Avery it resulted with a much higher risk: 36/1,000,000 (Wasserman and Olssen, 1990:105). On March 26, 1986, the Michigan Department of Public Health released a report stating that the risk of cancer from the Detroit incinerator's projected emissions would be 7/1,000,000. The next month Roy F. Weston, Inc., the consulting firm hired by the city of Detroit to perform an environmental impact analysis, released a projected risk level of 1/1,000,000 (Wasserman and Olssen, 1990:145-46). The MDNR eventually settled on a 36/1,000,000 figure, 19 times higher than any other risk level the State had ever approved. Because the scientific and policymaking community could not agree upon the risks posed by the incinerator, people lost confidence and trust in policymakers' ability to protect them from harm. This lack of confidence in risk assessment only energized people to intensify their mobilization efforts (Wasserman and Olssen, 1990:145-146).

A second event involved the potentially scientific irrationality of community people as perceived by the Michigan Air Pollution and Control Commission. Often policymakers assume that community people know very little about scientific matters and thus have little respect for the knowledge of community people. They feel that community activists are too emotional, irrational, or ill informed about such matters and that scientific decisions should be left to those who do science and policy. In 1984, this lack of respect for community people may have been shown when the Michigan Air Pollution Control Commission considered the Detroit incinerator application at a public hearing in Lansing (90 miles from Detroit). This meeting was held so far away that it made it difficult for people affected by or concerned about the incinerator to attend. When people protested against holding the meeting in Lansing, the Commission scheduled a public hearing on the incinerator permit in Detroit. Three hundred people attended this hearing. One hundred of them were turned away at what turned out to be a long and stormy night. Each side accused the other of politicizing the hearing with allegations of racism. Some people described this event as a three-ring circus; others claimed they were intimidated by people at the door and by people in the audience with hoots and catcalls. Still others from the Detroit area posited that people in Lansing were trying to prevent Detroit from solving its own problems. The hearing was also packed with many city officials and their supporters. Even though the hearing was a long and drawn out process, very little new technical information was added (Alter and Pickett, no date D). The hearing started at 7 p.m., yet public comments from concerned citizens were not allowed until 11 p.m., which showed a lack of respect for the community. This did not deter angry environmentalists and local residents. Some of them stayed and spoke out against the facility until 3:00 a.m. In the wee hours of the morning the representative of the state Attorney General Office suddenly told the commission that they had no authority to do anything to the existing permit because it would have required specific advance notice of the hearing (Alter and Pickett, no date D). Because of this, the lack of specific advance notice, all of the testifying against the incinerator was for naught. Most of the people had left for home. The commission then voted 9 to 1 in favor of the permit to build the incinerator despite the overwhelming opposition from community activists.

The lack of trust by the community emerged in discussions related to the use of the best available control technology. Activists assumed that Combustion Engineering and the City would use the best available control technology (BACT) to help ameliorate environmental conditions. But, BACT was not planned to be used to curtail incinerator emissions, which called into question whether the builders of the incinerator were concerned about the safety of local residents. In August 1983, MDNR received the Combustion Engineering's application. Electrostatic precipitators rather than scrubbers or baghouses were planned. In December 1985, the MDNR Air Quality Division sent a letter to Combustion Engineering and the City stating that they no longer considered electrostatic precipitators as being able to achieve the lowest emissions rates for particulates or as being the best available control technology for sulfur dioxide, hydrogen chloride, heavy metals, or chlorinated organics such as dioxins. The letter requested that Combustion Engineering and the City amend the permit application to include dry gas scrubbers and fabric filter collectors (Wasserman and Olssen, 1990:145). Environmentalists and community groups were suspicious of the health problems that could be caused by the emissions from the incinerator, but the lack of trust and suspicion was heightened further when activists posited that the Detroit incinerator was not using BACT. Environmentalists and community groups played an important role in exerting pressure on policy decision-makers to add baghouses and acid gas scrubbers to make the incinerator safer. The addition of scrubbers and baghouses was considered a partial victory even though activists were not successful in stopping the construction of the incinerator.

Lawsuits and countersuits were filed to stop the incinerator or make it safer. Details about the incinerator and safety issues had been overlooked which generated a ping-pong match of litigation and standoffs. The Detroit Audubon Society, North Cass Community Union, the Sierra Club, the Environmental Defense Fund, Sumpter Township, the Province of Ontario, and the City of Detroit all filed suits. Over the years, suits were filed to block the construction of the incinerator as planned, to apply the best available control technology to make incinerators safer, or to determine whether ash from the incinerator would be placed in regular landfills or in landfills designed for toxic waste. The city of Detroit filed suits to continue the construction of the incinerator. The court was the site of legal maneuvers, appeals, and counter-suits. When struggles take place in the courts, community activists often find themselves marginalized and disempowered. The court suits involving the Detroit incinerator were long and drawn out processes, and in the final analysis the decisions supported the best available technology and special landfills designed for toxic incinerator ash so that the Detroit incinerator could continue to operate. In this case, the legal strategy did not hamper the community activism and perhaps the activists did help the lawyers' standing in court. Mark Richardson of the Mt. Clemens County Prosecutors Office and Patrick Dungate of the Sierra Club felt that the legal strategies were effective.

Direct Action Nonviolence Against the Greater Resource Recovery Facility

The Detroit incinerator was one of the most hotly contested environmental struggles in the state of Michigan. Today it is located in an area that seems relatively quiet, and the Greater Resource Recovery Facility continues to operate without resistance. The incinerator spews thousands of pounds of toxic waste on the surrounding area, namely the Eastern Market, a major hospital complex, an elementary school, the African-American Art Museum, and Wayne State University. Among some of the poisonous substances emitted from the smokestack include lead, mercury, cadmium, chromium, arsenic, sulfur dioxide, carbon monoxide, and the deadly chemical compounds known as dioxins or furans. Although baghouses and scrubbers were added to the incinerator to reduce some of the pollutants emitted into the air, they failed to reduce the mercury and dioxin levels to any significant extent. Also sulfates and nitrates can cause acid rain; hydrochloric acid is a corrosive and a poison; heavy metal and dioxins can cause serious health problems, such as, birth defects, skin rashes, reproductive disorders, liver disease, and kidney cancer (Wasserman and Olssen, 1990:2). Even though the best available technology is being used, toxins still escape into the atmosphere.

On any given day the incinerator smells of acid depending on which way the wind is blowing, according to Ralph Franklin, one of the community activists who was intensively involved in the struggle to shut the plant down. Most of the pollution blows over into Canada, he said. Franklin feels that no one is monitoring the incinerator as it should be monitored, particularly since the MDNR made significant cutbacks in staffing shortly after Gov. John Engler was

Table 9.1: Health Indicators for the Incinerator Zip (48211), Immediately Surrounding Zips, the Rest of Detroit, and the Rest of Michigan

Health Indicator	Zip Code Group	Mean
Asthma index (> 1 is greater than expected)[a]	48211	2.14
	"downwind" of 48211	3.36
	rest of Detroit	1.95
	rest of Michigan	.88
Cancer index, 45-64 age group (> 1 is greater than expected)[b]	48211	1.48
	"downwind" of 48211	1.52
	rest of Detroit	1.28
	rest of Michigan	.95
% low birth weight babies [c]	48211	12.59
	"downwind" of 48211	13.82
	rest of Detroit	9.79
	rest of Michigan	3.78

[a] $F = 16.647$, $p < .001$
[b] $F = 7.834$, $p < .001$
[c] $F = 125.20$, $p < .001$

elected to office. Looking at the public health variables in our database, we can see the ill-effects of living near the incinerator. The incinerator itself is in zip code 48211, but very close to the borders of 48207. We identified three other zip codes abutting 48211 and basically "downwind" of the incinerator. The mean public health variables for these groupings of zip codes are at or near the incinerator, the rest of Detroit and the rest of Michigan is shown in Table 9.1. Living in the vicinity of the Detroit incinerator is not good for health!

In the 1980s Carol Izant and Ralph Franklin became increasing alarmed about the plans for the City to build an incinerator between the intersection of interstates 75 and 94 on Detroit's near East side. The Evergreen Alliance started when a collection of Cass Corridor poets, artists, and musicians organized themselves and joined with mainstream environmental activists and lawyers and the province of Ontario to keep the Detroit incineration off line. The members of the Alliance were proud of the fact that it was a leaderless organization where decisions were made by consensus. The Alliance used many tactics of nonviolent resistance to accomplish its goals and to make its collective opinions known. The Alliance successfully chronicled its issues in the electronic media, as well as through the use of direct-action, nonviolent demonstrations. These demonstrations included picketing outside of the plant, chaining themselves to the fence surrounding the incinerator, and sitting to block the front gates of the plant in protest of its operation. These actions precipitated mass arrests. The Alliance was creative in that it held a mock funeral to focus people's attention upon the number of causalities that would result from incinerator emissions. They used giant-sized puppets representing Mother Earth and animals to demonstrate the harm that would come if the incinerator was allowed to operate. The number of demonstrators at the site reached 600-900 on four different occasions. Greenpeace, a national environmental organization, was also involved in the struggle. At one point the members of Greenpeace hung banners of protest against the incinerator from the top of the Ambassador Bridge (Franklin, 2000). In other instances, members of the Mackinac Chapter of the Sierra Club mobilized over 150 people on several occasions to demonstrate against bill HB 4304, which exempted ash from the Michigan Hazardous Waste Management Act, 1979 PA 64. This bill was passed in the House on April 25, 1989 in spite of the protests (Wasserman and Olssen, 1990:115).

The Alliance and others demonstrated and disrupted public hearings on the incinerator. To broaden its area of influence, the Alliance went into the community and schools to educate people of the harms of the incinerator. The Alliance also brought in a lot of outside experts to speak at public forums about the dangerous impact of incinerator emissions. Franklin stated that the Evergreen Alliance was much influenced by the nonviolent occupation of a nuclear power site in Seabrook, New Hampshire, and the Green Party's nonviolent demonstrations against nuclear power plants in western Europe (Franklin, 2000).

When asked what victories, if any, resulted from these demonstrations, Franklin replied that the victories were partial, but of note. "The bureaucracy wore us out," he said. "The protests against the incinerator took over everyone's lives and protesters had full time jobs. We were fighting an uphill battle from the beginning," said Franklin. Members of environmental organizations such as the Audubon Society, the Sierra Club, and Clean Water Action originally were in support of the incinerator. Early on Greenpeace and the Alliance were the only environmental organizations that were against the incinerator with the Alliance standing alone in its protests from the very beginning. The partial victory after months of protesting was the forced shutdown of the incinerator until baghouses and scrubbers could be added for greater environmental protection. The ambient air quality would be even worse if it were not for the baghouses and scrubbers, reported Franklin. He went on to state that in the long run the struggle against the Detroit incinerator played a role in the eventual decline of incinerator construction nationwide. Pam Ortner, a longtime activist, stated that in Michigan activists have been very successful in closing down incinerators by forcing owners and regulators to find alternative means. Because of this, she feels people now have a greater awareness of the dangers of incineration, and people are recycling waste materials more than in the past. When asked to compare the legal strategies with the demonstrations of the Alliance, Franklin stated that although the legal strategies helped to open up meetings with decision-makers and helped in gaining access to information under the Freedom of Information Act, it was the demonstrations that were the most powerful and useful in raising people's consciousness. Although they were not able to shut down the incinerator, the Alliance was able to make it somewhat safer by forcing the decision-makers to use the best available technology in order to provide greater protection to the community (Franklin, 2000).

Why did environmentalists and local residents fail to block the construction of the incinerator? Perhaps part of the problem was that environmentalists and local activists were taking on the first black Mayor of Detroit, a Mayor who was very popular among the black residents of Detroit. Mayor Coleman Young was also labor-oriented with a radical past. His roots extended from the black community into the civil rights movement and the national Democratic Party. When Young took office he issued a warning to dope pushers, rip-off artists, and muggers saying it was time for them to hit 8 Mile Road (the northern border of the City) and leave Detroit. Young took office at a time when there was considerable hostility between black Detroit residents and whites in the suburbs. Although white people involved in the struggle lived in Detroit, most of them lived in the suburbs were members of environmental organizations. Collectively they did not have the clout or the resources to take on this Mayor. Also a considerable amount of strain existed between the police and the black community. Soon after he took office, Mayor Young abolished STRESS, the elite police unit responsible for killing a number of black youth in Detroit. He initiated an effective, yet controversial affirmative action program in the police department. He completed a variety of development projects in the downtown area and convinced people to vote for a raise in taxes during a time when there was a national tax revolt (Rich, 1989). Young was, for many years, the symbol of black pride, black leadership, black defiance, and black independence. To an extent, he was independent of the influence of the white suburbs. White environmentalists did not have the power to force Mayor Young to close down the incinerator.

It didn't matter if scientific rationality and moral arguments may have been on the side of the activists because Mayor Young had the power and support to complete his mission. He not only had the support of the community, but he had the resources of Detroit's government at his disposal. Young, a former State Senator, was well connected at the State Capitol. If he had not supported the incinerator, it never would have been built. Young basically felt that the incinerator could bring much-needed jobs to an area of high unemployment and crime. Depending upon the incinerator to bring jobs to Detroit was indeed a gamble. But early on there were signs that the gamble would fail. The incinerator not only consumed waste but it consumed money--hundreds of millions of dollars which will perhaps be its downfall (Collins, 2002). The incinerator is the City's largest debt (van Guilder, 2006), creating a massive economic burden for the City.

In 1990, an economist by the name of Leon Moses made an interesting observation about Robbins, Illinois, when it was marketing itself for an incinerator. He felt that despite offering potential economic opportunities, the incinerator could exacerbate the economic problems of a community.

> ...negative perceptions of the incinerator will probably keep other businesses from locating in town, except similar waste processing facilities. You will fail to attract because of the incinerator...And if more (businesses) do come, they'll come with what: More incinerators. You become the junkyard of the metropolitan area. (Goering, 1990)

Detroiters in support of their mayor felt environmentalists were against economic progress and jobs, particularly when they attempted to block construction of the incinerator. The question today is what has been the long-term effect of the incinerator on the economy and health of the community?

The Sumpter Connection

Sumpter is a rural township located within Wayne County, Michigan, about 35 miles Southwest of Detroit and 30 miles Southeast of Washtenaw County's Ann Arbor. Small churches dot the landscape on the main streets, and the howling of a hunting dog can often be heard in the distance. While the northern end of the township looks typically suburban, the southern end appears rural because of vast fields and small farmhouses. Sumpter Township is fairly expansive, with the majority of the 11,000 people residing in the city of Willow. Thirty-six percent of the township's population are under the age of 18. The median age is 26 years. Of the 3,000 families in the township, approximately 15 percent are African American. Sumpter is also poor. The per capita income is just over $7,000, with nine percent falling below the poverty level. Of all the residents in the township, 54 percent have graduated from high school, and 4 percent have attended four or more years of college (DeGannes, et al. 1991).

While legal and grassroots groups protested against the incinerator, the incinerator operators began six months of testing during which time the pollution control equipment was found to be inadequate along with some operational difficulties, thus causing plant shutdowns. As the weakness of the plant became more visible, controversy grew. Environmentalists and regulators questioned the toxicity of the incinerator ash that was dumped in Sumpter Township at a site owned by City Sand and Landfill Company. Greater Detroit Resource Recovery Authority (GDRRA) sent untested ash to the City Sand and Landfill Company although federal and state laws require the generator of waste to test material prior to disposal. This practice continued even though they had been notified and warned by the Environmental Defense Fund and MDNR that they were in violation of the law. Because GDRRA did not need a permit for managing incinerator ash, it continued to send toxic ash to Sumpter Township without the knowledge of MDNR. The Sierra Club notified MDNR of this, at which point GDRRA was ordered to halt the shipping, and Sumpter Township filed a court order to stop any hazardous waste from entering the City Sand and Landfill Company's disposal site. Over the next several months there was intense conflict over the tests. At one point the City of Detroit refused to give ash sample tests to MDNR because it wanted to use a different test, one that was rejected by the State. Then GDRRA claimed that ash could not be considered hazardous waste under the Resource Conservation and Recovery Act. While the State held fast to the validity of sample tests of the ash, the GDRRA would not give in but managed to obtain MDNR support on legislation exempting ash from hazardous waste laws (Wasserman and Olssen, 1990:109-112).

Sumpter Township, one of the poorest and least populated townships in Wayne County, is used by the Greater Detroit Resource Recovery Authority to dispose of its bottom ash. The northern part of Sumpter Township is still mostly urban and white, while the southern part remains more rural and African American, the site of the disposal of hazardous waste. Waste disposal is not new to this township because it has had a Wayne County landfill in operation for many years. The plan to increase the size of the landfill and use it to dispose of contaminated ash generated by the Detroit incinerator was of considerable concern to local residents. A debate ensued as to whether incinerator ash should be regulated as a hazardous waste or as solid waste. If incinerator ash was treated as toxic waste, then the expenses of its disposal would be prohibitive to municipalities that had heavily invested in resource recovery. The debate continued while ash from the Detroit incinerator was disposed of in the Sumpter landfill. This issue was settled when Rep. Michael Griffin (D-Jackson) proposed legislation to exempt incinerator ash, allowing it to be treated as solid waste. This legislation was passed with the support from MDNR and Detroit's Mayor Young, and was signed into law on May 12, 1989 (Wasserman and Olssen, 1990). All total there were two pieces of legislation that made it possible for incinerator ash to be treated as solid waste instead of hazardous waste.

Freddie, an African American man living in Sumpter Township, was not part of the negotiations that took place in public or in private, nor was he part of the passing of the legislation that exempted incinerator ash from the classification of hazardous waste, but he was affected by the landfill. A disabled veteran who was injured after the Korean War, he lived in Detroit at one time. He considered himself lucky when his Detroit landlord evicted him. A friend offered him a place to stay and work on his newly purchased horse farm in Sumpter Township on Elwell Road. Freddie felt very fortunate to have such a friend who allowed him an opportunity to raise horses. When Freddie was asked about the landfill across the street owned by City Management Corporation, he stated:

> I don't like having it here. It does no good to the community. I don't like the way it smells. The smell has gotten progressively worse in the four years that I've been living here. Sometimes it smells like chemicals, and then at other times it smells like rotting garbage. There are times when we wake up in the morning with clogged noses or throats. This area is permeated with a rotten odor. They keep the trash pretty much picked up, though, I can say that. At Thanksgiving and Christmas time the owners come around with the free turkeys. They're poisoning and feeding us at the same time (forwarded from DeGannes et al., 1991).

Freddie also expressed thoughts about the siting of these facilities as well. He felt that solid waste facilities were more likely to be found in rural communities like Sumpter because people lack the economic and political clout to resist such sitings. He felt these facilities had been placed where there are fewer people to make noise and kick up a fuss. Freddie believes racial factors have a lot to do with the siting of a facility, and that a black community would be chosen before a white one. Like Freddie, there are many others who feel they have been inconvenienced and unjustly targeted for waste disposal (DeGannes, et al. 1991).

Although the city of Detroit is predominantly black, it is using the predominantly black community of Sumpter Township for its waste disposal. This fact goes against the common notion of environmental racism because one black community is dumping its waste upon another one. However, the generators of waste in Detroit are mostly industries owned not by African Americans but by suburban whites. Would it have been possible for Detroit to dump its waste in a surrounding white community? Probably not. Perhaps there were no other options than to dump the waste in the black section of Sumpter Township. In many ways, although Coleman Young demonstrated a certain amount of independence, Detroit takes on the characteristics of a third world country in that the economic power exercised in Detroit is not by African Americans, but affluent whites residing outside the city.

Perhaps the lesson learned is that if environmentalists want to make an impact in inner cities of significant black populations, they must build a long-term relationship with the community rather than trying to muster the support of the black community in times of crisis. If the majority of black citizens of Detroit had been against the incinerator, perhaps it never would have been built. Environmentalists must ask themselves to what extent are they willing to make a long-term commitment to building relationships with the black and Arab communities. What kinds of long-term activities or projects can be used to build these lasting relationships? What kinds of relationships would lead to building sustainable, nurturing, and productive cities that are environmentally benign? There are no easy answers to these questions. Another lesson learned is that policymakers should involve community groups in discussions and respect their knowledge and their testimony. Community people should be actively engaged in the decision-making or their lack of involvement will only breed distrust and discontent.

10

THE MULTIFACETED NATURE OF POLLUTION, ENVIRONMENTAL CLEANUP AND ISSUES OF DISPARATE IMPACT AND HEALTH

Charles Morris and Elaine Hockman

Introduction and Overview

The issues involved in the siting of pollution-generating activities and the cleanup of already established pollution-generating sites are multifaceted. Some of the questions spawned by these issues include:

- Do economic benefits that may accrue for the host community offset costs in terms of air, water and soil contamination, noise and traffic?

- To what extent are distressed communities the targets of pollution siting?

- What are both the direct and indirect impacts of race and class on the siting of varying pollution sources such as landfills and hazardous waste?

- Might there be other factors, such as the population density and home ownership, that matter as much as income and race? and

- Is there really an association between pollution sources and adverse indicators of public health once other factors are taken into account?

Planners, who must consider the impact of siting on the local community, face these and other important questions. Drawing on our previous research (Hockman and Morris, 1998) we were able to show that:

a) Minority racial status remains a potent predictor of pollution siting even when other factors such as income, degree of home ownership, population density and other variables are considered;

b) Different sources of pollution, such as incinerator emissions and hazardous waste sites, are differentially impacted by social forces;

c) Proportionally little cleanup of hazardous waste sites has been carried out by the State of Michigan through the first half of the 1990s; and

d) There is a strong spatial association between pollution problems and, in particular, incinerator emissions, and rates of cancer and low birth weight.

This chapter builds on our previous research to advance our understanding of the dynamics of pollution siting and its social impact in four ways:

1) By the use of path analysis to measure direct as well as indirect effects of social forces on the siting of pollution sources;

2) By comparing how pollution impacts different minority communities in a state;

3) By the use of logistic regression to ascertain the social or racial biases, if any, that exist in site remediation over time; and

4) By an analysis of how different forms of pollution are related to rates of cancer, low birth weight, and asthma once other factors are taken into account.

Our models show that locations of pollution sources are influenced by distributions of minority racial status and wealth, both directly and indirectly. They demonstrate that different racial and ethnic minorities are unequally affected by the siting of different pollution sources. The status of hazardous waste site cleanup at three intervals over the course of six years are traced to see what kinds of biases exist in terms of remediation. Finally, the models show that no matter what form of public health indicator is used—cancer rates, low birth weight, or asthma rates—pollution has a measurable impact even when other factors such as age, race, and length of residence are taken into account.

Through the use of more precise multivariate statistics such as path analysis, we attempt to develop a fuller yet elegant description of the social processes that impact pollution siting. Such modeling, we believe, enables us to show how individual minority groups are differentially impacted by pollution. Path analysis enables us to see to what extent race and poverty interact with various sources of pollution in an adverse association with several indicators of stress on the public health.

Methodology

Although we have multiple measures available for the major domains under investigation, we have selected one variable per domain to use in multiple regression analyses. By selecting only one variable per domain or explanatory concept, we avoid a "hidden trap in ordinary least squares" that has been named the "phenomenon of differential repetitiveness" (O'Muircheartaigh and Payne, 1977). When there are different numbers of explanatory variables per concept included in the model, the concept represented by the most variables is apt not to show any significance, while the concept with the fewer variables is apt to show significance even if all explanatory variables have the same correlation with the dependent variable. Thus differential repetitiveness can lead to results that are statistical artifacts attributable to the number of measures used from each "substantive domain."

We use the following variables:

Minority Distribution: Because minorities are not evenly distributed across zip codes, each of the U. S. Census minority groups-black, Hispanic, Asian, and Native American-are analyzed separately in addition to analysis by total minority distribution. Our measures of minority distributions for each zip code are ratios of counts for the minority groups to the counts for white Non-Hispanics. The log ratio, rather than proportion minorities, was used in the statistical analysis because of extreme skew and severe leptokurtosis centered at the extremely small values. These ratios we use reflect minority distributions relative to the white, non-minority distribution. Higher values indicate strong presence of the minorities; lower values, strong presence of white, non-minority. Summaries of these ratios are shown in Table 10.1.

Economic Disadvantage—Public Assistance: Our previous research concentrated on median household income as the major indicator of economic status. For this current study, we are looking more directly at economic disadvantage and have selected the proportion of persons on public assistance as our measure of economic disadvantage. The mean proportion of persons on public assistance within a zip code was .09, with a range from 0 to .46. A log transformation of this variable was used for analysis because of extreme positive skew.

Length of Residence in the Zip—Tenure: An issue frequently raised in the environmental justice literature but not often addressed in the research literature (Been, 1994; Yandle and Burton, 1996) is that of temporal sequence. Did the pollution siting occur after the demographics of the area were established, or did the nature of the population change after the pollution siting? While we do

Table 10.1: Minority Distribution in Michigan Zip Codes Compared with White Distribution.

Minority Group	Mean Ratio of Minority Count to White Count	Range of Ratios
Black	.54	.00 to 93.96
Hispanic	.02	.00 to .85
Asian	.01	.00 to .31
Native American	.01	.00 to .62
All Minorities	.58	.00 to 94.31

not have direct observations on this important distinction, we have included for analysis an index of "tenure" to address this issue. The index was constructed by taking the ratio of the number of persons settling in the zip prior to 1960 to the number of persons settling there in 1989-90. Thus, when this index is greater than one, the old-timers outnumber the newcomers; when the index is less than one, there are relatively more newcomers than old-timers.

Pollution Measures: As in our earlier study, we investigate six pollution sources. These are:

- Toxic Release Inventory (TRI), 1989
- Act 307 Sites, 1990, 1995, and 1996
- Leaking Underground Storage Tanks (LUST), 1990
- Hazardous Waste Management Facilities, 1996
- Incinerators, 1996
- Landfills, 1996

Each of these pollution sources has been described in detail in Hockman and Morris (1996) and in Chapter 4 of this book. The distributions of these sources are shown in Table 10.2.

An index- "pollution density"-was computed for each zip code to represent the total pollution burden from these six sources combined, controlled for size of the zip code. The index was computed by summing the counts of the six pollution sources and dividing this sum by the area for the zip code. Thus this index represents pollution sources per square mile in the zip.

Measures of Public Health

Age—Adjusted Cancer Incidence: The number of new cancer cases

Table 10.2: Summary of Distribution of Pollution Sources for 873 Zip Codes in the State of Michigan.

Pollution Source	Mean	Range
1989 TRI citations	3.14	0 to 60
1990 Act 307 chemicals	7.97	0 to 193
LUST	6.81	0 to 72
Hazardous waste management facilities	.26	0 to 8
Incinerator citations	4.21	0 to 119
Landfills	.29	0 to 9

diagnosed in 1987, 1990, and 1993 in each of six age categories were made available to us from the Michigan Department of Public Health (MDPH). The age groupings were 1) less than 15 years of age, 2) 15-29, 3) 30-44, 4) 45-64, 5) 65-74, and 6) greater than 74 years of age. In our previous research we concentrated on total risk cancer rate (these are cancers known or suspected to be environmentally related) adjusted for population aged 65 or greater. In the current analysis we used cancer incidence ratios specific to each age group. These ratios were constructed as the ratio of the cancer rate for that age group in that zip to the cancer rate for that age group in the Michigan population from the 406 zip codes that presented cancer data from all three reporting years. The 367 zip codes not included among the cancer data were zips with fewer than 5,000 persons. When the age-specific cancer rate ratio is greater than one, the cancer rate in that zip code is greater than the corresponding state rate; when the age-specific cancer rate ratio is less than one, the cancer rate in that zip code is less than the corresponding state rate.

Although cancer rate indices were computed for all six age categories, we report in this chapter the results only for the 45-64 age group. This age group was selected for several reasons. The number of cancers jumps considerably between the first three age groups and this group. In other words, this age group is the first to show high cancer rates. Although the cancer rates are considerably higher in the last two age groups, these are also the age groups with decreasing population. It is hypothesized that, if pollution is truly having an adverse effect on health, there may be less than expected numbers of persons in the oldest age groups due to early death, thus leading to potential statistical artifacts when using cancer rates for zips with fewer older citizens than expected.

Low Birth Weight: The MDPH provided birth weight data from 1989, 1990, and 1991 for zips with at least 5,000 persons. The percentage of low birth weight babies born during the three-year period was computed for 425 zip codes. Low birth weight was defined as less than 2,000 grams. Low birth weight percentages ranged from 0 to 18%, with a mean of 4.3% for the 425 zip codes.

Asthma: The MDPH provided counts by zip code of asthma hospital discharges for primary and secondary diagnoses, 1989 to 1993, in Michigan children and youth from 1 to 14 years of age. The log of the rates per 1,000 served as our measure of asthma.

Analyses and Results

The current analysis was designed to assess 1) the effects of social forces upon the siting of pollution sources, 2) the effects of pollution upon public health indicators, 3) the impacts by racial distribution, and 4) to ascertain if social or racial biases exist in site remediation over time. Path analysis was used to address the first three purposes, while logistic regression was the intended procedure to address the fourth purpose.

The basic model for the path analyses is illustrated in Figure 10.1, where minority distribution and public assistance are hypothesized to influence residence tenure. In turn, these three social forces are hypothesized to influence pollution. All four of these forces then are hypothesized to contribute to public health. The equations were solved first for all minorities combined, for each of the three public health measures. These analyses were then repeated for each minority group. The path diagrams, with standardized path coefficients included, are shown for all minorities combined in Figure 10.2 (a, b). The results for the separate minority groups are shown in tabular form, Tables 10.3 - 10.6.

The analyses show that our model is a good one. In each and every path analysis, the multiple correlation with the public health variable as the dependent variable was significant-our variables significantly predict the health measures. Except for low birth weight, the chi square goodness of fit statistics showed that the data fit the model exceptionally well.

Path A- Race is a predictor of economic disadvantage, significantly so for blacks, Hispanics, and Native Americans.

Path B-Race as a predictor of residence tenure: As minority concentration, relative to white concentration, increases, the ratio of old-timers to new-timers favors the new-timers, as evidenced by the negative path coefficients.

Path C-Economic disadvantage as a predictor of residence tenure: As reliance on public assistance increases, so does the tendency to reside in the zip code over a longer period of time.

Path D-Residence tenure and pollution density: The net effect of these opposite results with respect to residence tenure ratio is that the tenure variable shows no relationship with pollution density. Minorities tend to move into environmentally adverse zip codes; those economically disadvantaged tend to remain there. However, for blacks and Asians, long term residence, as compared to recent influx, is significantly related to pollution density.

Path E-Race and pollution density: For each minority presence, there is a consistantly significant path between the minority concentration and pollution density, a direct path for blacks, Hispanics, and Asians, indirect for Native Americans-as the number of minorities relative to the number of whites in a zip code increases, so does the number of polluting factors per square mile.

Path F-Public Assistance: The results for the economic disadvantage variable as a predictor of pollution density were inconsistent. The path coefficients

Figure 10.1. Basic Path Diagram.

First part of the path diagram, Arrows A through F

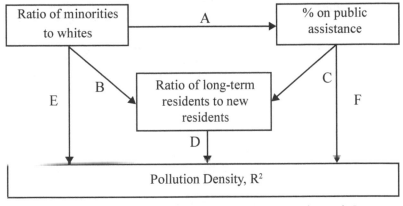

Second part of the path diagram, arrows G through I

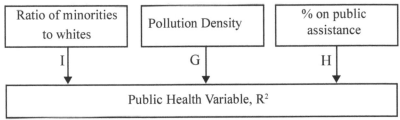

A   Race has a direct effect upon poverty.

B   Race has a direct effect upon residency duration.

C   Poverty has a direct effect upon residency duration.

D   Residency duration has a direct effect upon pollution siting.

E   Race has a direct effect upon pollution siting.

F   Poverty has a direct effect upon pollution siting.

G   Pollution siting has a direct effect upon health status.

H   Poverty has a direct effect upon health status.

I   Race has a direct effect upon health status.

for Asians and Native Americas were positive and significant, positive but not significant for Hispanics; for blacks, however, the coefficient was negative and significant. For Asians and Native Americans, pollution sources tend to follow poverty. For blacks, there was a tendency for less economic disadvantage to be related to greater environmental disamenities.

Path G-the influence of pollution density on public health: The results for the G paths were consistent and significant. As pollution density increases, so

Figure 10.2a. First part of the path diagram, Arrows A through F.

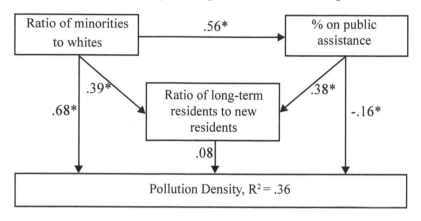

Figure 10.2b.—Second part of the path diagram, arrows G through I.

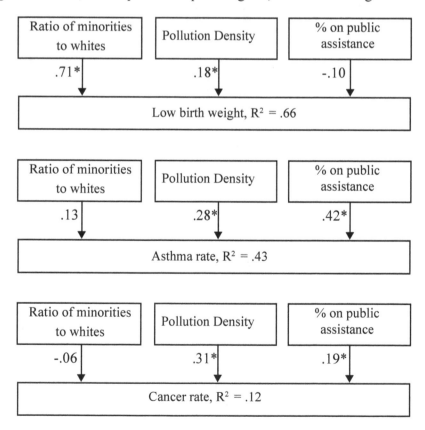

do the three public health problems of low birth weight, asthma, and cancer, regardless of race or public assistance.

Path H-the influence of economic disadvantage on public health: Consistent results were obtained for this part of the analysis, with reliance on public assistance significantly related to asthma and cancer in each minority group and to low birth weight in Hispanics, Asians, and Native Americans.

Path I-the influence of racial concentration on public health: The racial variable showed a consistent indirect influence on each public health variable. It was also a significant direct effect on low birth weight and asthma for blacks and Hispanics. The direct path between race and low birth weight was also significant for Asians.

Site Remediation

The fourth issue we wished to cover in the current research is a look at cleanup efforts for the Act 307 sites. Act 307 provides four categories of cleanup. These are, in order of cleanup progress:

1. No Action Taken

    No remedial plan has been approved.

    Evaluation, interim response activity, remedial actions, and/or operation and maintenance have not been undertaken.

2. Evaluation/Interim Response (EIR)

    Remedial Action Plan has not been approved.

    Interim response activity or evaluation is being provided by one of two sources, a) private funds provided by potentially responsible parties or other sources or b) state funds provided by the state of Michigan.

3. Final Cleanup (FCU)

    Remedial Action Plan has been approved.

    Remedial action has been or is being provided by one of two sources cited above.

4. Operation and Maintenance (OM)

    Cleanup completion/long-term maintenance is being provided by one of two sources cited above.

In looking at clean-up progress between 1990 and 1995 in a previous analysis, we found very little action, with too few sites to merit analysis against social measures for potential bias in cleanup. Indeed, we found that of 1992 sites, 80% showed no progress; 14% moved to a category representing some

Table 10.3: Ratio of Blacks to Whites Analysis Results for Three Public Health Variables.

Significance of Overall Public Health Models.

Statistic	Public Health Model		
	Low Birth Weight	Asthma	Cancer
Chi Square	2.799[a]	.522[a]	.071[a]
Squared Multiple Correlation	.623[b]	.430[b]	.123[b]

[a]$p > .05$
[b]$p <= .05$

Path Coefficients for Components Common across the Three Public Health Models.

Predictor (from)	Outcome (to)	Direct Path in the Model	Path Coefficients		
			Direct Effect	Indirect Effect	Total Effect
Ratio of Blacks to Whites	Public Assistance	A	.523*	--	.523
	Ratio of Old to New Residents	B	-.384*	.1921	-.191
	Pollution Density	E	.691*	-.0874	.604
Public Assistance	Ratio of Old to New Residents	C	.367*	--	.367
	Pollution Density	F	-.135*	.0321	-.103
Ratio of Old to New Residents	Pollution Density	D	.087*	--	.087

*$p<=.05$

Table 10.3 (continued): Path Coefficients Unique to Each Public Health Model.

Public Health Outcome Variable (to)	Predictor (from)	Direct Path in the Model	Path Coefficients		
			Direct Effect	Indirect Effect	Total Effect
Proportion of Babies with Low Birth Weight	Ratio of Blacks to Whites	I	.636*	.1385	.774
	Public Assistance	H	.044	-.0197	.024
	Pollution Density	G	.192*	--	.192
	Ratio of Old to New Residents	--	--	.0167	.017
Asthma Rate	Ratio of Blacks to Whites	I	.118*	.3958	.514
	Public Assistance	H	.427*	-.0294	.398
	Pollution Density	G	.286*	--	.286
	Ratio of Old to New Residents	--	--	.0250	.025
Cancer Rate	Ratio of Blacks to Whites	I	-.038	.2682	.231
	Public Assistance	H	.173*	-.0303	.143
	Pollution Density	G	.294*	--	.294
	Ratio of Old to New Residents	--	--	.0257	.026

*$p<=.05$

Table 10.4: Ratio of Hispanics to Whites Analysis Results for Three Public Health Variables.

Significance of Overall Public Health Models.

Statistic	Public Health Model		
	Low Birth Weight	Asthma	Cancer
Chi Square	4.605[b]	.049[a]	.065[a]
Squared Multiple Correlation	.453[b]	.430[b]	.127[b]

[a]p > .05
[b]p <= .05

Path Coefficients for Components Common across the Three Public Health Models.

Predictor (from)	Outcome (to)	Direct Path in the Model	Path Coefficients		
			Direct Effect	Indirect Effect	Total Effect
Ratio of Hispanics to Whites	Public Assistance	A	.455*	--	.4554
	Ratio of Old to New Residents	B	-.168*	.1921	-.0572
	Pollution Density	E	.422*	-.0874	.4513
Public Assistance	Ratio of Old to New Residents	C	.243*	--	.2431
	Pollution Density	F	.058	.0321	.0447
Ratio of Old to New Residents	Pollution Density	D	-.053	--	-.0529

*p <= .05

Table 10.4 (continued): Path Coefficients Unique to Each Public Health Model.

Public Health Outcome Variable (to)	Predictor (from)	Direct Path in the Model	Path Coefficients		
			Direct Effect	Indirect Effect	Total Effect
Proportion of Babies with Low Birth Weight	Ratio of Hispanics to Whites	I	.198*	.3023	.5004
	Public Assistance	H	.226*	.0197	.2455
	Pollution Density	G	.442*	--	.4421
	Ratio of Old to New Residents	--	--	-.0234	-.0234
Asthma Rate	Ratio of Hispanics to Whites	I	.101*	.3386	.4396
	Public Assistance	H	.437*	.0138	.4511
	Pollution Density	G	.309*	--	.3091
	Ratio of Old to New Residents	--	--	-.0164	-.0164
Cancer Rate	Ratio of Hispanics to Whites	I	-.090	.2259	.1362
	Public Assistance	H	.191*	.0138	.2047
	Pollution Density	G	.308*	--	.3079
	Ratio of Old to New Residents	--	--	-.0163	-.0163

*p<=.05

Table 10.5: Ratio of Asians to Whites Analysis Results for Three Public Health Variables.

Significance of Overall Public Health Models.

Statistic	Public Health Model		
	Low Birth Weight	Asthma	Cancer
Chi Square	2.148[a]	.001[a]	.309[a]
Squared Multiple Correlation	.526[b]	.424[b]	.124[b]

[a]$p > .05$
[b]$p <= .05$

Path Coefficients for Components Common across the Three Public Health Models.

Predictor (from)	Outcome (to)	Direct Path in the Model	Path Coefficients		
			Direct Effect	Indirect Effect	Total Effect
Ratio of Asians to Whites	Public Assistance	A	-.036	--	-.036
	Ratio of Old to New Residents	B	-.415*	-.0055	-.421
	Pollution Density	E	.677*	-.0835	.594
Public Assistance	Ratio of Old to New Residents	C	.152*	--	.152
	Pollution Density	F	.236*	.0270	.263
Ratio of Old to New Residents	Pollution Density	D	.178*	--	.178

*$p <= .05$

Table 10.5 (continued): Path Coefficients Unique to Each Public Health Model.

Public Health Outcome Variable (to)	Predictor (from)	Direct Path in the Model	Path Coefficients		
			Direct Effect	Indirect Effect	Total Effect
Proportion of Babies with Low Birth Weight	Ratio of Asians to Whites	I	.402*	.1389	.541
	Public Assistance	H	.375*	.0674	.443
	Pollution Density	G	.257*	--	.257
	Ratio of Old to New Residents	--	--	.0457	.046
Asthma Rate	Ratio of Asians to Whites	I	.002	.1875	.189
	Public Assistance	H	.475*	.0905	.565
	Pollution Density	G	.344*	--	.344
	Ratio of Old to New Residents	--	--	.0614	.061
Cancer Rate	Ratio of Asians to Whites	I	-.057	.1798	.123
	Public Assistance	H	.147*	.0819	.229
	Pollution Density	G	.312*	--	.312
	Ratio of Old to New Residents	--	--	.0555	.056

$*p <= .05$

Table 10.6: Ratio of Native Americans to Whites Analysis Results for Three Public Health Variables.

Significance of Overall Public Health Models.

Statistic	Public Health Model		
	Low Birth Weight	Asthma	Cancer
Chi Square	6.268[b]	.038[a]	.000[a]
Squared Multiple Correlation	.429[b]	.427[b]	.124[b]

[a]$p > .05$
[b]$p <= .05$

Path Coefficients for Components Common across the Three Public Health Models.

Predictor (from)	Outcome (to)	Direct Path in the Model	Path Coefficients		
			Direct Effect	Indirect Effect	Total Effect
Ratio of Native Americans to Whites	Public Assistance	A	.602*	--	.602
	Ratio of Old to New Residents	B	-.116	.1424	.026
	Pollution Density	E	-.033	.1655	.132
Public Assistance	Ratio of Old to New Residents	C	.236*	--	.236
	Pollution Density	F	.280*	-.0268	.253
Ratio of Old to New Residents	Pollution Density	D	-.113*	--	-.113

*$p <= .05$

Table 10.6 (continued): Path Coefficients Unique to Each Public Health Model.

Public Health Outcome Variable (to)	Predictor (from)	Direct Path in the Model	Path Coefficients		
			Direct Effect	Indirect Effect	Total Effect
Proportion of Babies with Low Birth Weight	Ratio of Native Americans to Whites	I	.050	.2297	.280
	Public Assistance	H	.268*	.1302	.443
	Pollution Density	G	.515*	--	.515
	Ratio of Old to New Residents	--	--	-.0583	-.058
Asthma Rate	Ratio of Native Americans to Whites	I	-.075	.3589	.283
	Public Assistance	H	.520*	.0872	.607
	Pollution Density	G	.345*	--	.345
	Ratio of Old to New Residents	--	--	-.0390	-.039
Cancer Rate	Ratio of Native Americans to Whites	I	.053	.1123	.165
	Public Assistance	H	.126*	.0699	.196
	Pollution Density	G	.276*	--	.276
	Ratio of Old to New Residents	--	--	-.0313	-.031

*$p <= .05$

progress toward cleanup, and 6% moved backwards to a less favorable clean-up status. Progress toward cleanup between 1995 and 1996 was even more discouraging. Of the 1831 sites with information for both 1995 and 1996, only six sites-less than 1%-moved to a more favorable status category. As there are multiple Act 307 sites per zip code and the sites within zip codes represent various combinations of clean-up status, it was not possible to conduct our planned logistic regressions to ascertain odds of progress toward cleanup, given various social indicators.

Discussion

Minority Status, Poverty, Residential Status and Public Health

Both minority status and poverty are associated with higher concentrations of pollution. And minority status, poverty, pollution density carry strong associations with low birth weight, asthma, and middle-age cancer. Blacks, Asians and Native Americans all tend to be relative newcomers to a zip. Each minority group save Native Americans has a strong relationship with pollution. Other differences arise. Asians and Hispanics who are poor tend to have positive significant paths in associating with cancer rates. But although the overall path between minority status and cancer rate is not directly significant, it plays an indirect role in its influence on pollution, whose impact on cancer rate is significant. Perhaps what is surprising is that there is as much overlap among minorities as there is. In particular, Asian Americans carry as much of a relationship to pollution as do African Americans. Perhaps the strength of Asian impact is related to heavy urban residential status. Of the variables we measure it is poverty and pollution exposure that matter most with respect to health. Given the significant statistical results, we have confidence that our model gives us a more accurate, multivalent picture of the dynamic of race, poverty, pollution and cancer.

The story repeats itself with low birth weight. Minority status and pollution both have strong positive effects on incidence of low birth weight.

A story begins to emerge that is related to the story told by environmental justice literature. However, the story that emerges here is more reflective of the complexities of a multivariate world.

First, race and class both appear to make their own unique contributions to the presence of pollution sources.

Second, an understanding of the presence of pollution is not adequately accounted for by a consideration of race and class alone. Zips characterized by more long term residential status also impact pollution, especially incinerators.

This is an important consideration. Although residential status has no direct impact on any of our public health measures, it does have an indirect effect through its path through pollution presence. That longer term residence status is related to greater pollution density tends to suggest that demographic patterns were well-established before pollution siting took place, adding yet another log to the environmental racism fire.

Third, each minority has its own story and is worthy of further research in itself. Each minority is impacted by pollution and by public health stress.[1] Blacks and Asians exhibit surprisingly similar path coefficients and direction in their paths. However, even here blacks have a stronger association with asthma and with low birth weight.

Fourth, pollution impacts rates of public health stress. The paths between pollution density and measures of public health stress were significant in every instance.[2] Regardless of the analytic tools we use, there remains a strong association between the presence of pollution and occurrence of public health stress. Areas that are more densely populated with toxicity in a small zip such as the industrial area of Southwest Detroit would conceivably pose more of a public health problem to residents than would an out-state zip that would have as many leaking underground storage tanks, but spread out over an area ten times the size.

Summary and Conclusion

When all is said and done, we are able to draw some new inferences. First, we cannot assume that every minority group in a community carries the same relationship to poverty, pollution siting and to public health problems. Nor can we be satisfied with a stereotypical image of a minority group in terms of its relation to environmental stress. Asian Americans, for example, even given their unique immigration history, show surprisingly similar associations with poverty, pollution and with adverse public health indicators as do African Americans.

Nor can we assume that direct relationships among phenomena are always the most important. Minority racial status as mediated through pollution carries a greater association with asthma rates than it does directly. The effects of race and social class ripple throughout the social system, impacting residential status, exposure to environmental toxins and perhaps to risk of contracting diseases such as asthma and cancer. Location of pollution sources in turn impacts who can live where. As we illustrate in this chapter, reality is not

---

[1] Although for Native Americans the impacts are more indirect than direct in their effects.

[2] Although not reported here, analyses were repeated for age-adjusted cancer rates in each of the remaining five age groups. Pollution density was a significant predictor in each case.

a bivariate correlation, nor even a multiple regression between two predictors and one dependent variable. Race and class associate with so many other facets of social life, which, in turn, associate with pollution. The critics of environmental justice research have a point. It isn't just economics that matter. Other variables matter. However, a consideration of both direct and indirect effects, as is done in this chapter, makes it clear that we are, after twenty years still in the initial stages of grasping all the ways in which race, class, and other factors relate to location of pollution sources.

Planners and policymakers face a daunting challenge. It is true that, as we acknowledge, one cannot draw causal inference about individuals' chances of contracting cancer or asthma because they live in the vicinity of an incinerator. However, the precautionary principle also must give us pause. If strong associations remain between the presence of pollution and the number of children who are born prematurely, if areas characterized by higher levels of sources of airborne contaminants are also areas where the asthma rates are also high even after race, poverty, and other social factors are taken into account, then it behooves planners and policymakers to insure that, at the least, no groups of citizens, either by race or class, be singled out in the decision as to where these environmentally adverse sources are sited.

We face vexing choices. After all, rates of cancer are not just numbers but individual human lives. The tragedy of higher rates of birth defects, of still birth, of debilitating asthma carry costs of all kinds-the very real costs in health care and to the work place, the cost in terms of human tragedy and loss, and the cost in terms of lost lives and lost opportunities for the next generation and the generation that follows. No longer will it do to view the presence or absence of pollution sources solely as an academic exercise.

11

JOBS AND ECONOMIC GROWTH VS. ENVIRONMENTAL PROTECTION DEBATE

Bunyan Bryant and Paul Mohai

No corporation of this state should be allowed to externalize costs so that it can make profits at the expense of worker health and the health of those in the community. Under no circumstance should the rights of people of the state be subjugated to the rights of corporations. A decent-paying job and a clean environment should be fundamental right for any person living in this state. We can have both. We can have a clean, safe environment and decent-paying jobs.

In the 1940s, when the mechanization of the farm pushed poor blacks and whites off the land in the South, many of them migrated to the North in search of jobs in the automobile and war industries. With these high-paying jobs they were able to afford luxuries that they never had before: they could own their own home, drive a new car, and send their children to college. For many years the automobile industry has been the backbone of the Michigan economy by employing thousands of workers. On average, these were indeed happy times. But things began to sour when foreign cars became competitive. The automobile companies suffered, because many consumers began to choose foreign cars over American ones since the former were superior to the latter. The big three—Ford, General Motors, and Chrysler—lost much of their competitive edge.

To rebound from foreign competition, the major automobile companies began to outsource to lower their wage costs. Industry as a whole and state government stepped up their attack on environmental regulations, claiming they were a disincentive to investment. To adhere to environmental regulations was too time consuming and cut too deeply into profit margins, and thus preventing them from making better products or cars. The automobile industry made it clear that workers would have to side with them against environmental protection or lose their jobs. It was clear that if workers chose environmental protection over jobs, the companies would pull up stakes and move to distant ports where labor was cheaper and environmental regulations weaker. Since the 1970s, when the Environmental Protection Agency was created and the Clean Air and Water Acts were passed by Congress, industry has been at the forefront fighting to weaken or dismantle environmental regulations. Even today industry has fought vigorously against the Corporate Average Fuel Economy (CAFE) standards, when adherence to such standards would go a long way to reduce greenhouse gases. Industry has gotten the Bush administration, through its energy plan, to relax many of the environmental standards that would be viewed to be favorable to it. Yet over the years it is ironic to note that even though many auto workers sided with industry against environmental regulations, their support gained them little security because of corporate restructuring, downsizing, and outsourcing. Even when companies were financially sound, workers still lost their jobs because of corporate restructuring.

The application of Title VI of the 1964 Civil Rights Act[1] to siting decisions has triggered a new round of debate on environmental regulations. Government agencies, particularly at the state and corporate levels, have embarked upon a campaign to defeat EPA's attempt to use Title VI in hazardous waste siting decisions. In the late 1990s, Gov. Engler and Russ Harding, director of the Michigan Department of Environmental Quality, and Mayor Dennis Archer of Detroit, joined forces in their attack on Title VI, claiming that its application to environmental decision-making would hurt the job market. It was during this time that environmental justice advocates were angered by Mayor Archer, an African-American, when he sided with business on this issue. When Archer took this position, they felt that Archer had betrayed the legacy of the civil rights movement.

But Title VI is only one of several pieces of legislation or rulemaking that the captains of industry and certain government officials are concerned about. They have been concerned about Judge Hayman's 1997 landmark decision that required the Michigan State Department of Environmental Quality to consider all pollution sources and their cumulative effects before issuing more permits in an area in Genesee County. The cumulative impact decision would require a new industry to weigh the environmental impact of all the industries in the siting area or get those industries in the target area to reduce their overall environmental impact before the new industry could locate there. While equal protection of the law has been a part of the political landscape, industry is concerned that government agencies, through the lobbying efforts of environmental justice activists, will be forced to apply equal protection of the law more vigorously in siting and hazardous waste cleanup decisions than in the past. In the 1990s,

---

[1] Title VI of the 1964 Civil Rights act is nondiscrimination in Federally assisted programs. One intent of Title VI was to prevent discrimination in hiring practices of corporations or government entities that received money from the Federal Government. A threat to withdraw such funds from corporations was often enough to reverse discriminatory practices. Title VI is used to apply to environmental inequality of siting decisions of state governments or agencies receiving federal assistance.

both CEOs and state government officials expressed concern about President Clinton's Environmental Justice Executive Order 12898, signed on February 11, 1994, requiring all major government agencies to design programs and strategies to ameliorate environmental injustice.

The application of civil rights and environmental justice legislation seems to threaten captains of industry to a point where they have intensified their efforts to undo the last several years of accomplishments. To strike back against environmental justice advocates, CEOs have engaged in Strategic Law Suits Against Public Participation (SLAPP suits), taking activists to court and charging them with disseminating false information. Even though the charges are often untrue and even though the corporation may lose in court, they still win because corporations will outspend their adversaries by staggering amounts of money. It is not only the legal expenses that hurt activists but also the amount of time consumed in preparing a defense against corporate power. SLAPP suits are ways in which corporate officials attempt to intimidate and disquiet their adversaries.

The Dilemma of Detroit Mayors

Governing a city requires jobs and a tax base for city services. Often the general public is led to believe that stringent environmental regulations will have a draconian effect upon both jobs and industry. If industry has to adhere to these regulations it will move its plants and jobs to other sectors of the world in search of cheaper labor, resources, and fewer environmental regulations, leaving cities impoverished, without jobs and city services, and vulnerable to crime and delinquency. Environmental protection laws are not detrimental to industrial competition because such laws can provide incentives to produce new industries and new jobs—jobs that increase people's self-esteem and personal significance. What mayor does not desire plentiful jobs and a robust economy?

---

[2] Environmental blackmail boils down to this: if a company is forced to internalize costs rather than externalize its costs onto people and the surrounding areas, then it threatens to close up shop and transport jobs to another section of the country or world. Workers are placed in the position of supporting externalized costs—costs they and their community will have to bear with respect to toxic-induced and aggravated disease. Governor Engler and Mayor Archer worked in concert. They believed that environmental regulations including Title VI were disincentives to investment and job creation. They were forcing workers and people of the state of Michigan to accept the externalization of costs in exchange for jobs. For more information on environmental blackmail see: D'Hondt, 1976; Renner, 1971; Francis, 1991; Kazis and Grossman, 1982; Bullard and Wright, (1987). Also, in 1990 powerful business interests employed aspects of environmental blackmail against the 1990 Clean Air Act, claiming that such regulations would cut into profits and cause adverse economic effects. Although modified by business interests, the 1990 Clean Air Act (CAA) was passed by Congress.

Table 11.1: Perception of Benefits from Hazardous Waste Facilities by Race.

Perceived Benefits	Black		White		Chi sq.
	N	% Perception of Benefits	N	% Perception of Benefits	
Contributes to Business	129	80	616	53	32.27813***
Tax Dollars for Community Services	127	76	610	59	12.76726**
Attract Industry	126	63	616	47	10.52056*

*   P<.001
** P<.0001
*** P<.00001

Table 11.2: Susceptibility to Environmental Blackmail: Potential Jobs and Job Protection by Race Percentages.

Perceived Benefits	Black		White		Chi sq.
	N	Black % Endorsing	N	White % Endorsing	
Favors Proposals for an Incinerator or Landfill	126	61	616	24	66.57090**
Hazardous Waste Facilities are Likely to Provide Jobs	127	79	619	65	9.69813*
Protect Jobs	126	44	594	25	16.70914**

*   P<.001
** P<.0001

Dismantling environmental regulations legitimizes the externalization[2] of the cost of production disproportionately onto low-income people and people of color. They in turn will pay a higher percentage of their income for the price of production through toxic-induced and aggravated disease and medical bills. To externalize cost is to subsidize industry, because the true cost of production which would include disease and health care costs are not factored into the equation. If a company internalizes the cost of production, then the true cost of production is borne by the company or the price is passed on to the consumer at large so that one group is not disproportionately burdened by environmental insults or health care problems.   People may want to pay higher prices for commodities if it meant they would live healthier lives. But a mayor who is short-sighted will support the externalization of costs as incentives for invest-ment and as a way of creating much needed jobs.   Perhaps the mayor felt that he had no alternative other than to pass the costs on to the poor and indigent because the companies were providing jobs now and perhaps he figured that the environment would take care of itself later. When workers are forced to choose between jobs and the environment, their predicament is a perfect example of what is called environmental blackmail.

But it is not just the mayor who is concerned about jobs; it is also the people he serves. People have suffered all too long from unemployment, unsafe neigh-borhoods, crime, and abject poverty In a study that was done in the Detroit area in the 1990s, an overwhelming majority of blacks (more so than whites) reported that hazardous waste facilities provide economic benefits and felt that a greater priority should be placed on the protection of jobs and industry. Comparison of responses from blacks and whites is presented in Tables 11.1 and 11.2.

Although environmentalists have warned local government agencies about the short-and long-term effects of pollutants, this is not new information to blacks, in that they are aware of the health and economic consequences of en-vironmental insults; they seem to be willing to risk sickness and perhaps even death in exchange for jobs and economic growth. A recent 2002 study by Pope, et al. reported that long-term exposure to fine particulate air pollutants in many metropolitan areas was a high-risk factor for cardiopulmonary mortality and that elevated fine particulate air pollutants were correlated with significant increases in lung cancer mortality. Blacks are willing to take their chances with the siting of hazardous waste facilities or proposals that favor incinerators and landfills, even though some pollutants are invisible and even though their exposure to these chemicals will perhaps have both short- and long-term health effects. To get blacks to lend their emotional support to environmental regulations is often done against a backdrop of their dire need for jobs.

Environmentalists can win the environmental blackmail argument if they are visionary and can hold firm to their belief that the biological capital that undergirds our social, economic and political institutions are at risk. Environ-mentalists can win this argument if they hold corporate feet to the political fire and demand and insist that they adhere to strict environmental regulations, forcing them to find creative and viable solutions. It is possible to have both a clean environment and jobs.

There are several reasons why environmental protection will increase the number of jobs and benefit the economy. In 1995, the size of the environmental protection industry was anywhere from $65 billion to $170 billion in early 1990s dollars (Rutledge and Leonard, 1991; U.S. Environmental Protection Agency, 1990; Silverstein, 1992a; 1992b). Competitiveness is fostered by environmental regulations because such regulations encourage companies to re-engineer their technology not only for pollution reduction, but also for lower product costs, efficiency, and for an improved and stable environment. While industry and state government officials seem to believe that environmental regulations will diminish the wealth of the nation, the regulations in fact transfer wealth from polluters to pollution-controllers and to pollution-reduction firms. Environmental regulations force companies to become more efficient and thus squander less of our precious biological capital. Stringent environmental regulations have ushered in a whole new set of pollution-control abatement industries.

In fact, Bezdek (1995) reports that since the 1960s, environmental protection and pollution abatement and control technology have grown to be a major sales-generating, profit-making and job-creating industry. In 1992, $169.8 billion were spent on environmental protection and created nearly 4 million jobs (1.9 million directly and 2.1 million indirectly) distributed throughout the economy (Bezdek, 1995).

Additional benefits of environmental protection have been made. Jeffrey C. Smith, executive director of the Institute of Clean Air Companies, Inc., made the following statement before the U.S. Senate Subcommittee on Manufacturing and Competitiveness on EPA's Revised National Ambient Air Quality Standards (NAAQS) for Particulate Matter and Ozone:

> In addition to the economic benefits accruing from implementation of the revised standards, such as improved worker productivity and reduced health care costs, implementation will also promote the air pollution control industry in the U.S., which creates jobs as compliance dollars are recycled in the economy. This industry is currently generating a modest trade surplus to help offset the billions this nation hemorrhages each month on international trade, and is providing technological leadership that can continue to be deployed in the fast-growing overseas markets for U.S. air pollution control technology (Smith, 1997:3).

He goes on to state:

> ...the Institute's best guess is that compliance with the ozone standard alone would create between 10,000 and 50,000 new jobs (in the pollution technology industry) after year (2000). Most of these are high paying jobs, such as those in engineering and construction (Smith, 1997:4).

Environmental protection (EP) is big business. EP spending today is even greater and will perhaps exceed the amount of money we spend on national defense. Or if EP were a corporation it would rank higher than the top Fortune 500 company. Management Information Services, Inc. (MISI) forecasts that real EP expenditures (1992 dollars) will increase from $170 billion in 1992 to $246 billion in 2000 to $292 billion in 2005 (Bezdek, 1995). In 1992, Bezdek reported that since the 1960s, spending to protect the environment has been growing three times faster than the gross domestic product. Because of the large amount of spending to protect the environment, a whole new industry has developed—an industry that has contributed immensely to economic growth and development. This is indeed a good sign and not a bad one for jobs and a robust economy.

Biological capital underlies the economic and social institutions of the state. Once this capital is squandered, so are the economic, political, and social institutions. Many companies in Michigan owe both their profits and their very existence to EP spending. In 1992, the jobs and sales created in Michigan by environmental protection expenditures created 188,000 jobs and $7.9 billion in sales and is still growing (Management Information Services, Inc., 1992). Conventional wisdom ignores the benefits that may be produced by environmental programs and policies—programs and polices that result in cleaner and healthier air and water for the state of Michigan and its people. In 1996, the Secretary of Interior, Bruce Babbitt spoke at the University of Michigan School of Natural Resources and Environment and said that where there was clean water, there were also economically viable cities. The Clean Water Act could have been an urban renewal act because of the economic growth associated with it. Environmental protection spending has not only been good for jobs and the economy, but it has held its own against economic recession. What is the evidence of environmental regulations resulting in jobs and a robust economy? We do not have to look very far to see that where there are strict environmental relations, there are jobs. While the U.S. economy in the late 1970s was reeling from inflationary shocks, record interest rates, the energy crisis, and anemic economic growth, spending on environmental protection grew by more than 60 percent ($55 billion to $90 billion) between 1975 and 1980. In 1980, while the United States witnessed the most severe economic depression in 50 years, with many industries experiencing depression-level problems, the EP spending increased by 22 percent— i.e., from 1980 to 1985 it increased by $20 billion (Bezdek, 1995).

There are several other instances where stringent environmental regulations have had a positive economic effect. Meyer (1992) reported that cities with ambitious environmental regulations had the highest level of economic growth. Other studies reported that pollution control measures had little or no effect on trading of goods and services or economic competitiveness (Leonard,

1989; Tobey, 1990; Porter, 1990; Cropper and Oates, 1992). In 1998, the U.S. Bureau of Labor Statistics reported that employers attributed 0.1 percent of all layoffs to environmentally related decisions (Forwarded from Lee, 1990). Even at the international level, environmental regulations have a positive effect. In late 1980s, Germany and Japan, which have the most stringent environmental regulations in the world, experienced a robust economy; profit-making activities were substantial and jobs were abundant. Environmental regulations forced the managers of corporations in these countries to be resourceful and creative.

Instead of spending large sums of money to fight regulators, industries in Germany (West Germany at the time) and Japan used that time and energy to develop pollution abatement control technology and have positioned themselves to corner the world market. Eastern Europe is in dire need of pollution control and abatement technology. As developing countries grow and develop, they will also need pollution abatement, control, and prevention technology. Michigan, with its factories and skilled labor force, is in a good position to build such technology and the international sale of such technology can help reduce the U.S. balance of payment deficit for years to come.

The argument that environmental regulations is a disincentive to investment is based upon the fact that the cost of production increases as more environmental restrictions impair the creation of goods and services. With good intentions, former Gov. John Engler and Russell Harding, former director of the Council for Environmental Quality, advanced this basic argument very successfully in their campaign against EPA and environmental organizations dedicated to environmental protection. Both Engler and Harding felt the economy could be stimulated by dismantling environmental regulations. Their arguments, buttressed by anecdotal evidence, was very convincing, particularly to people of color and low-income groups because joblessness disproportionately affects them. They were convincing because they felt that economic growth and con-siderably fewer environmental regulations are antidotes to poverty. The proper question, however, is not one of whether there should be economic growth, but what kind of economic growth. No citizen of this state, regardless of their race, ethnicity, or cultural background, should be forced to decide between jobs and a clean environment. No corporation of this state should be allowed to externalize costs so that it can make profits at the expense of worker health and the health of those in the community. Under no circumstance should the rights of people of the state be subjugated to the rights of corporations. A decent-paying job and a clean environment should be fundamental rights for any person living in this state. We can have both. We can have a clean, safe environment and decent-paying jobs. We must be firm in our resolve; we must not let corporations play workers against environmentalists or whites off against people of color. Jobs and a clean environment are a fundamental right for all. We must and can have both.

12

BERLIN & FARRO: PERHAPS MICHIGAN'S WORST TOXIC DISPOSAL SITE

Bunyan Bryant

We have been patient . . . . We have kept our windows shut in the sum-mer. We have often curtailed outdoor picnics, gardening, and other activities. We have watched our windows and cars become covered with industrial waste . . . . We have depended on the state regulatory agen-cies to protect the quality of our lives and they have failed us (Forward from Dempsey, 2001)

Background

In 1970, about half of the people who lived on South Moorish Road in Genesee County, bordering the 40-acre Berlin & Farro liquid waste incinerator and storage facility, no longer live there. They have moved away from this predominantly white farming area, or they have died. In 2000, Verna Courtemanche, at the time of this interview, was in her 80's and the 30 years she had been involved in this struggle were beginning to take their toll. Courtemanche had some digestive problems and these problems were less subtle than 33 years ago. Courtemanche stated that she was basically healthy, and her doctor didn't want to believe that any problems she might have may be related to where she lived. "I can remember when the government would come out to do testing in my front ditch. They came out with protective covering on and I screamed, 'I'm not protected and I live here every day'," she said. Men in protective covering failed to inspire confidence that she and her neighbors were safe from environmental toxins. Twenty-eight years ago her husband died of cancer. Although she felt strongly that there was a connection between his cancer and living in proximity to the landfill, she could not prove it.

The former Berlin & Farro landfill now lays fallow and is overgrown with weeds, surrounded by an old dilapidated fence. The property was purchased by the township government for $300.00, to prevent future development of the land. While doing so, however, they failed to heed the warnings of Courtemanche regarding the dangers of drainage from the landfill onto surrounding properties. And now that the people have been assured that the old landfill is safe, they are beginning to move into the area stated Courtemanche.

Courtemanche felt that she and her group of citizens, with their many protests--writing letters, attending and participating in public meetings, addressing the Department of Natural Resources, the Department of Health, the Governor's Environmental Review Board, and the Toxic Substance Control Commission--played a major role in shutting down Berlin & Farro by putting pressure on public officials. These officials in turn pressured the owners to stop the operation of the liquid waste incinerator, to clean up two lagoons and contaminated soil, and to remove thousands of buried drums from the site. The fact that owner Charles Berlin had to adhere to stricter standards forced him into bankruptcy. During the time of the struggle against Berlin & Farro, there were 100 people involved in the grassroots community organization "Citizens Against a Polluted Environment." Thirty to forty of them were regulars at meetings. Courtemanche believed that community activism proved to be a far more powerful strategy for cleanup, even though she felt the landfill was not clean to her satisfaction. She quickly reminded me that if it hadn't been for the political activism of the community "they would be much worse off than they are today" (Courtemanche, 2000).

EPA's Superfund Information System, the Comprehensive Environmental Response, Compensation, and Liability Information System (CERCLIS), cited June 1, 1975 as the date of discovery of the polluted site, with official entry onto its National Priorities List (NPL) on September 8, 1983. The final cleanup and excavation of soils, sediments, and aquifer materials began in December of 1995 and cleanup was completed in April of 1996, at a cost substantially lower than what was quoted (http://www.epa.gov/superfund/sites). Eleven years of Superfund management assistance ended on September 30, 1996 and on June 24, 1998, the site was removed from NPL. But in 2000, 30 years after waste disposal operations began and six years after the official end of cleanup, Verna Courtemanche still did not grow her own vegetables in her backyard and she depended on bottled water for drinking and cooking because she was convinced that the site was still a health threat. When the story broke in the early 1970s about the contamination of the landfill, it was impossible for Courtemanche to move unless she incurred a huge economic loss. She said today that was no longer the case because new development has increased the property values in the surrounding area. When asked why she hasn't moved since her property value has increased, she said that she would feel guilty, particularly if she sold her house to a family with young kids. Thoughtfully she joked, "Perhaps I could sell to an older couple, but not to families" (Courtemanche, 2002).

The Early Years

Born in 1938 to Clifton and Geraldine Berlin of Gaines Township, Charles Berlin grew up helping to work his father's farm. In 1956, he graduated from

Swartz Creek High School and three years later he was nationally honored in Kansas City as a "Future Farmer of America". Berlin owned a 40-acre farm on South Moorish Road and was in partnership with his father on a nearby 320-acre dairy farm (Braknis and Crawford, 1983). At the time, small farmers were struggling to survive economically, and it was easy for Berlin to look to the waste disposal business as a good way to get out of farming and into a business that was more lucrative. Hauling sewage for the City of Swartz Creek, Berlin was approached by General Motors officials in the late 1960s or early 1970s about the need for an industrial waste incinerator in the area. Berlin had the land and General Motors as well as other companies in the area would be steady customers. It seemed like a dream business venture that could not fail. In 1972, Berlin went into business with Frank Farro, a long-time township farmer whom Berlin had known for years. The disposal site covered 10 of the 40 acres owned by Berlin (Braknis and Crawford, 1983).

The Start of Berlin & Farro, Inc.

To obtain rezoning of this land from agricultural/residential to heavy manufacturing, Berlin and his wife Carolyn filed a request to change the zoning on 10 acres of their farmland on the West side of Moorish Road, across from their farm house. When the zoning proposal was presented, first to the Gaines Township Zoning Board, which conducted two meetings on their request during the summer of 1971, residents of the local area were not convinced of the merits of the operation, and large crowds attended both board hearings, held in the old township hall.

Representatives from the State Department of Public Health attended the hearings to answer questions from the public and board members. Although most people, including Melvin L. Brooks, the secretary of the township zoning board, felt it was an example of "spot zoning," Henry Jennings, township board member, expressed another view. He felt the local automotive plants were putting pressure on the state of Michigan to create a disposal site. When William Burton, another board member, expressed concern that people felt that an incinerator in the area would not work out, the township zoning board on July 12, 1971 denied Berlin's request. But Berlin was not deterred. He took his case to the Genesee County Zoning Board, and one month later county commissioners Preston Schmit, Gary Corbin and Edward McLogan in a 2-1 vote recommended against rezoning because it represented indiscriminate growth that would be harmful to the future of the township (Westerholm et al., 1985).

Because most of the public concern centered around the noise and traffic problems, resulting from operation of the site, the incinerator itself was not an issue. In those days the issue of pollution was not too much of a concern because it was often associated with economic development, and the phrase toxic waste did not have the same meaning it has today. Because of the public concern about the noise and traffic, the township board--not the township zoning board--was thus willing to listen to Berlin's request. They were willing to listen because rezoning was a way to expand the tax base in a township committed to farming. From Berlin's business investment of $220,000, this would yield approximately $3,500 a year in property taxes that could go to support local schools and government. One member of the township board was quoted as saying, "It would be private money fighting pollution, rather than public money" (Crawford, 1983:B3). Because of the need to handle factory waste from area industries, the township believed that the state supported the building of the incinerator. And although the residents did not want the incinerator, they had faith in the protective role of the state.

On September 7, 1971, after site planning concessions were made to appease nearby residents, a 10-acre site, located within Berlin's 40-acre farm, was approved for rezoning. The appeasement included fencing the site, locating the incinerator 500 feet from the road, and promising that the proposed waste incineration plant would be built on the property (Crawford, 1983). Additionally, the township board duly noted that the Department of Public Health's Air Pollution Control Commission (APCC) would monitor the operations and enforce state regulations.

The Residents Protests But to No Avail

On October 20, 1972, Berlin & Farro Liquid Incineration, Inc, officially began its burning operations by processing materials from two area Chevrolet plants. According to specifications, the incinerator was capable of burning 500 gallons an hour, although Berlin later told the Flint Journal that he could burn up to 1,000 gallons an hour (Braknis, 1983a). Emissions from the incinerator could be smelled up to four miles away. Residents stated that the incinerator operated 24 hours a day, creating the biggest odor problems in the afternoon and evening. Within a half mile radius residents complained of stinging eyes and burning throats, caused by smoke and airborne soot all of which ruined outdoor activities and caused some of them to stay inside with windows closed. Incomplete combustion resulted from operating the incinerator beyond its recommended burning capacity, creating and releasing smoke and particulate matter above acceptable levels. When certain chemical and/or plastics are burned they produce dioxin, a chemical that is more dangerous than the pre-burned chemicals or toxins themselves. In fact dioxin is the most toxic man-made organic chemical. Initially Berlin & Farro was allowed to store up to 40,000 gallons of waste on the site, apparently in tanks. Several months later the company obtained a permit to bury solid waste, specifically empty barrels, on the Southwest corner of the adjacent 30 acres owned by Berlin and his wife (Braknis, 1983a).

In June of 1973, less than a year after commencement of the waste burning operations, the first citizen meeting was called at the Gaines Township Hall to protest against the pollution and to press the State to take action against Berlin & Farro. Throughout 1973 and 1974, local and state health departments, and the Air Quality and Environmental Enforcement Divisions of the MDNR and the Pollution Emergency Alerting System of MDNR were the target of a number of complaints. These were some of the same agencies that had previously promised that they would take immediate action in response to complaints levied by individual citizens. But time passed with no relief for Berlin's neighbors. Citing the lack of manpower and/or expertise in this area, state and local officials seemed unable or unwilling to take action to remedy the situation. Because of this unresponsiveness, the faith and trust that people had in state agencies to protect them from environmental harm eroded and quickly destroyed. Many residents gave up on state agencies and began to create new avenues to address the problem at the local level. One such avenue occurred when Gaines Township adopted the state of Michigan's air pollution regulations as a local ordinance, and then officially informed Berlin & Farro that it was in violation of the new ordinance. When Berlin & Farro was ordered to stop, Berlin disregarded the notice and continued business as usual. To respond to Berlin's defiance, the township board countered by filing a lawsuit against the company in August 1973 (Westerholm et al. 1985). Due to the lack of progress, the suit was dismissed four years later.

The State Takes Action But to No Avail

In September 1973, legal action was initiated against Berlin & Farro by the State of Michigan for air pollution violations. Two months later, the air pollution suit brought against the company by Gaines Township was set aside due to the MDNR's involvement. Then in January 1974, Berlin & Farro's waste storage license was renewed, based upon the County Board of Health recommendation, despite the legal actions and complaints filed against the company. In March of 1974, a final Consent Order, containing 11 specific stipulations that required corrective action by Berlin & Farro was issued by the MDNR. Although Charles Berlin informed the MDNR that he had ordered a scrubber for the incinerator, the financial limitations on the part of the company would delay its installation. Therefore, all 11 stipulations of the Consent Order were violated during 1974 and 1975, including Berlin & Farro's commitment to install air pollution control equipment to help sequester toxins. A complaint by one person stated that the burner was smoking terribly and soot was found on the snow in his field and no corrective action had been made. The state thought that it would get the company to improve its performance by relying upon the philosophy of cooperation rather than confrontation with business (Dempsey, 2001). Meanwhile, the residents of the area continued to complain, in person, to the APCC and the Governor's Environmental Review Board.

It was later revealed that Berlin had constructed two unauthorized lagoons on the property. But because the State knew about them and never issued any violations, Berlin therefore claimed that they were not a problem. While the South lagoon contained 1,000,000 gallons, the North lagoon contained 1,500,000 gallons of unspecified wastes. In March of 1974, various overflows from these lagoons into Slocum Drain and Swartz Creek were documented by county inspectors. When the inspectors gave the company seven days to correct the problems, Berlin ignored the deadline and the MDNR failed to take any action. Remarkably, in December 1975, the MDNR Water Resources Commission reissued a permit to Berlin & Farro for controlled waste storage. Despite the continued contamination problems from the lagoons, in February 1976, the MDNR Water Resources Division reissued a landfill permit to the company (Westerholm, et al. 1985).

On September 16, 1975, a final Cease and Desist Order was issued by Howard Tanner, who at the time was the Director of the MDNR (Westerholm et al. 1985). This Cease and Desist order not only required the termination of all incinerator use and prohibited the hauling of liquid waste to the site, but it required Berlin & Farro to develop a plan for cleanup of liquid wastes within 30 days. An appeal by the company was filed at the District Superior Court and the court upheld the Order. While all of this was going on, the Genesee County Prosecutor's Office initiated a lawsuit against the company and obtained a restraining order to shut down its operations. These orders were also violated and the landfill continued to be used until late 1975.

During April 1976, subject to conditions such as removal of the unauthorized lagoons, tanks, and drums present on the property, the MDNR renewed Berlin & Farro's liquid waste hauling license. Throughout 1976 and 1977, Berlin ignored these conditions as well as continued orders from MDNR to: 1) stop contaminated flows through on-site agricultural field drains to Slocum and Kimball drains, 2) clean out lagoons, 3) remove all the drums, and 4) excavate the tanks used for storage. Finally, to force the company to comply, Michigan's Attorney General's Office issued a civil lawsuit. A partial agreement was reached and the Genesee County Circuit Court ordered the company to remove the lagoons and underground tanks, provide fencing around the lagoons, seal the contents with dirt, and conduct a hydrological study. In addition, the company was to post a $500,000 bond to insure that those conditions would be met. But still the company refused to comply with the order. As late as April 1981, the lagoons were not only still open and unfenced, but groundwater contamination was also detected. Sometime in 1977, Frank Farro sold his portion of the company to Charles Berlin and left the firm (Westerholm, et al. 1985).

Berlin Goes Bankrupt: The State is Left with a Mess

In May 1980, Berlin & Farro filed for bankruptcy under Chapter 11 under the United States Bankruptcy Act (Braknis, 1983). Also in May, to detect if any of the residents should receive medical care, the Toxic Substance Control Commission (TSCC) proposed testing for chromosome damage due to chemical exposure. However, this testing was never done. In addition, soil testing by Dr. Norman Zimmerman of the TSCC in February 1981 showed unacceptable levels of highly toxic chemicals such as pentachlorobenzene, C-53, C-54, hexachlorobenzene, and tetrarchloropentadiene on property adjacent to the site. Contaminated surface water due to natural drainage patterns crossed over onto Guy Slocum's property West of the Berlin site, continued into the Slocum Drain, and eventually emptied into the Flint River (Westerholm et al., 1985). In addition, there were 11,000 cubic yards of soil containing highly toxic materials that posed a serious health threat to people in the area. Because these chemicals were dangerous, and some of which are known to cause cancer, liver damage, and brain damage, Governor William Milliken, acting upon the recommendation of the state TSCC, declared the Berlin & Farro site a "toxic emergency" in May of 1981 (Braknis, 1983:B6). Although Milliken declared this site to be an emergency, not much was expected to happen because the State had only a limited amount of State and federal money at the time. No money was ever set aside for emergency situations and this rendered the declaration meaningless.

Efforts to Cleanup the Site are Derailed

The belated involvement of the EPA, which has lengthy and strict procedures to be followed before it will fund chemical dump cleanups, stalled the cleanup effort at the site. When EPA finally allocated the money, the weather postponed the cleanup several months (Braknis, 1983:B6). Cleanup at the site was also blocked by disputes. In October 1981, Clifton Berlin (the father of Charles Berlin) was embroiled in a dispute with EPA. Clifton refused to give EPA access to the site to stop the runoff due to heavy rains until an unspecified fee was paid by EPA to Clifton Berlin. Questions of property ownership stalled EPA efforts because Charles Berlin owed three years worth of back taxes. In order to establish land ownership and to gain access to the land, the State sued Charles, his wife Carolyn, Clifton Berlin, and the Peter Marsh Agency, which had started the foreclosing proceedings. Clifton Berlin was finally declared the property owner when he paid the back taxes. In addition to the conflict over property ownership and access, controversy ensued over the proper place for waste disposal. Sen. Phil Arthurhultz (R-Whitehall) tried to block the attempts of MDNR to send the waste from Berlin & Farro to a Muskegon-area site. Concurrently, a heated debate ensued between TSCC and MDNR, each accusing the other of irresponsibility and not responding adequately to the problem. Toward the end of 1981, the Hooker Chemical and Plastics Corporation entered into an agreement with the Attorney General's Office and the MDNR to dispose of 15,200 cubic yards of contaminated waste by trucking it to its vault in Montague, Michigan (Westerholm, et al. 1985).

A Site Cleanup Program is Proposed

In March of 1982, John Magyar of the TSCC reported that a total of four tanks containing approximately 26,000 gallons of C-56 had been recently discovered buried at the site. To gather citizen input upon a proposed cleanup plan, a public hearing was held two months later in Gaines Township. Officials from both the MDNR and the Department of Public Health (DPH) were present to answer questions about the proposed cleanup plan. The TSCC agreed with the citizens' demands for an immediate cleanup, but not without adding the following stipulations: 1) residents were to be evacuated during the cleanup, 2) toxic wastes were to be disposed of off the site as opposed to on-site containment, 3) groundwater monitoring would continue for at least two years, and 4) cleanup would start immediately, regardless of whether EPA had supplied Superfund money. Four tanks plus a fifth tank containing C-56 were removed by November of (1982). In the process of removing the tanks, it was then discovered that the soil was contaminated by C-56 to a depth of 15 feet. The true extent of this problem will perhaps never be known, because the testing stopped at 15 feet (Westerholm et al., 1985).

Verna Courtemanche, in January of 1983, noticed that for no apparent reason, cleanup work had stopped on the site. When she called the supervisor of the cleanup site and was not satisfied with his reasons for the work stoppage, she continued to ask questions. Drawing upon her knowledge of other sites around the country, she asked the supervisor, already knowing the answer to her question, if he had found cyanide. He answered that there was only a little and that he had found the remnants of a drum and stated that he didn't know if there was more and had stopped work. She politely thanked him and said she would have to share this information with the residents and the press (Westerholm, et al., 1985). Through a little research on her own, Courtemanche had found out that both cyanide and hydrochloric acid were present on the site.

When the residents in the surrounding area learned in early 1983 that hydrochloric acid and cyanide might be burned at the site, they became even more outraged. Also, people could be killed or harmed if the two chemicals during their removal reacted with one another, causing toxic fumes that drifted and engulfed people in the area. In March, the newly elected Governor James Blanchard decided to cover the site and stopped the cleanup until fall when the chance of chemical reactions would be minimized due to the cooler weather.

Work Stoppage Angers Residents: The Courts Order Cleanup

The residents in the area became angry when the state stopped the cleanup of the site. Charles Mueller, a local state representative and township lawyer James Bovie filed a lawsuit in Judge Judith Fullerton's Genesee County Court in support of the angry residents (Dempsey, 2001).

Mueller believed that Blanchard was relying upon faulty advice from staff members who had no scientific or natural resource backgrounds. Immediate cleanup was demanded by the lawsuit. Despite the protests from opposition lawyers, Judge Fullerton was able to clear her deck of other cases and convened court on a Saturday in order to resolve this most important issue and she was determined to hold court until the issue was resolved. After weighing the evidence, Judge Fullerton decided in favor of the immediate cleanup. She ordered on April 16, 1983, that 30 homes near the Gaines Township site be evacuated during the cleanup. She appointed James Truchan of the MDNR's environmental enforcement division to administer both the clean up and the evacuation activities, with the latter to be done within three days.

While the evacuation took place, the controversy continued. At one point Truchan told the court that he felt the evacuation was unnecessary, even though men working on the site were wearing protective clothing and respirators. When Claudia Kerbawy of MDNR's Groundwater Quality Division, stated that the threshold for odors outside the immediate evacuation area (approximately one-half mile) would be well below health hazards, John W. Shaffer of the MDNR Air Quality Division estimated that one mile would be necessary to ensure a safe level. On April 20, A-1 Disposal Company evacuated 30 families and began the cleanup. On April 22, when three more families complained of odors, they too were evacuated. Those families that remained complained about dust, not odors. The dust may have been from the heavy traffic of trucks carrying disposal waste or the movement of dirt on the site. It is unknown to what extent any transported toxins became airborne with the dust. The impact of the cleanup on those people who were not evacuated may never be determined. By the end of May, the residents were allowed to return home. The cleanup had taken much longer than anticipated (Westerholm et al., 1985). And when the evacuated families returned home, they still had questions about safety. Demanding to know the risks to their health, after finding out through the press that MDNR and EPA were going to remove another 4,000 exposed drums of waste, they physically blocked the road leading to the site. To explain the cleanup plans, agencies hastily scheduled a meeting the next day (Dempsey, 2001).

Health Problems Associated with the Site

In 1983, a lawsuit was filed on behalf of 28-year-old Jeff Bendle of Swartz Creek, whose parents claimed his severe mental illness was related to his exposure to toxic chemicals while working at Berlin & Farro 10 years earlier. Bendle's parents claimed that his severe mental illness was induced by exposure to toxic chemicals at the site. According to lab reports, Bendle's tissues held a high level of hexachlorabenzene, a compound reportedly found at the dumpsite and identified as the cause of a rare mental disease. Bendle was institutionalized and the MDNR tried to locate the approximately 100 one-time employees of Berlin & Farro to inquire about their health status (Morse, 1983).

Michelle Holmes was born in March 1983 to Cliff and Chris Holmes. Both Cliff and Chris believe that Michelle's illness is related to the contamination from the Berlin & Farro site. Doctors believe that she suffers from Acquired Immune Deficiency, a disease that is sometimes linked to exposure to modern day chemicals. When Michelle was tested by Dr. Paula Davy, M.D., an Ann Arbor doctor specializing in chemically-related disorders, she reported that the tests indicated that Michelle's illness could have occurred because of exposure to the chemically polluted air near the Berlin & Farro site. Michelle was besieged with vomiting, diarrhea, and constant crying right after she was born and her inability to fight off disease may be related to exposure to chemicals. When the Homes family moved to Flint, Michelle's symptoms had started to diminish. However, when the family returned to Cliff's mother's house to visit, Michelle again reacted violently and was taken to the area hospital. The doctors were not optimistic about her future because she has only a slim chance to build up her immune system (Westerholm, et al. 1985; Gustafson, 1983).

As the Cleanup is Finished-A Larger Problem Surfaces

In May of 1983, many of the residents thought the problem was over when the surface contaminants were finally removed. But many people began to wonder what, if any, effect the long-term dumping of liquid into an open pit would have on the groundwater. A study conducted by D'Appolonia Waste Management Services of Pittsburgh for the Michigan Department of Natural Resources reported groundwater and soil contamination 700 feet south of the defunct dumpsite. The study not only found water contamination in an aquifer at a depth of 14 feet, but soil contamination in other areas up to a depth of 156 feet. More than 50 toxic chemicals were found at the site (*Detroit Free Press*,

1983). Because area residents used well water, most of them were now forced to purchase bottled water for their drinking and cooking. Private testing was done on some water supplies to determine whether they were contaminated. One person, who lived one mile from the site, reported that the arsenic levels were initially measured at .046 parts per million (ppm) in 1982 and by 1983 had risen to .073 ppm (Gruber, 1984).

Verna Courtemanche and neighbor Lottie Fitzki both had wells closest to the site and shared the distinction of having the highest levels of arsenic. Arsenic is used in a variety of manufacturing processes by firms that sent waste to the site throughout the 1970s. It is used to make a variety of pesticides and insecticides. In 1980, the United States Department of Interior did a geological survey that indicated the highest level of arsenic naturally occurring in state groundwater was .032 ppm. Courtemanche was told by James Lahtie of the state Department of Health that if the high arsenic levels she suspected were true, that he would definitely not drink the water. David Wade, toxicologist consultant for the DPH's Division of Environmental Epidemiology stated that he did not consider the reported amounts to be dangerous (Gearino, 1983).

By 1984, while the state had contributed another $1.4 million and while EPA contributed $9 million, the companies that used the disposal facility agreed to pay $14 million after being threatened with a lawsuit under the federal Superfund toxic waste cleanup law. The list of waste generators was a veritable "Who's Who" of Michigan's industry. They included notables such as General Motors with its Flint automobile assembly plant topping the list. Other contributors included the Chrysler Corporation, Ford Motor Company, Dow Corning, Consumers Power Company, and Detroit Edison. In 1998, after fifteen years of cleanup, the EPA and MDNR declared the site to be clean-almost 25 years after the first complaint about Berlin & Farro was filed (Dempsey, 2001).

Analysis

The analysis of this environmental crisis runs much deeper than the controversy over the Berlin & Farro disposal site. This crisis is rooted in the post-World War II era when Michigan's major manufacturing industries began generating mammoth amounts of hazardous waste-metals, such as chromium from plating plants, solvents and paints, and wastes from automobile manufacturing. Oftentimes waste was used to fill in low areas that included wetlands and other natural areas. While most of the focus was on the accumulation of profits, very little thought was given to the accumulation of waste or its safe disposal. This story is no different from the situation the nation over. Any social structure of accumulation must focus not only on profit-making, but also upon waste-making or the results will be similar to Berlin & Farro.

What was thought to have been a simple problem and solution turned into one of the most complicated environmental problems the State will perhaps ever witness. Why was Berlin & Farro allowed to stay open as long as it was? Berlin himself has maintained that he cooperated with state officials and took corrective actions as instructed and has been wrongfully accused, blamed for problems at the site and unjustly forced out of business by the State and the media. He reported that he did not feel guilty of anything and that he had disposed of the waste properly. He further questioned, that if he were in violation of something, then why was he not jailed (Braknis and Crawford, 1983). Perhaps the blame lies not with Berlin so much as with the State of Michigan, which allowed him too much freedom to play off one agency or department or division against another. Berlin himself was adroit at manipulating the system by defying court orders or Cease and Desist orders or by just ignoring their existence. All the while, local residents continued to be threatened and spoke out that their illnesses were associated with the Berlin & Farro site. The residents in fact subsidized this renegade industry by paying for externalized costs as reflected in health care bills, and taxpayer dollars. There are many reasons why this situation lasted as long as it did. One general reason is that modern scientific results have outstripped our ability to understand or to dispose of the by-products of scientific outcomes in the form of waste in ways that are safe. Another reason is that the State of Michigan was understaffed and under-programmed due to budget cuts. Also,"(v)ital programs to control discharges of toxic substances in our air and water, to carefully manage hazardous waste and to clean up environmental contamination cannot be provided...." (Tanner, forwarded from Peterson, 1983a:B2). Yet another reason is that the state was not only understaffed but many staff members did not have the necessary training either in the enforcement or scientific realm. One additional reason was that this was a classical problem of inter- and intra-agency coordination.

With approximately 20 agencies, bureaus or divisions,[1] oftentimes the left hand was oblivious to what the right hand was doing. In 1983, according to then Governor James Blanchard, in a statement to the Detroit News, poor communication and petty jealousies among state agencies were to blame for the delay in the cleanup. "After weeks of finger pointing, Blanchard was quoted as saying that he finally persuaded three agencies to meet and sign an agreement on a site cleanup" (Cummins and Gearino, 2002:A1). Howard Tanner, Director of the MDNR at the time, made some interesting comments regarding the organizational structure of the state government. He reported that in addition to the Natural Resource Commission, there were five other commissions that were

---

[1] Over the span of time that Berlin-Farro was in operation, the following agencies, divisions, or bureaus were involved: Department of Public Health, Department of Natural Resources, Gaines Township Zoning Board, Gaines Township Board, State Air Pollution Control Commission,

autonomous or semi-autonomous that were accused of not talking to one another or "playing ball" together. "It is terribly difficult to run an agency where two or three offshoots are independent . . . . The Natural Resources Commission has no input into other commissions . . . . (and) (I)f two bureaus can't agree on a joint project, they can come to me and I can resolve it. Not so with differences between bureaus and environmental commissions" (Tanner, forwarded from Peterson, 1983a:B2).

Tanner went on to say that although the Division Staff also serves the Air Pollution Control and Water Resources Commissions in pollution control and compliance functions, they get direction from two sources-from commission orders and from Tanner through the bureau chief's directives. A staff employee could be taking contradictory directions from a member of another commission and a bureau chief. For example, the APCC must utilize staff from the Bureau of Environmental Protection in order for the former to exercise its pollution control duties.

When the Air Pollution Control Commission was transferred from the State Department of Public Health to the MDNR, the director of Public Health was made permanent chairman of APCC (Peterson, 1983a). The Air Pollution Control Commission was in Public Health when it gave Berlin & Farro its incinerator license. When it became apparent that the commissions could not enforce the applicable water and air regulations, Tanner went to then Governor William Milliken to ask for enforcement powers to be transferred to the Natural Resources Commission. Governor Milliken signed an executive order, in 1976, to complete the transfer of power (Peterson, 1983a). However, by the time the transfer of power had taken place, the enforcement division had to begin from scratch in order to build a case against the company. And, as with most state agencies, the divisions were understaffed with respect to preventive enforcement. Most of the time officials were busy fighting other problems and work on Berlin & Farro distilled down to making token gestures such as revoking permits. It was only after media, legislative and judicial attention, that substantive agency action occurred. By the time the MDNR finally began to enforce the regulations they had lost the respect of the local citizens and this complicated matters too. When the site became a media topic, both State Rep. Charles Mueller and Judge Fullerton became highly involved in championing the rights of local citizens.

Water Resources Commission of the MDNR, the County Health Department, the County Health Board, the state Attorney General's Office, Toxic Substances Control Commission, Genesee County Circuit Court, MDNR Enforcement Division, Air Quality and Enforcement Division of MDNR, the Polluting Emergency System of the MDNR, the Governor's Environmental Review Board, the MDNR Water Resources Division, District Superior Court, Genesee County's Prosecutor's Office, the Governors Office, U.S. Environmental Protection Agency, and at least two state Representatives.

Both were elected officials and were perhaps responding to political pressure to evacuate families nearest the site. Because of weather factors, the MDNR proposed cleaning up the site during the winter because cold temperatures would reduce the volatilization of organic compounds in the lagoons. But anything MDNR said or did had little credibility by that point; they had lost control of the process. Through a court order, they were forced to evacuate the residents and conduct the cleanup immediately. Also, the problem of confusion and interagency coordination permeated the lower echelons of the state as well. At the lower level, staff were inadequately trained in legal or administrative processes and were placed in charge to regulate facilities they knew nothing about. Staff were not trained to be enforcement-oriented people (Truchan, forwarded from Westerholm et al., 1985).

But inter-agency coordination was not the only problem. There were co-ordination problems within the MDNR itself. Peterson (1983a) reported that the problem was that there were too many managers in the MDNR and that environmental teammates had been accused of not talking to each other. "Problem is in the MDNR itself, MDNR divisions are not coordinated. They are not talking to each other" (Freeman forwarded from Peterson, 1983a:B2). When Tanner issued a final Cease and Desist Order on September 16, 1975 that effectively stopped all incineration and hauling of waste to the site and remedial action, Berlin appealed the order and a lengthy administrative hearing ensued. In 1978, Tanner reissued to the company a permit anyway for hauling waste from the site, not to the site. But the company hauled more waste to the site, even though it was not supposed to do so. The license was finally taken away on July 1, 1981. Freeman, the assistant attorney general who had drafted the Cease and Desist Order, said it was absolutely amazing and mind boggling, that he was not consulted about license renewal.

This situation was not only confusing to staff, but also to the public. Frequently a person must deal with a number of bureaus and commissions to get an answer. It is no wonder that people have been frustrated in their dealings with regulatory agency personnel and scientists. In the process of trying to get the regulatory agencies to do their job, Courtemanche felt patronized and belittled, viewed as an irrational and paranoid citizen when she was in search of answers to questions so she could make informed decisions. She was given the run-around, put on hold and lied to by government, making her doubtful of government. Courtemanche reported that over the years she had complained, requested, begged, written letters, attended public hearings, screamed, yelled and cried. She reported that she had run the gamut of frustration, uncertainty, doubt, anger, mistrust, stress, and fear. But she was mainly concerned about fear. She was not only afraid of the immediate possibilities of contaminated air and water or possible fire and explosion, but she was also afraid of the long-range effects of ingestion of toxins over the years in which she had been exposed (Westerholm et al., 1985). This preoccupation with finding ways to cope, oftentimes in the face of scientific uncertainty, can affect one's personal and family relations. Courtemanche felt that people began to doubt themselves and began to think that they were crazy for raising these issues.

But Courtemanche is not alone because hundreds of people in communities across the nation have become frustrated, angry and distrustful of government as their demands for certainty and immediate solutions have gone unanswered. In another incident in the state of Michigan, where parents found that the elementary school had been build upon top of a landfill, they demanded that the school be closed. While many of the parents wanted to close the school to protect the health of their children, others argued that if the school closed, their property values would quickly decline and wipe out their life savings invested in their homes. They felt there was no absolute proof that what was found on the playground of the school was harmful. The argument boiled down to health vs. economics. For example does one close down the school to protect the health of children or does one keep it open to protect property values from falling in the surrounding area? This demand to close the school tore the community asunder. In some instances, it split families where daughters were against mothers and sons against fathers. Although the school was closed in the absence of conclusive proof of harm and the children were moved to another school, it was not without a price that people paid in terms of personal relationships. Often people have to pay the high price of sacrificing personal relationships, because professionals from regulatory agencies, scientists, and policymakers are often baffled about what to do to protect people from environmental harm. They often cannot speak with certainty or clarity to bring comfort, security to those who feel they are at risk.

The question is "can this happen again?" Perhaps not to the extent that it did with Berlin & Farro, where you had approximately 20 government entities at varying levels involved. This was definitely a unique situation. But frustration can be encountered by people attempting to bring attention to an environmental "wrong." Today various forms of toxic waste may have surpassed our ability to monitor or dispose of them properly. As hundreds and perhaps thousands of new chemicals come onto the market each year, many of them will bypass our senses of sight, smell, taste, sound, and will go undetected. Getting regulatory agencies to respond in the future where the harm of chemicals or their disposal may be harder to detect could be just as frustrating as Courtemanche's experiences. Perhaps one way to deal with these problems is that industry must have a foolproof way of disposing certain chemicals or products before it markets them. Another way is for industry to refrain from using chemicals or products in the production cycle that are inconsistent with the earth's life-cycle or harmful to the biophysical environment.

———————————————

13

IN CONCLUSION

Bunyan Bryant and Elaine Hockman

Our species must be prepared to make some basic and more fundamental change if we are to survive the 21st Century. We must build cities and production systems that mimic nature. In nature there is no waste because the waste from one life form becomes the food for another. As in nature we must build cities and production systems so that the waste from one industry becomes the raw materials for another (Anderson, 1998).

Although this book is based upon the 1990 census data, we feel that very little has changed over years. With the exception of different characters, the state of Michigan may be worse off today than when these data were collected. This book not only provides useful information to policymakers in government and in the private sector, but it provides useful baseline data for future studies so that systematic comparisons can be made between the outcomes of this study with future ones. Now that new census data are available it would be useful to test out the hypothesis that environmental conditions in Michigan are worse than they were at the time of the 1990 census. Now for the summary discussion.

To build sustainable cities requires that we face up to the race question and we must face up to people who are disproportionately burdened by environmental hazards. To build sustainable and environmentally just communities requires more than a reactive problem-solving approach. It requires that we stop producing chemicals that are not found in nature and chemicals that are toxic and persistent. It requires us to allocate resources so that the cities can be cleaned up and made more livable. If it looks "bad," smells "bad," and sounds "bad," it should be cleaned up and the situation rectified without having to prove causality.

The data are clear. We have shown that when we compare the average black and white person in the Detroit area, the former equally strongly agreed with their white counterparts on a wide range of abstract environmental issues. Yet when these two groups were compared on quality of life issues, blacks reported significant differences than their white counterparts. Perhaps this difference is related to the possibility that blacks live in neighborhoods that have deteriorated more than white neighborhoods and therefore are more concerned about quality of life issues.

We discovered that disproportionate amounts of environmental hazards are found in predominantly people of color and low-income communities. Although the quantitative studies presented in this book fail to demonstrate causality, they do nevertheless prove what many people have been saying all a long: that people of color and low-income groups experience a greater number of toxic and hazardous chemical or facilities in their neighborhoods as compared with their more affluent white counterparts. Several studies we include in this book show that there is a direct independent and positive correlation of minority concentrations with the presence of environmental insults. That is to say, as the number of minorities within a zip code increases, so do the number of toxins and/or hazardous waste facilities.

We have also shown that minority concentrations have influenced siting in two ways: first a direct path and second an indirect path through median household income. When people's household income is low, they are more apt to be minority, and if they are minority, they are more apt to live in communities overburdened with environmental insults. Race has both a direct and through income an indirect influence upon siting.

When it is demonstrated over and over again that people of color tend to live in areas where they shoulder a greater body burden of environmental insults and when it has been shown that these insults may have negative effects upon their health, we thus feel that regardless of whether the waste disposal or polluting industries were located there before people moved in, the problem needs to solved. We also feel that race and poverty may be a greater causal effect than any other factor in explaining exposure to environmental toxins or hazards. More affluent white populations live in cleaner and more wholesome neighborhoods, have better access to health care, are usually healthier, and are better educated. Working on issues of poverty and racism is perhaps the long-term solution to environmental injustice. Although environmental regulations may influence the development of new pollution-abatement and control technology, and although more jobs may be created, this by itself is not enough to eradicate economic poverty. We must also work to eradicate the poverty of the spirit, and the mind. We must work hard to eradicate the multiple forms of institutional racism.

But in the short-term our efforts to eradicate poverty and racism do not mean we tolerate the arguments of government officials and corporate executives that there is "no proof of harm" in exposure to environmental toxins. Community groups should continue to organize to protect their communities against environmental harm by combining science with community organizing or the mobilization of large numbers of people to protest against policymakers or policies that would result in a negative environmental impact. Community groups have found that a combination of the above strategies have proven to be most effective. In our struggle to protect our communities, we must not get caught in the free will and determinant arguments but we must continue to operate from the precautionary principle of taking action to clean and restore our communities to make them free of toxins, even though scientific certainty about the cause of pollution or diseases has not yet been proven.

Even though this book focuses more on the plight of African-Americans, we also recognize the plight of Hispanic, Arab, Asian, and Native American populations. Because many of these populations are small in Michigan, many of them were not picked up in significant numbers in the zip codes. If one were to observe where the Hispanic, Arab, and Native American populations live, one would find that they are most likely to be disproportionately burdened by environmental pollutants just as blacks. In agricultural regions, migrant workers, most of whom are Hispanic, are often exposed to a variety of harmful pesticides and herbicides as they work the land to bring food to our tables.

Because policymakers or scientists often cannot speak with certainty of the health impacts of toxins or are unable to offer immediate solutions to environmental problems, community people often experience a crisis of confidence. They come to believe that they cannot depend upon policymakers or scientists for correct information. They come to distrust them because the "experts" speak in language that is difficult to understand and assume that the experts either lack the answers to community problems or have something to hide. In this book we have not only presented the statistics, but we have also presented the pain, anger, concerns, fears, and distrust that people experience in trying to find reasonable solutions to their problems. The Berlin-Farro is a case in point, where Verna Courtemanche and those she represented could not get clear answers from government policymakers or scientists. Because she was put on hold, shouted at, and called a meddling Gray Panther by government officials, and because it took a number of years of struggle to get the government to respond to the problem adequately, Courtemanche and other community people lost confidence in government. There are countless stories that could be told in Michigan alone about people's struggles with government and the corporate sector to protect their communities against environmental harm.

Although this book does not address specific chemicals that cause specific health problems, it does make the associations between those industries that spew poison chemicals into air and water and on to the land, and the residential closeness of people of color and low-income groups to these polluting facilities. But all of us are exposed to chemicals. We are exposed to thousands of synthetic chemicals, and we have no idea of the extent of their single or synergistic effects. Yet, we do know that some of these chemicals have been known to cause birth defects and deformities, cancer, respiratory diseases, life-long impaired mental functioning, low-sperm count, and sterilization (Colburn, 1996).[1]   We believe that some of these chemicals may be responsible for the violence and aggressive behavior reported on the six o'clock news. To attempt to determine causality would be a research nightmare costing billions of dollars. To study the combined effects rather than the singular effects of these toxins would be even more complex. For example, to determine the singular effect of cigarette smoking and lung cancer took more than 30 years of debate before laws and policies could be made regarding the harmful effects of cigarette smoking. In the meantime millions of people became ill or died. Something similar to the long and protracted cigarette debate could happen in regard to chemicals whose causal relationships have not yet been proven. Under these circumstances, we must use the precautionary principle in order to take action to reverse harmful environmental trends when cause and effect cannot be proven. The precautionary principle should not only be an integral part of policymaking decisions, but it must also be actively enforced.

Other questions raised in the literature of the disproportionate impact of environmental hazards on people of color include: Was the nuisance there first and the people moved to the nuisance or vice versa? Was it a biased siting decision or a discriminatory housing market (Been, 1994)? While whites were able to save enough money to move from contaminated areas, blacks were left with fewer options to move out to cleaner and healthier areas even if they had the financial resources to do so. Or because of housing discrimination, their options limited them to polluted areas as places to move into and live. The argument presented above is one of determinism and less so of free will. Because science is based upon the determinist model, it leads those of us who are interested in environmental injustice as a scientific area of inquiry to ask the following questions: Why do blacks live in segregated areas? Why do they lack political power? Why do they live in areas that are economically poor and where land values are cheap? We doubt this is by chance alone. That is to say, if people of color were more equally distributed throughout Michigan, then the economic argument—not the race argument—would perhaps carry more explanatory weight.

The southeastern part of Michigan is heavily industrialized. It would definitely be a challenge for environmental justice activists to help solve environmental problems in the area. Over the years the plants and foundries of the automobile industry in particular have contributed to the lion's share of pollutants in communities in which people of color and low-income people reside.

---

[1]   For more information on the health effects of chemicals, see Theo Colburn's work.

In recent years, Americans have become more environmentally aware, and in recent years local and state decision-makers would like to make cities sustainable. At one level, there are those who want to make Detroit attractive enough to reverse the tide of out-migration and in fact encourage whites to return to the city to prevent future urban sprawl. Environmentalists and others have voiced concern that the out-migration has destroyed prime agricultural lands, forest lands, and wetlands. This trend must be reversed. Yet, some blacks are leery about whites returning to the city because their increased numbers in the city will curtail black political power.

Several short-term solutions come to mind to help ameliorate environmental conditions and move us toward sustainable cities. Because many cities are blighted and poor, the federal government should implement a domestic Marshall Plan similar to the one that helped Europe back to its feet following World War II. This plan not only strengthened Europe's economy but strengthened America's economy, too, because U.S. business now had someone to trade with. We feel that in the long run such a plan for the state of Michigan, particularly Detroit and similarly affected cities would strengthen the economy of Michigan as a whole as well as the rest of the nation. Part of the funds for such a plan would go to new product design and/or to re-engineer products to make them environmentally benign. Along with the Marshall Plan the Michigan National Guard should be activated to help cleanup the blight and to revitalize our cities to help make them sustainable and livable. While the National Guard might be at the forefront of this environmental cleanup, we must also enlist citizens in this effort. Industries must provide workers with a choice of working a five day-week or a four-day week with the fifth day devoted to community service.[2] These cleanup activities should be seen as the moral equivalent of war.

Several other short-term solutions could also be implemented. For example: 1) New companies wanting to locate in an area must perform a cumulative impact statement to measure the overall amount of pollution increase resulting from their operations. New companies should not move into an area unless they can get other companies to reduce their overall toxic emissions. 2) All companies should practice extensive conservation such as recycling, reducing, and reusing programs in order to cut down the waste stream. The more we conserve, the less waste we produce requiring disposal. 3) Companies should use nontoxic waste in their production cycle to cut down on the amount of toxins to be disposed of at the end of the cycle. 4) The Environmental Protection Agency should enforce the principle equal protection of the law regardless of the income or racial characteristics of communities. EPA should not only increase its own staff

---

[2]   For other forms of creative work, see Jeremy Rifkin's *The End of Work*, Matthew Fox's *Reinventing Work* and Robert Theobald's *Guaranteed Income*.

to do a better job of environmental protection, but it should train high school teachers to teach their students about monitoring the air, water, and land to help the agency to carry out its mission. Students can become additional monitors to help with environmental protection and at the same time learn about chemistry, biology, and civics and the importance of an interdisciplinary approach to social and environmental problem-solving

Although tradable emissions have been recommended to solve our environmental problems, the Environmental Justice community is skeptical of that practice. To use the market to solve our problems by emissions-trading is highly suspect among environmental justice advocates, because the market got us into this position in the first place and the environmental justice activists do not have confidence that the market will get us out of this predicament. Although emissions may be reduced in the aggregate, they are not reduced in the specific. In fact, specific conditions often become worse than before because one industry is allowed to trade with another for emissions-reduction credits outside its immediate area, which allows it to continue to pollute at previous or even increased pollution levels. The question is: what happens to the people who live in the immediate vicinity where the pollution continues at its present levels or even increases? In short, emissions-trading is not a solution.[3] A combination of strategies, including command and control, should be at work to solve this most important problem.

Although corporate CEOs claim that market strategies will enhance creativity in solving environmental problems, one can make the same argument for command and control or environmental regulations. Environmental regulations have forced companies to become creative. For example, while West Germany and Japan led the world in strict environmental regulations in the 1980s, they also had the most robust and productive economies as compared with other nation-states. Environmental regulations have been responsible for a whole new industry of pollution abatement and control technologies— technologies that are much needed throughout the world, particularly in the Eastern European countries and other countries throughout the world as they develop economically and increase the volume of pollution. This new industry will not only generate jobs for an intelligent work force in Michigan, but it can help the nation with its balance of payment deficits (Bedzek, 1995).

But an even more fundamental problem is the fossil fuel economy that the world embarked upon well over a century ago. In order to deal with the environmental crisis and the crisis of environmental injustice, we must jettison

---

[3] For more information on emissions trading see Robert N. Stavins's *Economics of the Environment.*

the fossil fuel economy. Our species must be prepared to make some basic and more fundamental change if we are to survive the 21st Century. We must build cities and production systems that mimic nature. In nature there is no waste because the waste from one life form becomes the food for another. As in nature we must build cities and production systems so that the waste from one industry becomes the raw materials for another (Anderson, 1998). Recycling and product redesigns are not enough. We must be willing and able to change the whole system in order to build an environmentally just and sustainable society in which people can interact with confidence that their environment is safe, nurturing, and productive. The people of Detroit and Flint and the state of Michigan can become leaders in this area. Michigan has an intelligent work force that can build a new State that can serve as a model for other states and countries throughout the nation and world. The state of Michigan has outstanding universities and together with an intelligent workforce, they can help build neighborhoods that are healthy and productive. We can build more efficient mass transit systems. We must find ways to use the sun and wind and other environmentally benign energy sources to power our industry and cities and set as a goal to never mine the Earth for coal or drill for another drop of oil (Anderson, 1998).

At the same time, the knowledge that comes from our university researchers and from inventors must always be questioned. Although much of that knowledge may be sustainable in the short-run, it may be unsustainable in the long run. Universities must help us define sustainable knowledge if we are to survive on the planet. Many would say these goals are too lofty and unattainable, but if we do not attain them then we have only ourselves to fault. We must be visionary and bold in our actions. We must make our mistakes now and not in the future. It is much better to plan the future than to blunder into it. Our country spent lavishly to reach the Moon, and succeeded in a short time. Surely we can do as much for ourselves and the state of Michigan. In doing so, we will surely make a difference for those of future generations.

But protecting the biophysical environment is only half of the problem. The other half of the problem is overcoming the abject poverty and racism that mark our social and economic landscape. To date numerous studies, whether they are local, regional, or national or whether they were designed properly or improperly overwhelmingly point to race as the greater explanatory variable as compared with income in the location of environmental insults. Although we should focus on toxic cleanups to ensure our health and our sanity, the greater causes of environmental injustice are perhaps poverty and racism. Affluent whites often live in communities that are pristine and free of toxins. They are usually healthier, experience better access to health care, and are better educated. [4]

We must keep our eyes on the prize; we must work hard to understand the legacy of racism and how its historical aspects shape present race relations. Diligent work can eradicate the vestiges of racism and poverty in our midst. No one in our society, no matter what color, should live in unsafe environments or be forced into a position to choose between jobs and environmental protection or between jobs and health care protection. No one should be without a decent home, a safe place to work with decent wages and a decent neighborhood in which to live.[5] Once we free people from poverty and extricate them from the jaws of racism, they will be better off both environmentally and physically. Once we achieve environmental and economic justice our state will flourish as never before.

---

[4] Barry Commoner addresses this issue in his article entitled "How Poverty Breeds Overpopulation."

[5] We should review the possibility of a national health care program that includes a public option and the creative use of urban land trusts and food and housing and business cooperatives to help us eradicate poverty. We must give people a choice of working five days or four days with the fifth day of work devoted to helping in the community to make life better for people or devoted to healing people or healing the planet.

REFERENCES

Acuña, R. (1988). *Occupied America: A History of Chicanos*. New York: Harper & Row.

AFL-CIO. (1993, July 2). Pesticide Findings Vindicate UFW. *The California News.*

Aguirre-Molina, M. and C. W. Molina. (1994). Latino Populations: Who Are They? In Molina, C. W. and M. Aguirre-Molina, (Eds.), *Latino Health in the U. S.: A Growing Challenge*. Washington DC: American Public Health Association.

Alter, D. and G. Pickett. (No date). *Solid Waste Management in Detroit.*

Part B. An unpublished paper.

_____. (No date). *Solid Waste Management in Detroit. Part D.* An unpublished paper.

Analysis of the Air Toxics Provisions Contained in the Proposed Clean Air Act Amendments. (1990). Prepared for: The Business Roundtable and the Clean Air Working Group: Pittsburgh, PA. CONSAD Research Corporation. 1-33.

Anderson, R. C. (1998). *Mid-Course Correction*. Atlanta, GA: The Peregrinzilla Press.

Anderton, D. L., et al. (1994). Environmental Equity: The Demographics of Dumping. *Demography*, 31(2), 229-248.

Anita: Interview in March (1995).

Antonio: Interview in March (1995).

_____: Interview in April (1995).

Aponte, R. (1994). *Michigan's Hispanics: A Socio-Economic Profile. Statistical Brief No. 1*. East Lansing: Julian Samora Research Institute.

Asch, P. and J. J. Seneca. (1978). Some Evidence of the Distribution of Air Quality. *Land Economics,* 54(3), 278-297.

Askari, E. (1994, July 11). Location of Incinerators Shows Racial Bias, Study Charges. *Detroit Free Press*, 1 A and 2 A.

Associated Press. (1995, February 4). EPA to Investigate Genesee Twp. Incinerator. *Flint Journal*. Saturday, C1.

Babbie, E. (1989). *The Practice of Social Research*. Fifth Edition. Belmont, California: Wadsworth Publishing Company.

Bailey, C. et al. (1989, September). Public Opinions and Attitudes Regarding Hazardous Waste in Alabama: Results from Three 1988 Surveys. *Rural Sociological Series No. 14*. Auburn, Ala.: Auburn University, 1-128.

Been, V. (1994). Locally Undesirable Land Uses in Minority Neighborhoods; Disproportionate Siting or Market Dynamics? *The Yale law Journal* 03(1383): 1383-1422

Berry, B. J. L. (1977). *The Social Burdens of Environmental Pollution: A Comparative Metropolitan Data Source*. Cambridge, MA: Ballinger Publishing Company.

Bezdek, R. H. (1992), February. *Employment and Business Opportunities in the Environmental Protection Areas During the 1990s*. Washington D.C.: Management Information Services, Inc. Background Paper for Environment and Employment. An Interactive Symposium for Labour, Business, and Environmentalists. Ottawa, Canada, 1-17.

Bezdek, R. H., R. M. Wendling and J. D. Jones. (1989). The Economic and Employment Effects of Investment in Pollution Abatement and Control Technology. *Ambia: A Journal of Human Environment* 18(5): 274-279.

Bezdek, R. H. (1995). The Net Impact of Environmental Protection on Jobs and the Economy. In Bryant, B. *Environmental Justice: Issues, Policies, and Solutions*. Washington, D.C.: Island Press.

Blalock, H. M. et al. (1964). *Causal Inferences in Nonexperimental Research*. Chapel Hill: University of North Carolina.

Boerner, C. and T. Lambert. (1995). Environmental Injustice. *The Public Interest*, 118, 61-82

Bollen, K. A. (1989). *Structural Equations with Latent Variables*. New York: A Wiley-Interscience Publication.

Bourke, L. M. (1991). *Anticipating a Hazardous Waste Facility in Rural Utah Communities: Economic and Environmental Perceptions*. Logan: Utah State University. A Thesis submitted in partial fulfillment of the requirements for the degree of Master of Science in Sociology.

Bowen, W. M., M. J. Salling, E. J. Cyran, and H. A. Moody. (1993), May. *The Spatial Association between Race, Income, and Industrial Toxic Emissions in Cuyahoga County, Ohio*. A paper prepared for the annual meetings of the

Association of American Geographers, Atlanta, Georgia. Cleveland, OH: Levin College of Urban Affairs, Cleveland State University.

Bowen, W. M., M. J. Salling, K. E. Haynes, and E. J. Cyran. (1995). Toward Environmental Justice: Spatial Equity in Ohio and Cleveland. *Annals of the American Association of Geographers*, 85(14), 623-640. December.

Boyd, R. and N. D. Uri. (1991). Costs of Improving the Quality of the Environment. *Journal of Policy Modeling*, 13(1), 115-140.

Braknis, G. (1983, April 10). Berlin & Farro: Continuing Story of Failures, Fears. *The Flint Journal*, B1 and B6.

Braknis, G. and K. Crawford. (1983, April 10). The "Future" Turned Sour. *The Flint Journal*, B1.

Bronkema, D. (1986). December. Is Environmental Control an Expense or an Investment?" *EPA Journal*, 12(10), 30-31.

Brown v. Board of Education of Topeka, 347 U.S. 483 (1954).

Bruno, K. et al. (1999). *Greenhouse Gangsters vs. Climate Change*. San Francisco: Corpwatch.

Bryant, B. and P. Mohai. (Eds.), (1992). *Race and the Incidence of Environmental Hazards: A Time for Discourse*. Boulder, CO: Westview Press.

Bryant, B. and E. M. Hockman. (1995). *Hazardous Waste and Spatial Relations According to Race and Income in the State of Michigan*. University of Michigan, Ann Arbor (unpublished book).

Bryant, B. and P. Mohai. (1990). The Michigan Conference: A Turning Point. *Environmental Protection Agency Journal*, 18(1), 9-10.

Bryant, B. (Ed.), (1995). *Environmental Justice: Issues, Policies and Solutions*. Washsington, D.C.: Island Press.

Buist, A. S. and Vollmer, W. M. (1994). Preventing Deaths From Asthma. *The New England Journal of Medicine*, 331(23), 1584-1585.

Bullard, R., P. Mohai, R. Saha, B. Wright. (2007). *Toxic Wastes and Race at Twenty 1987-2007: A Report Prepared for the United Church of Christ Justice & Witness Ministries*. Cleveland, Ohio: United Church of Christ.

Bullard, R. (1992). Urban Infrastructure: Social Environmental and Health Risks to African Americans. *The State of Black America*. New York: National Urban League.

_____. (1990). *Dumping in Dixie: Race, Class and Environmental Quality.* Boulder, CO: Westview Press.

Bullard, R. and Wright, B. H. (1986). The Politics of Pollution: Implications for the Black Community. *Phylon,* 47, 71-78.

_____. (1987). Environmentalism and the Politics of Equity: Emergent Trends in the Black Community. *Mid-American Review of Sociology,*12(2), 21-38.

_____.(1987b). Implications of Toxics in Minority Communities. *Proceedings of the Conference on Community Toxic Pollution Awareness for Historically Black Colleges and Universities.* Tallahasse, FL: Legal Environmental Assistance Foundation.

Burch, W. (1976). The Peregrine Falcon and the Urban Poor: Some Sociological Interrelations. In Richerson, P. and J. McEvoy (Eds.),, *Human Ecology: An Environmental Approach.* Belmont, CA: Duxbury Press.

Bureau of the Census. (1990). *1990 Census of Population and Housing; Summary Tape File 3. Economic and Statistics Administration.* Washington, D.C.: U.S. Department of Commerce.

Bureau of Economic Analysis. (1975). Capital Expenditures by Business for Air, Water, and Solid Waste Pollution Abatement, 1974 and Planned 1975. *Survey of Current Business,* July, 55(7), 15-20.

Burke, L. M. (1993). Race and Environmental Equity: A Geographic Analysis in Los Angeles. *Geographic Information Systems,* 3(9),44-50.

Carey, J. (1986, August/September). A Breath of Fresh Air for the Economy. *National Wildlife,* 24(5), 37.

Caron, J. A. (1989). Environmental Perspectives of Blacks: Acceptance of the 'New Environmental Paradigm'. *Journal of Environmental Education.* (P.20).

Ceasar. Interview in March (1995).

Center for New Community. (2001). *State of Hate: White Nationalism in the Midwest 2000-(2001).* Oak Park, Illinois: Center for New Community.

CEHCs, (Children's Environmental Health Centers). (2009). *Important Alert: Facts About Southwest Detroit Projects Currently Under Discussion.* U. S. Environmental Protection Agency. Retrieved from http://www.epa.gov/ ncer/childrenscenters/southwestdetroit.html

Chakraborty, J. (2002). Acute Exposure to Extremely Hazardous Substances:

An Analysis of Environmental Equity. *Risk Analysis*, 21(5), 883-883.

Colburn, T. D., D. Dumanoski, and J. P. Myers. (1996). *Our Stolen Future*. New York, NY: Dutton.

Collins, L. M. (2002). The Huge Smokestack Burns Big Bucks and Spews Bad Fumes. Retrieved 2010 from http://www.metrotimes.com/editorial/story. asp?id=3053.

Commission for Racial Justice. (1987). *Toxic Wastes and Race in the United States: A National Report on the Racial and Socio-Economic Characteristics of Communities with Hazardous Waste Sites.* New York: Commission for Racial Justice, United Church of Christ.

Commoner, B. (1975). How Poverty Breeds Overpopulation. *Ramparts*, 13(10), 21-25, 58-59.

Cook, A. A. (1986, Fall). The Ohio Story: The Economic and Employment Benefits of Controlling Acid Rain. The *Amicus Journal*, 5-7.

Costner, P. and J. Thornton. (1990). *Playing with Fire*. Washington, D.C.: Greenpeace.

Council on Environmental Quality. (1971). *The Inner City Environment. The Second Annual Report of the Council of Environmental Quality.* Washington, D.C.: U. S. Government Printing Office.

Craig, S. C. (1979). Efficacy, Trust and Political Behavior. *American Politics Quarterly*, 225-239.

Crawford, K. (1982, April 10). From a Patch of Farmland to a Contaminated Dump. *The Flint Journal*, B3.

Cropper, M. L. and W. E. Oates. (1992). Environmental Economics: A Survey. *Journal of Economic Literature*, 30(2), 675-740.

Croxton, F. E. and D. Cowden, (1955). *Applied General Statistics*. Englewood Cliffs, New Jersey: Prentice -Hall.

Cummins, E. and D. Gearino. (1983, April 12). Berlin Toxic Cleanup Awaits Court Ruling. *The Flint Journal*, A1-A2.

Cushman, J. H., Jr. 1997, September 29. U. S. Reshaping Cancer Strategy as Incidence in Children Rises: Increase May Be Tied to New Chemicals in Environment. *New York Times* (Late New York Edition): A1.

Davidson, P. R. (2003). Risky Business? Relying on Empirical Studies to Assess Environmental Justice. In Visgilio, G.R. and D.M. Whitelaw (Eds.), *Our Backyard: A Quest for Environmental Justice.* New York: Rowman and Littlefield Publishers

DeGannes, K. et al.(1991). *Sumpter Township Study: The Effects of Two Incinerator Ash Facilities on a Community.* An unpublished paper. University of Michigan School of Natural Resources and Environment.

Dempsey, D. (2001). *Ruin and Recovery.* Ann Arbor: University of Michigan Press.

Denton, N. A. and D. S. Massey. (1988). Residential Segregation of Blacks, Hispanics, and Asians by Socio-economic Status and Generation. *Social Science Quarterly,* 69(4), 797-817.

D'Hondt, F. (1976). *Jobs vs. Environment: Must There Be a Conflict? Working for Environmental and Economic Justice and Jobs.* A National Action Conference at the Walter and May Reuther UAW Family Education Center. (May), 2-6.

The Detroit Free Press. (1983, November 25). *Toxic Waste was Detected 700 Feet from Dump. 12A.*

The Detroit News. (1986, March 28). *Who's Running the Store?* Section A.

Downey, L. (1998). Environmental Justice: Is Race or Income a Better Predictor? *Social Science Quarterly,* 79(4), 766-778.

Duncan, O. D. and B. Duncan. (1955). Residential Distribution and Occupational Stratification. *American Journal of Sociology,* 60, 493-503.

Dungate, Patrick. Interview in summer of (2000).

Elmer-Dewitt, P. (1992). Rich vs. Poor. *Time,* 139(22), 42-46, 51, 54,56.

Ember, L. (1990). Groups Disagree on Costs, Benefits of Clean Air Bills. *Chemical and Engineering News,* 68(6), 23.

Environmental Protection Agency and Underground Injection Practices Council. (1990). *Injection Wells: An Introduction to Their Use, Operation and Regulation.* Washington, D.C.

Environmental Racism: It Could Be A Messy Fight: A Planned Incineration in California has Led to an Unusual Law Suit. (1991, May 20). *Business Week.*

Ember, L. (1990). Industry Fears Lost Jobs from Clean Air Bills. *Chemical and Engineering News,* (March 5) 68(10).

Erickson, D. (1991). Sustainable Jobs. *Scientific American,* 265(5), 127-128.

Faber, D. R. (2002). Unequal Exposure to Ecological Hazards: Environmental Injustice in the Commonwealth of Massachusetts. *Environmental Health Perspectives.* (April), 100, 277-288.

Forester, J. (1989). *Planning in the Face of Power.* Berkeley, CA: University of California Press.

Fox, M. (1994). *The Reinvention of Work: A New Vision of Livelihood for our Time.* New York, NY: Harper San Francisco.

Francis, P. et al. (1991). *Environmental Blackmail: Identifying those who may be Vulnerable.* Environmental Inequity in the Detroit Tri-county Area: A Report of the 1990 Detroit Area Study. Masters Practicum. Ann Arbor: University of Michigan School of Natural Resources.

Franklin, Ralph. (2000). Detroit Incinerator Interview. Interview held in Detroit, MI.

Freeman, A. M. (1972). The Distribution of Environmental Quality. In Knesse, A.N. and B.T. Bower. (Eds.), *Environmental Quality Analysis.* Baltimore, MD: Johns Hopkins University Press for Resources for the Future.

Freudenberg, N. (1984). *Not in Our Backyards!: Community Action for Health and the Environment.* New York: Monthly Review Press.

Frey, W. H. (1992). Minority Suburbanization and Continued "White Flights" in the U.S. Metropolitan Areas: Assessing Findings from the 1990 census. *Research Report No. 92-247,* Population Studies Center, University of Michigan.

Gamson, W. A. (1968). P*ower and Discontent.* Homewood, IL: Dorsey Press.

Garfield, Mike (2000). Informal conversation

Gelobter, M. (1988). *The Distribution of Air Pollution by Income and Race.* Paper presented at the Second Symposium on Social Science in Resource Management. Urbana, IL. June.

Gelobter, M. (1992). Toward a Model of 'Environmental Discrimination'. In Bryant, B. and P. Mohai. (Eds.),. *Race and the Incidence of Environmental Hazards: A Time for Discourse.* Boulder, CO: Westview Press.

Gelobter, M. (1988). *The Distribution of Air Pollution by Income and Race.* Paper presented at the Second Symposium on Social Science in Resource Management. Urbana, IL. June.

Georgakas, D. and M. Surkin. (1998). *Detroit: I Do Mind Dying.* Updated Edition. Cambridge, MA: South End Press.

Geschwind, S. A. et al. (1992). Risk of Congenital Malformations Associated with Proximity to Hazardous Waste Sites. *American Journal of Epidemiology,* 135(11), 1197-1207.

Gershman, J. (1991). *Trading Freedom: How Free Trade Affects Our Lives, Work, and Environment.* San Francisco: Institute for Food and Development Policy.

Geskey, S. M. (1995). *Environmental Racism in Michigan: A State Law Toolbox Emphasizing Michigan Constitution of 1963.*

Goering, L. (1990, June 18). Robbins Future Remains Hazy: The Incinerator May Not Clean Up Town's Economic Woes. *The Chicago Tribune.*

Gianessi, L., H. M. Peskin and E. Wolff. (1979). The Distributional Effects of Uniform Air Pollution Policy in the US. *Quarterly Journal of Economics* (May), 281-301.

Goldman, B. A. and L. Fitton. (1994). *Toxic Wastes and Race Revisited: An Update of the 1987 Report on the Racial and Socio-economic Characteristics of Communities with Hazardous Waste Sites.* Washington, DC: Center for Policy Alternatives.

Goldman, B. A. (1994). *Not Just Prosperity: Achieving Sustainability with Environmental Justice.* This document was commissioned for the National Wildlife Federation Corporate Conservation Council's Synergy 1994 Conference, February,1994, Washington, DC.

_____. (1991). *The Truth about Where You Live: An Atlas for Action on Toxins and Morality.* New York: Times Books/Random House.

Goodman, R. (1979). *The Last Entrepreneurs: America's Regional Wars for Jobs and Dollars.* New York: Simon and Schuster.

Grossman, R. and G. Daneker. (1977). *Jobs and Energy.* Washington, DC: Environmentalists for Full Employment.

Gruber, S. (1984, November 15). Wells Near B&F Will be Tested Again for Arsenic. *The Flint Journal,* A1-A2.

Gustafson, C. (1983, October 8). Berlin Residents Air Frustrations, Share Study Results. *The Flint Journal,* A1 and A2.

Hansen-Kuhn, K. and S. Hellinger. (no date). *Look Before You Leap.* Washington, DC: The Development Group for Alternative Policies.

Harding, A. K. and M. L. Greer. (1993). The Health Impact of Hazardous Waste Sites on Minority Communities: Implications for Public Health and Environ-Mental Health Professionals. *Journal of Environmental Health*, 55(7), 6-10

Harrison, D., Jr. (1975). *Who Pays for Clean Air: The Cost and Benefit Distribution of Automobilie Emissions Standards*. Cambridge, MA: Ballinger.

Hawken, P. (1993). *The Ecology of Commerce: A Declaration of Sustainability*. New York: Harper Business.

Hawken, P., A. Lovins and L. H. Lovins. (1999). *Natural Capitalism*. New York, NY: Little, Brown and Company.

Hazilla, M. and R. J. Kopp. (1990). Social Costs of Environmental Quality Regulation: A General Equilibrium Analysis. *Journal of Political Economy*, 98(4), 853-873.

Higgins, R. (1993). Race and Environmental Equity: An Overview an Environmental Justice Issues in the Policy Process. *Polity*, XXVI (2), 281-300.

Hockman, E., and C. Morris. (1998). Progress Toward Environmental Justice: A Five-Year Perspective of Toxicity, Race and Poverty in Michigan, 1990-(1995). *Journal of Environmental Planning and Management*, 41(2), 157 - 176.

Holden, A. (2000a). The Activist: Southeast Michigan Group of the Sierra Club. *Sierra Club*, March/April/May, 18(l), 1-4.

Impact of Federal Pollution Control and Abatement Expenditures on Manpower Requirements. (1975). Washington D.C.: Bureau of Labor Statistics Bulletin # 1836,1-59.

Jencks, C., and S. E. Mayer. (1990). Residential Segregation, Job Proximity and Black Job Opportunities. In Lynn, L.E. Jr., and M.G. McGeary. (Eds.),, *Inner-City Poverty in the United States*. Washington, DC: National Academy Press.

Jenkins, J. C. (1983). Resource Mobilization Theory and the Study of Social Movements. *Annual Review of Sociology*, 9, 527-553.

Jobs at Risk: Updating the Economic Effects of the Proposed Clean Air Act Amendments. (1990). Prepared for: The Clean Air Working Group. Pittsburgh, Pennsylvania: CONSAD Research Corporation. 1-32.

Jordon, V. (1978). Energy Policy and Black People. *Vital Speeches of the Day*, XLIV(11), 341-344.

Jorgenson, C. and P. Wilcoxen. (1990). Environmental Regulations and U.S. *Economic Growth*, 2(2), 314-340.

_____. (1990). Interporal General Equilibrium Model of U.S. *Environmental Regulation,* 12(4), 715-744.

Jose: Interview in March (1995).

Katz, J. H. (1978). *White Awareness: Handbook for Anti-racism Training.* Norman, OK: University of Oklahoma Press.

Kazis, R. and R. Grossman. (1982). *Fear at Work: Job Blackmail, Labor, and the Environment.* New York: The Pilgrim Press.

_____. (1983). Job Blackmail: It's Not Jobs or the Environment. In Green, M.J., M. Waldman, and R. Massie, (Eds.), *The Big Business Reader: On Corporate America.* New York: The Pilgrim Press.

Kay, J. H. (1997). *Asphalt Nation.* New York: Crown Publishers, Inc.

Kerner Commission. (1968). *Report of the National Advisory Commission on Civil Disorders.* Washington, D.C.: U. S. Government Printing Office.

Koren, H. S. and M. J. Utell. (1997). Asthma and the Environment. *Environmental Health Perspectives,* 105(5), 534-537.

Krannich, R. S. and R. L. Little. (1983). August. *Household Expenditure Patterns and the Leakage of Economic Resources in the Lake Powell Area.* Paper Presented at the Annual Meetings of the Rural Sociological Society, Kentucky.

Kruvant, W. J. (1975). People, Energy, and Pollution. In Newman, D. K. and D. Day. (Eds.), *The American Energy Consumer.* Cambridge, MA: Ballinger.

LaBalme, J. (1987). *A Road to Walk, A Struggle for Environmental Justice.* Durham, NC: The Regulator Press.

Lamoglia, J. (1991), March. Disposal Services Profit Despite Recession. *HR Magazine on Human Resource Management.* 41-42.

Lang, D. M. and M. Polansky. (1994). Patterns of Asthma Mortality in Philadelphia From 1969 to 1991. *The New England Journal of Medicine,* 331(23), 1542-1583.

LaVeist, T. A. (1993). Segregation, Poverty and Empowerment: Health Consequences for African Americans. *Milbank Quarterly,* 71(1), 41-64.

Lavelle, M. and M. Coyle. (1992). Unequal Protection. *The National Law Journal,* 15(3), 1-43.

Lee, C. (1992). In Bryant, B. and Mohai, P. (Eds.), *Race and the Incidence of Environmental Hazards: A Time for Discourse.* Boulder, CO: Westview Press.

Lee, T. (1990). Here Comes the Pink Slip. *American Demographics,* 12(3), 46-49.

Legislative Services Bureau of the State of Michigan. (1994). *Michigan Environmental Response Act and Related Administrative Rules.*

Leone, R. A. (1986). *Who Profits: Winners, Losers, and Government Regulation.* New York: Basic Books, Inc., Publishers.

Leonard, H. J. (1989). *Environment and the Poor: Development Strategies for a Common Agenda.* New Brunswick, NJ: Transaction Books.

Lott, E. (1994). Review Essay: Race Matters. *Social Text,* 40 (Fall), 39-50.

Management Information Services, Inc. (1991, October 14). U.S. Environmental Spending to Exceed National Defense Budget. *News Release.* Washington D.C., 1-3.

Management Information Services, Inc. (no date). *1985 Private Environmental Investments Create New Industry with $19 Billion in Corporate Sales, 167,00 Jobs.* News Release. Washington D. C.

Management Information Services, Inc. (1992). Environmental Protection Spending Total $170 Billion and Creates 4 Million Jobs. Washington, D.C.: *MISI.* December.

Marin, G. and Marin, B. V. (1991). *Research with Hispanic Populations.* Newbury Park, CA: Age Publications

Markham, W. and E. Rufa. (1997). Class, Race, and the Disposal of Urban Waste: Locations of Landfills, Incinerators, and Sewage Treatment Plants. *Sociological Spectrum,* 17, 235-248.

Massey, D. S., A. B. Gross. and M. L. Eggers. (1991). Segregation, the Concentration of Poverty and the Life Changes of Individuals. *Social Science Research,* Vol. 20, 397-420.

McCarthy, J. D. and M. N. Zald. (1977). Resource Mobilization and Social Movements: A Partial Theory. *American Journal of Sociology,* 82, 1212-1241.

McCaull, J. (1977). Discriminatory Air Pollution. In Birch, W. K. (Ed.),, *Readings in Sociology, Energy and Human Society: Contemporary perspectives.* New York: Harper and Row.

McDonald, L., and J. A. Powell. (1993). *The Rights of Racial Minorities: The Basic ACLU Guide to Racial Minority Rights.* 2nd ed. Cardondale: Southern Illinois University Press.

McDonough, W. and M. Braungart. October. (1998). The Next Industrial Revolution. *The Atlantic Monthly.* 82-92.

Mehnert, E., C. Gendron, and R. Brower. (1990). *Investigation of the Hydraulic Effects of Deep-Well Injection of Industrial Wastes.* Department of Energy and Natural Resources, Illinois State Geological Survey, Hazardous Waste Research and Information Center (HWRIC).

Meyer, S. M. (1992). October. *Environmentalism and Economic Prosperity: Testing the Environmental Impact Hypothesis.* A Study by the Massachusetts Institute of Technology, Project on Environmental Policies and Policy.

Michigan Environmental Response Act. Environmental Response Division, Michigan Department of Natural Resources. *Act 307 of the Public Acts of 1982,* 820-838.

Michigan Solid Waste Industries. (no date). *Working Together to Keep our Communities Clean.* Retrieved June 16, 2010 from Website: http://www.michiganwasteindustries.org/about/industry-background/faq-frequently-asked-questions/

Miller, G. T., Jr. (1988). *Living in the Environment: Fifth Edition.* Belmont, CA: Wadsworth. M.

Minnesota Issue Watch. (2002). *Great Lakes Governors Urged to Establish Joint Environmental Report Card.* Retrieved from http://www.gda.state.mn.us/issues/resource.html?Id=2345

Mohai, P. and B. Bryant. (1992). Environmental Racism: Reviewing the Evidence. In Bryant, B. and P. Mohai (Eds.),. *Race and the Incidence of Environmental Hazards: A Time for Discourse.* Boulder, CO: Westview Press.

Mohai, P. and B. Bryant. (1992). Environmental Injustice: Weighing Race and Class as Factors in the Distribution of Environmental Hazards. *University of Colorado Law Review,* 63(4), 921-932.

Montgomery, L. E. and O. Carter-Pokras. (1993). Health Status by Social Class and/or Minority Status: Implication of Environmental Equity Research. *Toxicology and Industrial Health,* Sept/Oct. 9(5), 729-773.

Moore, C. and C. Miller. (1994). *Green Gold: Japan, Germany, the United States, and the Race for Environmental Technology.* Boston, MA: Beacon Press.

Morello-Frosch, R. et al. (2002). Environmental Justice and Regional Inequity in Southern California: Implications for Future Research. *Environmental Perspectives,* 100, (April), 149-154.

Morris, C. and E. Perle, (1996) *Statistical Model of Hazardous Waste Sites and Their Spatial Correlates*. Proceedings of the Conference on the Small City and Regional Community, University of Wisconsin-Stevens Point: Foundation Press.

Morse, S. (1983). Civic Lesson for Children of Swartz Creek. *Detroit Free Press*. March 18, 1B-2B.

Musial, R. (1995, February 4). EPA to Investigate Choice of Flint Power Plant Site. *Detroit Free Press*, 9A.

Motavalli, J. (2001, March-April). Zero Waste. *E: The Environmental Magazine*, 12(2), 27-33.

Mouat, L. (1981, September 24). Trash: Cheap Energy or Heap of Trouble. *Christian Science Monitor*.

National Research Council. (1977). Manpower for Environmental Pollution Control Analysis Studies of USEPA. USEPA, 5, 1-477.

National Resources Defense Council. (no date) Retrieved April 14, 2003 from the National Resources Defense Council Web site: http://www.nrdc.org/air/pollution/bt/MI.asp

Oakes, J., D. Anderton, and A. Anderson. (1996). Longitudinal Analysis of Environmental Equity in Communities with Hazardous Waste Facilities. *Social Science Research*, 25, 125-148.

Orfield, G., F. Monfort and R. George. (1987). *School Segregation in the 1980s: In States and Metropolitan Areas*. Report by the National School Desegregation Project to the Joint Center for Political Studies.

O'Neal, J. (1995, April 7). The Flint Woodburning Plant. Presentation to the School of Public Health, University of Michigan, Ann Arbor, Michigan.

O'Muircheartaigh, C. A. and C. Payne (Eds.), (1977). *The Analysis of Survey Data, Volume 2: Model Fitting*. Chichester: John Wiley & Sons, Ltd.

Ortner, Pam. Interview in summer of (2000).

Orr, R. H. (1974). The Additive and Interactive Effects of Powerlessness and Anomie in Predicting Opposition to Pollution Control. *Rural Sociology*, 39, 471-486.

Orum, A. M. (1974). On Participation in Political Protest Movements. *Journal of Applied Behavioral Science*, 10(2), 181-207.

Peña, D. and J. Gallegos. (1993). Nature and Chicanos in Southern Colorado. In Bullard, R. and B.F. Chavis (Eds.), *Confronting Environmental Racism: Voices from the Grassroots.* Boston: South End Press.

Pastor, M., J. Sadd, and J. Hipp. Which came First? Toxic Facilities, Minority Move-in and Environmental Justice. *Journal of Urban Affairs*, 23(1), 1-21.

Perfecto, I. and B. Velasquez. (1992). Farm Workers: Among the Least Protected. *EPA Journal* 8(March/April) 13-14.

Pershagen, G. and L. Simonato. (1990). Epidemiological Evidence on Air Pollution and Cancer. In Tomatis, L. (Ed.),, *Air Pollution and Human Cancer.* Berlin: Springer-Verlag.

Peterson, Kenneth L. (1983a, April 10). The Toxic Waste Mess; Could it Happen Again? *The Flint Journal.* B2.

Peterson, Kenneth L. (1983b, April 10). "Superfund" for Super Perils. *The Flint Journal.* B8.

Pine, J. C., B. D. Max and A. Lakshmanan. (2002). The Examination of Accidental-Release Scenarios from Chemical-Processing Sites: The Relation of Race to Distance. *Social Science Quarterly.* March, 83(1), 317-332.

PIRGIM (Public Interest Research Group in Michigan). (2004). *Detroit Ranks 3rd for Worst Air Pollution among Major U.S. Cities.* Retrieved from http://www.great-lakes.net/lists/enviro-mich/2004-09/msg00132.html

Pope, C. A., III (2002). Lung Cancer, Cardiopulmonary Mortality and Long-term Exposure to Fine Particulate Air Pollution. *JAMA.* 287(9). Retrieved from http://jama.ama.assn.org/issues/v287n9/rfull/joc11435.html

Porter, M. E. (1990). *The Competitive Advantage of Nations.* New York: The Free Press.

Prout, L. R. (1992). The Toxic Avengers. *EPA Journal*, 18(March/April) 48-49.

Public Act 64. (1979). Hazardous Waste Management Act. *Michigan Public and Local Laws*, (1979), 179-198.

Public Act 641. (1978). Solid Waste Managment Act. *Michigan Public and Local Laws*, (1979), 2437-2451. Amended in 1994 as PA 451.

Renner, M. (1991). September. *Jobs in a Sustainable Economy: World Watch Paper 104.* Washington, D.C., 5-58.

Rich, W. C. (1989). *Coleman Young and Detroit Politics.* Detroit, MI: Wayne State University Press.

Richardson, Mark, Interview in summer of (2000).

Rifkin, J. (1995). *The End of Work: The Decline of the Global Labor Force and the Dawn of the Post Market Era.* New York, NY: Putman Publishing Group.

Rochin, R., A. Santiago and K. Dickey. (1989). Migrant and Seasonal Workers in Michigan's Agriculture: A Study of their Contributions, Characteristics, Needs, and Services. *Institute Research Report No. 1* . East Lansing: Julian Samora Research Institute.

Roper, C. and B. van Guilder. (2006, August 31). *Stabenow Trash Deal a Big Win in Michigan.* Retrieved from http://www.great-lakes.net/lists/enviro-mich/2006-08/msg00238.html

Rogers, D. L. and D. A. Whetten. (1982). *Interorganizational Coordination. Theory, Research, and Implementation.* Ames: Iowa State University Press.

Rotter, J. B. (1966). Generalized Expectancies for Internal Versus External Control of Reinforcement. *Psychological Monographs General and Applied,* 80, 1-28.

_____. (1975). Some Problems and Misconceptions related to the Construct of Internal Versus External Control of Reinforcement. *Journal of Consulting and Clinical Psychology,* 43, 56-57.

Rusk, D. (1993). *Cities Without Suburbs.* The Woodrow Wilson Center Press: Washington, DC..

Russell, D. (1989). Environmental Racism: Minority Communities and their Battle Against Toxins. *The Amicus Journal,* 11(2), 22-32.

Rutledge, G. L. and M. L. Leonard. (1991) September. Pollution Abatement and Control Expenditures, 1987-89. *Survey of Current Business.* 46-50.

Santiago, A. M. (1991). The Spatial Dimensions of Ethnic and Racial Stratification. *Research Report* No. 91-230, Population Studies Center, University of Michigan.

Schneidman, M. (1994). Michigan: Land of Landfills. *Michigan Toxics Watch,* 5(3), 6-9.

SEMCOG, (2008). *Ozone Action Season Begins; More Ozone Days Possible as EPA Lowers Standards.* Retrieved from http://www.semcog.org/OAseason_5-1-08.aspx

Shavelson, L. (1988, Nov. 6). The Nightmare Stays with Us: Dread and Death in McFarland, California. *This World,* 10-11.

Silverstein, M. (1992a, February 18). In Economics 'Green' is Gold. *The Christian Science Monitor,* 19.

Silverstein, M. (1992b, May 28). Bush's Polluter Protectionism Isn't Pro-Business. *The Wall Street Journal,* A19.

Smith, J. C. (1997, September 24). *Testimony of the Institution of Clean Air Companies, Inc. Before the U.S. Senate Subcommittee on Manufacturing and Competitiveness on EPA's Revised NAAQS for Particulate Matter and Ozone.*

Simon, C. A. and G. L. Avery. (1986, April 9). *Department of Natural Resources Air Quality Division Staff Report.* Report submitted by Simon and Avery.

Statistical Abstract of the United States. (1992). 112th Edition. *The National Data Book.* U.S. Department of Commerce, Economics and Statistics Administration Bureau of the Census. U.S. Department of Commerce.

Stavins, R. N. (Ed.), (2000). *Economics of the Environment: Selected Readings. Fourth Edition.* New York: W. W. Norton & Company.

Steingraber, S. (1997). *Living Downstream: An Ecologist Looks at Cancer and the Environment.* Reading, MA: Addison-Wesley Press.

Stobbe, M. (1992a, October 23). Planned Wood-burning Project Draws fire. *Flint Journal,* B1.

_____. (1992b, October 28). Residents Angry Over Power Plant Proposal. *Flint Journal,* B1.

_____. (1992c, November 17). Medical Society Opposes Power Plant. *Flint Journal,* C1.

_____. (1992d, November 22). Wood-burning Plant Fueling Controversy. *Flint Journal.* A1.

_____. (1992e, December 2). State OKs Power Plant; Neighbors vow appeal. *Flint Journal,* A1.

Syme, S. L. (1987). Social Determinants of Disease. *Annals of Clinical Research,* Number 19, 44-52.

Syme, S. L. and L. F. Berkman. (1976). Social Class, Susceptibility and Sickness. *American Journal of Epidemiology,* 104(1), 1-8.

Terry, R. (1970). *For Whites Only.* Grand Rapids: William B. Eerdmans Publishing Company.

Theobald, R. (1967). *The Guaranteed Income.* New York, NY: Anchor Books.

Tobey, J. A. (1990). "The Effects of Domestic Environmental Policies on Patterns of World Trade: An Empirical Test." KYKLOS, 43(2), 191-209

Tomboulian, A., P. Tomboulian, K. Metzger, D. Towns, and L. Hands. (1995). *Tri-County Detroit Area Environmental Equality Study.* U. S. Environmental Protection Agency and United Way Community Services for Southeastem Michigan.

Truax, B. (1990). Minorities at Risk. *Environmental Action.* January/February, 20, 19-21.

Truchan, J. (1986, March 14). Interview of James Truchan of the Michigan Department of Natural Resources.

Unger, D. et al. (1992). Living Near a Hazardous Waste Facility: Coping with Individual and Family Distress. *American Journal of Orthopsychiatry,* 62(1), 55-70.

United Church of Christ. (1987). *Toxic Wastes and Rare in the United States: A National Report on the Racial and Socio-economic Characteristics of Communities with Hazardous Waste Sires.* New York: Commission for Racial Justice, United Church of Christ..

US. Environmental Protection Agency (EPA). (1989, June). *The Toxics-Release Inventory Executive Summary.* Washington, D.C..

_____. (1976, April 12). 1975 Fourth Quarter Report of the Economic Dislocation Early Warning System.

_____. (1990). Environmental Investment: The Cost of a Clean Environment. Washington, D.C., November, Report Number: EE-0294B.

United States Census Bureau. *1990 Census of Population and Housing.*

United States Department of Commerce, Economics and Statistics Administration Bureau of the Census. (1992). *Statistical Abstract of the US, (1992).* 112th Edition. The National Data Book. Washington, DC: U.S. Government Printing Office.

United States General Accounting Office. (1983). *Siting of Hazardous Waste Landfills and their Correlation with Racial and Economic Status of Surrounding Communities.* Washington D.C.: U. S. General Accounting Office.

U.S. Environmental Protection Agency (EPA). (1992). *Environmental Equality; Reducing Risk for All Communities. 2 Vols. EPA230-R-92-008 and EPA230-R-92-008A.* Washington, DC: Policy, Planning and Evaluation, U.S. Environmental Protection Agency.

Valdes, D. (1992). *Divergent Roots, Common Destinies? Latino Work and Settlement in Michigan. Occasional Paper No. 4.* East Lansing: Julian Samora Research Institute.

van Guilder, B. *Detroit's Solid Waste Crisis.* Retrieved 2010 from http://www. ecocenter.org/recycling/documents/detroit_sw-crisis_nomap.pdf

Wang, X., H. Ding, L. Ryan, and X. Xu. (1997). Association Between Air Pollution and Low Birth Weight: A Community-Based Study. *Environmental Health Perspectives,* 105(5), 514-520. May.

Wasserman, A. and K. Olssen. (1990). *Banning the Burn: A Political Economic Framework for Reducing the Environmental and Public Health Hazards Posed by Incinerators.* A Master's Practicum submitted in partial fulfillment of the requirements for the Degree of Master's of Science. School of Natural Resources at the University of Michigan.

Wendling, R.M. and R. H. Bezdek. (1988). Acid Rain Abatement Legislation-Costs and Benefits. Omega International Journal of Management Science, 17(3), 251-261.

Wernette, D.R. and L.A. Nieves. (1992). Breathing Polluted Air. *EPA Journal,* 18 (March/April) 16-17.

Wernette, D. R. and L. A. Nieves. (1991, June 27-28). *Minorities and Air Pollution: A Preliminary Geodemographic Analysis.* Presented at the Socio-economic Research Analysis Conference. .

West, P., et al. (1992a). Invitation to Poison? Detroit Minorities and Toxic Fish Consumption from the Detroit River. In Bryant, B. and Mohai, P. (Eds.),, *Race and the Incidence of Environmental Hazards: A Time for Discourse.* Boulder, CO: Westview Press.

West, P., J. M. Fly, F. Larkin, and P. Marans. (1992b). Minority Anglers and Toxic Fish Consumption: Evidence from a State-Wide Survey of Michigan. In Bryant, B. and P. Mohai (Eds.),, R*ace and the Incidence of Environmental Hazards: A rime for Discourse.* Boulder, CO: Westview Press.

Westerholm et al. (1985). *Berlin-Farro: The History of a Toxic Waste Site.* Ann Arbor: An unpublished paper submitted in partial fulfillment of a class requirement.

White, M. J. (1988). Segregation and Diversity Measures in Population Distribution. *Population Index,* 52(2), 198-221.

Wilson, A. (Ed.), (1998). *Green Development: Integrating Ecology and Real Estate.* New York: John Wiley & Sons, Inc.

Wilson, S. M. et al. (2002). Environmental Injustice and the Mississippi Hog Industry. *Environmental Health Perspectives*, 110, 195-201.

Yandle, T. and D. Burton. (1996). Reexamining Environmental Justice: A Statistical Analysis of Historical Hazardous Waste Landfill Siting Patterns in Metropolitan Texas. *Social Science Quarterly,* 77(3), 477-491.

Zeiss, C. and J. Atwater. (1987). Waste Facilities in Residential Communities: Impacts and Acceptance. *American Society of Civil Engineers Journal of Urban Planning and Development.* May, 113(1), 19-34.

Zubrinsky, C. and L. Bobo. (1996). Prismatic Metropolis: Race and Residential Segregation in the City of Angels. *Social Science Research,* 25, 335-374.

Zupan, J. M. (1973). *The Distribution of Air Quality in the New York Region.* Baltimore, MD: Johns Hopkins University Press.

Index

BUY A SHARE OF THE FUTURE IN YOUR COMMUNITY

These certificates make great holiday, graduation and birthday gifts that can be personalized with the recipient's name. The cost of one S.H.A.R.E. or one square foot is $54.17. The personalized certificate is suitable for framing and will state the number of shares purchased and the amount of each share, as well as the recipient's name. The home that you participate in "building" will last for many years and will continue to grow in value.

Here is a sample SHARE certificate:

YES, I WOULD LIKE TO HELP!

I support the work that Habitat for Humanity does and I want to be part of the excitement! As a donor, I will receive periodic updates on your construction activities but, more importantly, I know my gift will help a family in our community realize the dream of homeownership. **I would like to SHARE in your efforts against substandard housing in my community!** *(Please print below)*

PLEASE SEND ME _____ SHARES at $54.17 EACH = $ $_____

In Honor Of: _____

Occasion: (Circle One)   HOLIDAY   BIRTHDAY   ANNIVERSARY

       OTHER: _____

Address of Recipient: _____

Gift From: _____ *Donor Address:* _____

Donor Email: _____

I AM ENCLOSING A CHECK FOR $ $_____ PAYABLE TO HABITAT FOR HUMANITY OR PLEASE CHARGE MY VISA OR MASTERCARD *(CIRCLE ONE)*

Card Number _____ Expiration Date: _____

Name as it appears on Credit Card _____ Charge Amount $ _____

Signature _____

Billing Address _____

Telephone # Day _____ Eve _____

PLEASE NOTE: Your contribution is tax-deductible to the fullest extent allowed by law.
Habitat for Humanity • P.O. Box 1443 • Newport News, VA 23601 • 757-596-5553
www.HelpHabitatforHumanity.org

Printed in the USA
CPSIA information can be obtained
at www.ICGtesting.com
JSHW082159140824
68134JS00014B/322